STOLEN SONG

STOLEN SONG

HOW THE TROUBADOURS BECAME FRENCH

ELIZA ZINGESSER

CORNELL UNIVERSITY PRESS
Ithaca and London

Support for the publication of this book was provided by Columbia University through a Lenfest Junior Faculty Development Grant.

First published 2020 by Cornell University Press

Library of Congress Cataloging-in-Publication Data

Names: Zingesser, Eliza, 1984– author.
Title: Stolen song : how the troubadours became French / Eliza Zingesser.
Description: Ithaca [New York] : Cornell University Press, 2020. | Includes bibliographical references and index.
Identifiers: LCCN 2019017308 (print) | LCCN 2019019425 (ebook) | ISBN 9781501747649 (pdf) | ISBN 9781501747632 (epub/mobi) | ISBN 9781501747571 | ISBN 9781501747571 (cloth)
Subjects: LCSH: Troubadour songs—Influence. | Literature, Medieval—Provençal influences. | Poetry, Medieval—History and criticism. | Provençal poetry—History and criticism. | French literature—To 1500—History and criticism. | Troubadours. | Quotations in literature—History and criticism.
Classification: LCC PC3304 (ebook) | LCC PC3304 .Z55 2020 (print) | DDC 809.1/4—dc23
LC record available at https://lccn.loc.gov/2019017308

For my mother

Contents

Illustrations

Acknowledgments

It is my pleasure to acknowledge here the many interlocutors from whom this book benefited. I am indebted to Sarah Kay for her incisive and brilliant comments on the earliest version of *Stolen Song*. I am also grateful to Simone Marchesi and Anna Zayaruznaya for their astute remarks and suggestions on that version. Anna, as is her wont, went well beyond the call of duty as a reader. Her warmth and intellectual generosity remain an inspiration. I am also indebted to several others who read or kindly answered questions about portions of this book: Teo Barolini, Susan Boynton, Emma Dillon, Eleanor Johnson, Jennifer Saltzstein, Marion Uhlig, and especially Marilynn Desmond, who read a large portion of the book in draft. In other venues, parts of the project have been improved by the comments and questions of Matilda Tomaryn Bruckner, Bill Burgwinkle, Ardis Butterfield, Christopher Davis, Eglal Doss-Quinby, Mary Franklin-Brown, Marisa Galvez, Simon Gaunt, Miranda Griffin, Philipp Jeserich, Christopher Lucken, Wayne Storey, and Court Wells. Jena Barchas-Lichtenstein and Nicholas Limerick provided helpful bibliographic suggestions in the field of linguistic anthropology. Anne Levitsky transposed two motets into Finale for the musical examples in chapter 5. I am grateful to all of my brilliant students at Columbia, but I should single out Clara Beccaro and Sias Merkling, who worked as my research assistants.

Sections of this book were written under the collegial auspices of Clare Hall, Cambridge, where I was a research fellow, and at the Institute for Research in the Humanities at the University of Wisconsin, Madison, from which I was very fortunate to receive a Solmsen Fellowship. In Cambridge, discussions with Bill Burgwinkle, Emma Dillon, Jane Gilbert, Miranda Griffin, Philipp Jeserich, and Marilynn Desmond were both helpful and a pleasure. In Madison I profited from the advice and feedback of Catherine Bates, Susan Stanford Friedman, Bethany Moreton, Lucy Traverse, Scott Trudell, and Pamela Voekel. I am also thankful for a blissful stay at the American Academy in Rome made possible by the Michael I. Sovern/Columbia Affiliated Fellowship.

For allowing me to consult the manuscript sources discussed here (or reproductions thereof), I am indebted to the librarians of the Biblioteca Apostolica Vaticana, the Bibliothèque nationale de France, the Institut de recherche et d'histoire des textes, and the Pierpont Morgan Library. At the Vatican, the supremely gracious Paolo Vian made possible the consultation of two manuscripts which would normally have been unavailable. Carmela Vircillo Franklin generously smoothed my path at the Vatican and in Rome more broadly.

Parts of chapter 4 were drawn from "Pidgin Poetics: Bird Talk in Medieval France and Occitania," *New Medieval Literatures* 17 (2017): 62–80. They are reproduced here courtesy of the publisher, Boydell and Brewer Ltd. Parts of "Francophone Troubadors: Assimilating Occitan Lyrics in Medieval France," published in *Medieval Francophone Literary Culture Outside France: Studies in the Moving Word*, ed. Dirk Schoenaers and Nicola Morato (Turnhout, Belgium: Brepols, 2018), 371–87, appear throughout the book by permission of the publisher.

Cornell University Press has been a pleasure to work with at every step of the way. I am especially indebted to Mahinder Kingra, editor extraordinaire. Many thanks, too, to Lori Rider, who copyedited the manuscript with the utmost care, and to my production editor, Karen Laun.

I am also grateful to many friends and colleagues, especially Karen Bishop, Clémence Boulouque, Julie Crawford, Pierre Force, Hannah Freed-Thall, Jonathan Hirsh, Eleanor Johnson, Isabel Köster, Ève Morisi, Jillian Porter, Emily Kate Price, Karen Quandt, Joanna Stalnaker, and Renata Szczepaniak. Sabrina Cohen was a paragon of patience, perseverance, and rigor when I most needed it. My deepest appreciation goes to Brooke, whom I met toward the end of this project, but whose love and support enabled its completion, and to my mother, to whom my debt is beyond words.

Abbreviations and Sigla

Bibliographic Data

PC	Catalog of troubadour lyric compiled by Pillet and Carstens (*Bibliographie der Troubadours*. Halle: M. Niemeyer, 1933)
RS	Catalog of trouvère lyric by Raynaud and Spanke (*Raynauds Bibliographie des altfranzösischen Liedes. Neu bearbeitet und ergänzt von Hans Spanke*. Leiden: E. J. Brill, 1955)
VdB	van den Boogaard's catalog of rondeaux and refrains (*Rondeaux et refrains du XIIe siècle au début du XIVe*. Paris: Klincksieck, 1969)

Manuscript Abbreviations and Sigla

Arras 657	Arras, Bibliothèque municipale, MS 657 (French *A*)
Bern 389	Bern Burgerbibliothek, Hs. 389 (French *C*, Occitan *h*)
Douce 308	Oxford, Bodleian Library, MS. 308
BnF fr. 795	Paris, Bibliothèque nationale de France, Manuscrit français 795 (Occitan *Y*)
BnF fr. 837	Paris, Bibliothèque nationale de France, Manuscrit français 837
BnF fr. 844	Paris, Bibliothèque nationale de France, Manuscrit français 844, also known as the "Chansonnier du Roi" (French *M*/*Mt*, Occitan *W*)
BnF fr. 846	Paris, Bibliothèque nationale de France, Manuscrit français 846, also known as the "Chansonnier Cangé" (French *O*)
BnF fr. 1802	Paris, Bibliothèque nationale de France, Manuscrit français 1802
BnF fr. 12581	Paris, Bibliothèque nationale de France, Manuscrit français 12581
BnF fr. 12615	Paris, Bibliothèque nationale de France, Manuscrit français 12615, also known as the "Chansonnier de Noailles" (French *T*)
BnF fr. 12786	Paris, Bibliothèque nationale de France, Manuscrit français 12786
BnF fr. 20050	Paris, Bibliothèque nationale de France, Manuscrit français 20050 (French *U*, Occitan *X*)

BnF fr. 24406	Paris, Bibliothèque nationale de France, Manuscrit français 24406 (French *V*, Occitan *n*)
BnF fr. 25532	Paris, Bibliothèque nationale de France, Manuscrit français 25532
Montpellier Codex	Montpellier, Bibliothèque interuniversitaire, Section Médecine, MS. 196
Thott 1087	Copenhagen, Det Kongelige Bibliotek, Thott 1087 (Occitan *Kp*)
Vat 1490	Vatican City, Biblioteca Apostolica Vaticana Reg. Lat. MS. 1490 (French *a*)
Vat 1659	Vatican City, Biblioteca Apostolica Vaticana, Reg. Lat. MS. 1659 (Occitan *η*)

Manuscripts and Sigla of the *Roman de la violette*

A Paris, Bibliothèque nationale de France, Manuscrit français 1553
B Paris, Bibliothèque nationale de France, Manuscrit français 1374
C Saint Petersburg, National Library of Russia, Fr. Q. v. XIV. 3 (olim 53)
D New York, Pierpont Morgan Library, M. 36

Manuscripts and Sigla of Richard de Fournival's *Bestiaire d'amour*

The *sigla* assigned here are drawn from Segre's edition, whenever possible, and—in the case of manuscripts discovered after this edition—from Christopher Lucken's unpublished doctoral dissertation (University of Geneva, 1994).[1] I have assigned a siglum to the Saint Petersburg fragment.

A Paris, Bibliothèque nationale de France, MS fr. 25566
B Paris, Bibliothèque nationale de France, MS fr. 412
C Paris, Bibliothèque nationale de France, MS fr. 12786
D Paris, Bibliothèque nationale de France, MS fr. 12469
E Paris, Bibliothèque nationale de France, MS fr. 1444
F Paris, Bibliothèque nationale de France, MS fr. 24406
G Paris, Bibliothèque nationale de France, MS fr. 15213
H Dijon, Bibliothèque municipale MS 526
I Paris, Bibliothèque Sainte-Geneviève MS fr. 2200
J Arras, Bibliothèque municipale, MS 139 (anc. 657)

1. My thanks to Christopher Lucken for sharing this material with me.

K Brussels, Bibliothèque royale de Belgique, MS 10349–414
L London, British Library Harley 273
M New York, Pierpont Morgan Library MS 459
O Oxford, Bodleian Library Douce 308
P Florence, Biblioteca Medicea-Laurenziana, Plut. LXXVI, 79
Q Florence, Biblioteca Medicea-Laurenziana, Cod. Ashburnhamiani 123 (Fondo Libri 50)
R Private collection (Heribert Tenschert), available in facsimile[2]
S Geneva, Bibliothèque publique et universitaire, Fonds *Comites Latenses,* no. 179 [*Ex libris* Sion Segre-Amar. Contains only a fragment of the *Bestiaire,* ending with p. 26, l. 2 of Segre's edition.]
T Turin, Biblioteca nazionale universitaria, 1660 L.III.22 [Manuscript badly burned in a fire in 1904. Transcription available at the IRHT in Paris, not assigned a siglum by Segre]
V Vienna, Österreichische Nationalbibliothek MS 2609
W Milan, Biblioteca Ambrosiana I. 78 sup.
Y Milan, Biblioteca nazionale Braidense, AC.X.10 [manuscript badly damaged and only partially legible]
Z fragment preserved in St. Petersburg, described in Lozinski, "Un fragment du *Bestiaire d'amour* de Richard de Fournival," *Romania* 51 (1925): 561–68

2. I have followed Bianciotto's suggested siglum of *R* for this manuscript because, as he notes, Roy's proposed *T* duplicates the siglum of the Turin manuscript (Richard de Fournival 2009, 100).

STOLEN SONG

Introduction

Troubadour poetry occupies a unique place in the French literary canon. It is the only corpus composed in what would today be described as a "regional language" (currently known as Occitan) to have found a place within the hallowed walls of the canon, at least as measured by syllabi and reference works such as Lagarde and Michard, or, more recently, Denis Hollier's *A New History of French Literature*. But troubadour poetry has not just infiltrated the modern canon. It is sometimes implicitly framed as the very point of origin for this canon, featuring in the first week of many a survey course.[1] Numerous other works in regional languages would make more comfortable bedfellows with the familiar suspects in Lagarde and Michard. Troubadour song was, after all, written not just in a vernacular distinct from French but in a period when Occitania was not yet part of France. To include it in the canon thus involves a retrospective imposition of France's current geographical boundaries. This might not seem like an unreasonable way of proceeding in writing the literary history of France, but in survey courses the troubadours are routinely the *sole* writers taught that used France's regional languages. What makes matters even worse is that Occitania was not just *not yet French*. The region was in fact at

1. Admittedly, the perspective is different in Italy, where the troubadours are often thought of in relation to the Sicilian school and thus to the origins of Italian literature.

war with the French Crown and the (mostly) francophone armies that had moved southward in a war known as the Albigensian Crusade (1209–29). This conflict led ultimately to the annexation of many parts of Occitania by French forces, but such an outcome would have been unforeseeable to participants in the Crusade, regardless of the side on which they fought. There was, consequently, not much that could be construed as French, whether linguistically or culturally, about troubadour poetry at the time it was composed. Indeed, many troubadours penned songs of protest against French invaders. And yet the story of our current misprision of troubadour song as French begins in the earliest stages of its transmission in francophone space. Far from being treated as a foreign entity, Occitan lyric was already considered "native" in French sources, even long before Occitan-speaking territories were officially annexed to France. To tell this story of assimilation, the process through which Occitan song was domesticated, this book surveys the two types of medieval material—songbooks and lyric-interpolated narratives—that quote or compile Occitan song in native francophone territory.[2] *Stolen Song* charts the ways in which the linguistic and cultural specificity of Occitan lyric was actively effaced in its medieval reception in the northern territories of what is now France, allowing it to pass as part of a French literary tradition. It also documents the emergence of a parallel corpus of what might be considered fake troubadour song. These songs, which were composed by francophone poets, deployed linguistic coloring to evoke Occitan in less prestigious genres and with pseudo-primitive elements. They thereby produced a vision for francophone audiences of a foreign culture (Occitan) as rustic, while genuine troubadour songs were silently purloined and reframed as part of French literary history.

Some preliminary definitions are in order, since even terms as simple as "France" and "song" prove more complex in a medieval context than in a modern one. I turn first to the former. The setting of *Stolen Song* is both larger and smaller than the space occupied by France on contemporary maps. In medieval usage, the term "France" could mean anything from the territory of the Franks, to the region controlled by the French king, to the area known today as the Île-de-France. For the purposes of this book, I have tried to avoid using the term "France" in favor of francophone territories. By this I mean any territory in which Old French was spoken as a native language, even in coexistence with other languages. These parameters allow for the inclusion

2. I use the term "songbook" rather than the more common "chansonnier" in order to avoid suggesting the Frenchness of a form that was not especially French. On songbooks in medieval Europe, see Marisa Galvez's recent study (2012).

of England (whence one songbook in the corpus hails) and the Morea in the Peloponnese (which had a francophone ruler). Such parameters would also have allowed for the inclusion of the Crusader states and Flanders, had any manuscripts survived from these territories that included Occitan song.[3] The francophone territories under consideration here are thus not politically unified, and to claim a "French" provenance for a songbook or narrative here (or to indicate assimilation into a "French" context) does not in any way indicate a relationship to the French Crown or to any unified political space at all.

Like medieval "France," the space of Occitania resists easy demarcation. It is generally understood today as the region extending from the Pyrenees to the Alps and northward to the Auvergne and the Limousin. This corresponds to the space singled out by the medieval poet Albertet, who includes within its perimeters Gascony, Provence, the Limousin, the Auvergne, and the Viennois (Harvey and Paterson 2010, 100). But Albertet describes this space as belonging not to the Occitanians but to the Catalans. On the other side of the fence, under the rubric of "Franses," or French, he places not just Capetian allies but the francophone Plantagenets, describing these northern regions as "la terra dels dos reis."[4] Occitania corresponds in part to the administrative unit of the "Septem Provinciae" in Roman Gaul, although the cultural and linguistic specificity of medieval Occitania is only partially related to the Roman presence in the region.[5] This area represents something between the southern third and the southern half of the current French Hexagon.[6] Throughout these pages, I use the term "Occitania" rather than

---

3. I have excluded Italy on the grounds that, with the exception of Angevin territory (which did not see the compilation of any songbooks including Occitan), French seems to have been a literary rather than a spoken language there. As I show in the conclusion, the dynamics of the reception of troubadour song in Italy are fundamentally opposed to those in francophone territories.

4. Albertet's description takes place in a *tenso* or debate poem between him and the poet Monge. The first stanza establishes a distinction between the two peoples: "Monge, cauzetz, segon vostra siensa, / qual valon mais, Catalan ho Franses? / Et met de sai Guascuenha e Proensa / e Lemozi, Alvernh'e Vianes, / e de lai met la terra dels dos reis" (Monge, choose, using your knowledge, who are worth more, the Catalans or the French? And I put on this side Gascony and Provence and the Limousin, Auvergne and Viennois, and on the other side I put the land of the two kings) (PC 16.17) (Harvey and Paterson 2010, 100). PC numbers throughout this book refer to Pillet and Carstens's catalog of troubadour lyric (Pillet and Carstens 1933). All translations are mine unless otherwise indicated.

5. The traditional account of the linguistic division between what is now northern and southern France is that the Germanic invasions had more of an influence in the North than the South, both linguistically and culturally. Roman law, for example, survived in Occitania for much of the Middle Ages. This view of Germanic influence is now thought to be oversimplified. In any case, the linguistic divide follows no clear political or geographical frontier (Lodge 1993, 73).

6. The Loire River is sometimes described as the point of demarcation between the two territories, which would situate the linguistic divide as far north as Nantes, Angers, and Tours. Others

"southern France" whenever possible in order to avoid suggesting the existence of a nation that had not yet come into being.

Like the French-speaking territories from which the songbooks and narratives that compile and quote the troubadours came, the historical Occitania was politically diverse. Until the Albigensian Crusade, the powerful political players in Occitania included the dukes of Aquitaine, the counts of Toulouse, and the kings of Aragon-Catalonia. Generally speaking, the western part of Occitania (and, indeed, much farther north) was controlled by the dukes of Aquitaine, who were nominal vassals of the Capetian kings (which may have contributed to a sense of ownership of troubadour song). On Eleanor of Aquitaine's marriage to Henry II of England in 1152, this territory fell under the control of the Plantagenets. Poitou, however, was reannexed by Philip Augustus in 1204. The counts of Toulouse—technically also vassals of the French king—held most of the Languedoc, with some territories falling under the control of Ramon Berenguer IV, count of Barcelona (Paterson 1993, 1). The part of Provence beyond the Rhone lay within the kingdom of Burgundy, which in turn was one of the realms of the Holy Roman Empire.[7]

Despite the variegated political landscape of both halves of what is now France, there is some evidence of a perceived cultural unity within Occitania as early as the eleventh century. For instance, Rodolfus Glaber complained of the influx of barbarous people resulting from King Robert II of France's marriage to Constance of Arles in 1001. Rodolfus refers to these people through their regions of origins—Auvergne and Aquitaine—but he clearly perceives them as part of the same cultural space (Paterson 2011, 2). But it is after the eleventh century, and in the aftermath of the Albigensian Crusade, that a sense of a pan-Occitan identity emerged most clearly. It was only in this period that the French language came to be distinguished from Occitan in municipal documents, through labels such as *langue du roi* and *roman*. The space of Occitania is also described through its shared language in these documents via the term *patria linguae occitanae* (Paterson 2011, 3, 5; 1993, 3). As the above quotations make clear, language was often at the heart of articulations of pan-Occitan culture during this period. The Catalan Raimon Vidal, in his treatise on vernacular lyric composition, the *Razos de trobar* (ca. 1190–1213), advises aspiring composers to adopt the language of "Lemosy,"

---

would place it closer to Poitiers and Limoges. Where one positions the boundary depends on the linguistic features used to establish it. The situation "on the ground" was much closer to a continuum than a sharp divide (Lodge 1993, 72).

7. Bernard Hamilton (2008) gives a detailed account of the political situation in Occitania at the time of the Albigensian Crusade.

a term he deploys in reference to areas well beyond the Limousin, including Provence, Auvergne, and the Quercy.[8] The troubadour Paulet de Marseilla also articulates a claim for Occitan identity that pivots on language, using the term "lenguatge" (language) to mean something akin to homeland.[9] Raymond VII of Toulouse likewise posits a community rooted in a shared language, interpellating residents of the Languedoc via this trait: "Homines nostre ydiome, videlicet de hac nostra lingua" (Men of our idiom, that is to say, of our language). I have dwelled on these moments of linguistic self-consciousness, and of cultural self-consciousness rooted in language, because it is not a given that medieval imaginings of the linguistic map of what is now France overlap with our own. Nevertheless, as the above comments suggest, there is clear evidence of a perceived linguistic divide between Occitania and what is now northern France as early as the eleventh century and especially in the aftermath of the Albigensian Crusade.

What is more, the boundary between French and Occitan, or *langue d'oïl* and *langue d'oc*, to use Dante's terms, seems to be coterminous for many authors with a choice of form.[10] Dante, for his part, associates what we could call narratives—compilations from the Bible, histories of Troy and Rome, Arthurian tales, and "many other works of history and doctrine" (Dante Alighieri 1996, Book 1, p. 10)—with the French language.[11] By contrast, his

8. "qant ieu parlarai de 'Lemosy,' qe totas estas terras entendas et totas lor vezinas et totas cellas qe son entre ellas" (when I speak of 'Limousin,' I mean all those lands and the neighboring lands, and all those that are between them) (Marshall 1972, 4, vv. 59–64).

9. The term appears in Paulet's "L'autrier m'anav'ab cor pensiu" (PC 319.6), composed around 1265. "L'autrier" is a political *pastorela* regarding Charles of Anjou's claim to Provence. A clear supporter of Peter of Aragon, the shepherdess first asks why Charles of Anjou kills Occitanians who have done him no wrong: "Mas, si·us platz, senher, digatz mi / del comte que Proensa te / per que los proensals ausi / ni·ls destrui, qu'ilh no·ilh forfan re?" (But, if you please, sir, tell me why the count who holds Provence kills Provençaux and destroys them, when they have committed no crime?). She then refers to someone who expelled the French from their domain: "tro que·ls agues mes en l'or / [lacuna] e·l gites de nostre *lenguatge* for" (until he had expelled them and thrown them out of our homeland). In his edition of this piece, Martín de Riquer (1975, 3:1452) comments that "*lenguatge* parece estar en el sentido de comunidad idiomática" (*lenguatge* seems to have the sense of linguistic community).

10. One or both of the terms appear in Dante's *Vita nuova, De vulgari eloquentia,* and *Convivio.* Admittedly, Dante's view of the languages of *oc* (generally understood as Occitan and Catalan), *oïl* (French), and *sì* (Italian) as separate languages is somewhat complicated by his view of them as part of the same "tripartite system" (see Dante Alighieri 1996, Book I, 8).

11. "Allegat ergo pro se lingua *oïl* quod propter sui faciliorem ac delectabiliorem vulgaritatem quicquid redactum sive inventum est ad vulgare prosaicum, suum est: videlicet Biblia cum Troyanorum Romanorumque gestibus compilata et Arturi regis ambages pulcerrime et quamplures alie ystorie ac doctrine" (Thus the language of *oïl* adduces on its own behalf the fact that, because of the greater facility and pleasing quality of its vernacular style, everything that is recounted or invented in vernacular prose belongs to it: such as compilations from the Bible and the histories of Troy and Rome, and the beautiful tales of King Arthur, and many other works of history and doctrine) (trans. Botterill).

treatise presents Occitan as the language of vernacular poetry. Although Dante does quote a few selections of Old French lyric, it is Occitan poets whom Dante quotes most often and with the most reverence. Dante further addresses the prestige of Occitan in his *Convivio*, defending Italian against those who prefer Occitan: "Mossimi ancora per difendere lui [i.e., the vernacular] da molti suoi accusatori, li quali dispregiano esso e commendano li altri, massimamente quello di lingua d'oco, dicendo che è più bello e migliore quello che questo; partendose in ciò de la veritade" (I was moved to defend it from many of its accusers who disparage it and commend the other vernaculars, especially the language of *oc*, calling that one more beautiful and better than this one, departing in this from the truth) (Dante Alighieri 1979, sec. I.10).[12] Raimon Vidal makes a similar case for the prestige of Occitan as a poetic language, mentioning French in relation to the narrative genre of romance as well as in relation to what is perhaps the most narrative of all poetic genres, the *pastourelle*: "La parladura francesa val mais et [es] plus avinenz a far romanz et pasturellas, mas cella de Lemosin val mais per far vers et cansons et serventes" (the French language is better suited and more beautiful for making romances and *pastourelles*, but that [language] of Limousin is better for making songs and *cansos* and *sirventes*) (Marshall 1972, 6). So strong was the association between Occitan and song (or poetry) that the author of the *Doctrina d'acort*, a poetic treatise, refers to the Occitan language merely as "chanz."[13] The same author advocates maintaining the linguistic purity of Occitan in poetic composition and explicitly advises against mixing the language with French, as we will see shortly. The chronicler Philippe Mousket (1215–83) chose to give a quasi-divine underpinning to the generic and linguistic divide between French and Occitan, arguing that when Charlemagne separated his conquests, he gave Provence as a fief to the minstrels and jongleurs who had followed his army. Just as the territory of Provence is passed from generation to generation, he explains, so is the gift of poetic composition.

Dont departi Karles les tieres,
Qu'il avoit conquises par gières [. . .]
Li manestrel et li jougleur
Orent Prouvence, si fu leur.
Par nature encor çou trouvons,

12. My translation.

13. Terramagnino da Pisa, *Doctrina d'acort* (Marshall 1972, vv. 131, 146, 147, and passim).

> Font Provenciel et cans et sons
> Millors que gent d'autres païs
> Pour çaus dont il furent nays.
>
> (Mousket 1836, vv. 6274–75, 6298–6304)

> When Charlemagne divided the lands he had conquered through war [. . .] the minstrels and jongleurs had Provence. Through nature still we find this, that the Provençaux make better melodies and lyrics than people from other countries, because of those from whom they were born.

Mousket posits poetic composition as part of an Occitan heritage—indeed, as the defining feature of generation on generation of Occitanians. One of the claims of this book is that, alongside the appropriation and domestication of genuine troubadour songs, this talent for song was ultimately reimagined as the foundation of *French* rather than Occitan identity. As we will see in chapter 5, one French poem with Occitanizing linguistic traits imagines a lineage for France that ultimately goes back to the siren and the nightingale.

Unsurprisingly, the question of linguistic choice seems to have come to the fore for many thinkers in the wake of the Albigensian Crusade. Probably composing in the aftermath of the war, the author of the tale "Frayre de joy et sor de plaser" declines to employ the French language because he associates it with cultural oppressors: "Sitot Francess a bel lengatge / No·m pac en re de son linatge, / car son erguylos ses merce / [. . .] Per qu'eu no vull parlar frances" (Even though the French have a beautiful language, their lineage does not please me, for they are proud and without mercy; [. . .] for this reason, I do not wish to speak French) (Thiolier-Méjean and Notz-Grob 1997, vv. 1–3, 6). Perhaps because he is composing a narrative text rather than a lyric poem, this anonymous author feels the need to explain his decision not to opt for French. His reasoning hinges on the cultural freight of the French language in the aftermath of the Albigensian Crusade.

Hostility toward the French is also expressed in troubadour poetry of the period. The dual-authored *Song of the Albigensian Crusade* is the lengthiest of these poetic responses. Even in the first section of the poem, which is sympathetic to the crusader cause, the French are described as "aicela gens estranha" (that foreign people) (Zink 1989, 152). And the author of the second section, who is much more critical of the French, describes them as aggressive by their very nature: "E Frances, per natura, deu conquerir primers / E conquer tant que puja pus aut c'un esparviers") (And a Frenchman, by nature, must conquer first of all, and conquer so much that he thinks himself higher than a sparrow hawk) (408). Hostility is also evident in the corpus of Occitan lyric poetry. Two troubadours, Tomier and Palazi, composed three inflammatory sirventes in order to encourage Occitanians fighting for the independence of their lands during the campaigns in the Bas-Rhône. One of their pieces denounces the "Franses" and exhorts Occitanians to avenge their comrades (Aurell 1989, 47). Similar animosity is evident in an anonymous sirventes, "Vai Ugonet, ses bistensa" (PC 461.247, ca. 1213). In this piece, the poet exhorts Peter II of Aragon to defend his vassals from the French (Riquer 1975, 3:1702–4; Léglu, Rist, and Taylor 2014, 88–89). French cultural identity had become synonymous with deceit, at least for one troubadour writing in the aftermath of the Treaty of Paris in 1229, as a result of which Count Raymond VII of Toulouse was forced to surrender most of his possessions to the French king and the papacy. In response to these events, Bernart de la Barta composed "Foilla ni flors" (PC 58.4) in defense of the count. He alludes to the false peace resulting from the treaty as a "patz de clercs et de Frances" (peace of clerks and Frenchmen) (Léglu, Rist, and Taylor 2014, 102–3; Chambers 1979, 51–54). Another Bernart, this one Bernart Sicart de Marvejols, expressed similar discontent at the results of this treaty in "Ab greu cossire," lamenting that wherever he goes, he sees Occitanians meekly addressing the French as "sir."[14] Like the troubadours just quoted, Boniface de Castellana did not brook such oppression easily; his poem "Si tot no·m es fort gaya la sazos" (PC 102.3), dramatically dedicated to the "Provenzals paubres e cossiros" (poor and anxious Provençaux), supported the rebellion against the French at Marseille in 1262 (Parducci 1920, 503).[15] Examples could well be multiplied here, but it should already be clear that troubadour song was both a privileged medium of political resistance to the French during and in the aftermath of the Albigensian Crusade and a critical site for thinking about cultural and linguistic difference from the French.

During precisely the period in which these troubadours penned their songs of protest, francophone compilers and writers transcribed some of the troubadours' (less political) songs on expensive parchment, in songbooks,

14. The relevant passage (stanza 2) reads as follows: "Vas on que·m vire, / Aug la corteza gen / Que cridon 'Cyre' / al Frances humilmen" (wherever I turn I hear courtly people who cry out 'sir!' to the French humbly) (Riquer 1975, 3:1202–6; Léglu, Rist, and Taylor 2014, 103–4). The word used here—"cyre"—may represent an attempt at reproducing French (in Occitan, one would expect "senhor"), suggesting that Occitanians sometimes interacted with the French in the French language.

15. For a broad overview of Occitanian reactions to the Albigensian Crusade, see chap. 1, "Le Déferlement des croisés," in Aurell (1989).

and in lyric-interpolated romances.[16] Perhaps because of the diaspora that the Crusade produced, with many troubadours leaving for what is now Italy, most troubadour songbooks were compiled outside of Occitania in the thirteenth and fourteenth centuries. According to one count, of the forty-one major troubadour songbooks, twenty-seven are of Italian origin (Riquer 1975, 1:12–14). Nine songbooks, the topic of chapter 1, were compiled in francophone territories (mostly what is now northern France but also the Morea and Anglo-French England) in the thirteenth and fourteenth centuries. The keen interest in troubadour song on the part of Italians likely resulted both from the prestige of troubadour song in the European sphere, as shown above, and from the actual physical presence of troubadours in Italian courts. Likewise, the fascination with their art on the part of francophone audiences may have resulted from the additional contact brought about by the Albigensian Crusade.[17] These francophone songbooks diverge from their Italian counterparts considerably. If, in Italy, troubadour song was treated as a prestige corpus and Occitan as a language worthy of study, in francophone territories troubadour song was assimilated to make it look French and the cultural alterity of troubadour song thoroughly eclipsed. Alongside the songbooks, three narratives by francophone authors attest to the transmission of troubadour song in French-speaking territories. These are, in chronological order, Jean Renart's *Roman de la rose* (early thirteenth century), Gerbert de Montreuil's *Roman de la violette* (ca. 1225), and Richard de Fournival's *Bestiaire d'amour* (ca. 1250). This material evidence—the compilation and quotation of troubadour song—represents the most concrete trace of contact between francophone audiences and Occitan lyric.

There are, of course, less concrete pieces of evidence of contact between francophone audiences and the troubadours, or at least their songs. Many critics have postulated that the heyday for troubadour art was Eleanor of Aquitaine's court. Eleanor was in fact the granddaughter of the first known troubadour, Guilhem IX, duke of Aquitaine and Gascony and count of Poitou. Eleanor married Louis VII, king of France, in 1137. Her entourage would have provided a receptive audience for the performance of such poetry in the North.[18] One Norman chronicle suggests that Eleanor continued to

16. Lyric-interpolated romances are romances in which songs are quoted, usually in the context of performance. The canonical study of these texts remains Maureen Boulton's (1993). Ardis Butterfield's (2002) *Poetry and Music in Medieval France* also touches on many lyric-interpolated romances.

17. Ardis Butterfield (2009) has explored the impact of war on theories and deployment of language in an Anglo-French context.

18. One major proponent of this theory was Louis Gauchat, who, following Paul Meyer (1890, 3), argued that imitation between lyric in *langue d'oïl* and that in *langue d'oc* began when

speak Occitan with her barons (Gauchat 1893, 376). It has also been suggested that the enduring northern survival of troubadour lyric is a result of the patronage of Eleanor's two daughters, Marie de Champagne and Aélis de Blois (Lejeune 1958, 1954). According to this theory, their patronage spread Occitan lyric arts farther north via their respective courts (Nelson 1995, 255). Marie's court may have hosted Conon de Béthune and Bertran de Born, an encounter to which Lejeune attributes Conon's borrowings of troubadour rhyme schemes (Lejeune 1958, 325). Blois was frequented by Gaucelm Faidit and Raimbaut de Vaqueiras, in addition to trouvères such as Gace Brulé and Huon d'Oisy (Lejeune 1958, 328), Guillaume de Ferrières, and Le Vidame de Chartres (Bracken 2002, 100). The court of Geoffroy II, duke of Brittany (1158–86), may also have been the site of encounters between troubadours such as Bertran de Born, Guiraut de Calanson, Gaucelm Faidit, Peire Vidal, Raimon Vidal, and *langue d'oïl* poets Guiot de Provins and Gace Brulé (Lejeune 1958, 323). Lejeune views the role of the courts of Eleanor and her descendants as so pivotal in the transmission and cultivation of Occitan poetry in the North that she describes these environments as the site of a "bilingual civilization" (332). Like Lejeune, Pierre Bec hypothesized that interaction between the troubadours and trouvères was at its height in the Aquitaine and the domains controlled by the Plantagenets (Bec 1986, 9). In support of his case, he points to the number of famous troubadours who were active in these areas. These include, by his reckoning, Guilhem IX, Jaufre Rudel, Marcabru, Peire Rogier, Rigaut de Berbezilh, Bernart de Ventadorn, Peire d'Alvernha, Guiraut de Bornelh, Arnaut Daniel, Arnaut de Mareuil, Bertran de Born, Gaucelm Faidit, Gui d'Ussel, and others. Bec points out that the only famous troubadours who were *not* from areas under the control of the Plantagenets are Raimbaut d'Aurenga, Raimbaut de Vaqueiras, and Folquet de Marselha (10).

Other proposed scenarios in which troubadours may have come into contact with trouvères (and, indeed, with lyric poets of other linguistic traditions) include international festivals such as the one held at Mainz in 1184, which was attended by Guiot de Provins as well as some troubadours (Cain Van D'Elden 1995, 264). Bernard Cerquiglini agrees that international *foires* were a source of contact between troubadours and trouvères, and he goes so far as to propose that a sort of pidgin between French and Occitan may have been spoken there as well as in wars and for business purposes (Cerquiglini

---

Eleanor of Poitiers was queen of France (1137–52) (Gauchat 1893, 376, 390). Ruth Harvey (2005) has expressed skepticism regarding this theory. She suggests that contact may have occurred in northern Italy—notably in Montferrat—rather than in the Plantagenet realm (Harvey 1995, 211).

1983, 19, 23). The Eastern Crusades may also have provided an occasion for contact between speakers of French and Occitan. There is one extant stanza by the trouvère Hugues de Berzé addressed to Folquet de Romans, in which Hugues asks Folquet to join him in the war, and this piece may be indicative of more widespread exchange (Meyer 1890, 6). Some historical evidence suggests movement of French and Occitan speakers between courts. One of Robert de Sorbon's sermons, for instance, reports that Folquet de Marselha heard one of his songs performed at the court of the king of France by a jongleur (Folquet de Marseille 1910, 112). Arnaut Daniel also reports being in the presence of the French king, alluding to the coronation of Philip Augustus (1180) in his song "Doutz brais e critz" (PC 29.8).[19] And, in the other direction, that francophone poets frequented Occitania is clear from such incipit as Perrin d'Angecourt's "Quant partis sui de Provence" ("When I Left Provence") and the anonymous "Au repairier que je fis de Provence" ("Upon my return from Provence") (Meyer 1890, 5).[20]

Stolen Song's main goal is not to provide additional evidence of contact between francophone audiences and troubadour song. Nor is it to investigate further the historical circumstances surrounding such contact, or to examine the particularities of each act of copying of a song, where the alteration of lyrics likely occurred for a combination of reasons (garbled performance, scribal error, etc.). It is, instead, to examine closely the corpus outlined above—the songbooks from francophone territories that compile troubadour song and the narratives that quote them—with an eye to what sets them apart within the broader European transmission of troubadour song. The questions underlying this study are: Why, against a backdrop of political antagonism between (largely) francophone forces and Occitan armies in the Albigensian Crusade, did francophone compilers and writers circulate troubadour song? How was troubadour song treated by medieval francophone compilers and authors? To what use(s) was it put? Was it framed as part of a foreign cultural and linguistic tradition? Did francophone

19. The allusion is in the *tornada* (Arnaut Daniel 1961, 302).

20. Evidence of contact of a more indirect variety—literary imitation—is more abundant. Many studies have focused on contrafacta, pairs of poems that share the same metrical structure, rhyme scheme, or music. The poets involved in these exchanges include the Châtelain de Coucy and Bernart de Ventadorn (Rossi 1979), Conon de Béthune, Guiraut de Bornelh, and Bertran de Born, and Thibaut de Champagne and Rigaut de Berbezilh (Nelson 1995, 259). On the practice of contrafacture in Occitan and French, see Bonse (2003), Chambers (1952), and Räkel (1977). Asperti (1991) has studied Occitan contrafacta of French lyrics. Several other articles have argued for cases of formal imitation between the troubadours and trouvères (Bec 1998; Marshall 1979). Dijsktra (1998) has argued for mutual influence of crusade lyrics. Jung (1986, 1992) focuses on intertextual clusters rather than clear contrafacta. Jeanroy (1889a, 1889b, 1898) proposed a few potential cases of translation rather than imitation. On the troubadours' possible influence on Chrétien de Troyes, see Meneghetti (1984).

compilers and authors evince interest in particular troubadours and/or genres, and, if so, why?

I want to conclude here with a few words on the conceptual blurriness surrounding one of the key terms of this study, "Occitan." As discussed earlier in this chapter, if the identity of the "French" seems to have coalesced for the troubadours during and in the aftermath of the Crusade, the evidence for a conception of Occitan culture as unified linguistically is less abundant. Though certain writers (such as Philippe Mousket, quoted above) clearly had a sense of Occitan song as part of a particular cultural practice, it is worth pointing out that, in the absence of a widely accepted label for the language we today call Occitan or a space we would today call Occitania, medieval conceptions of "troubadour song" would necessarily have been very different from our own. It is, for instance, not at all obvious that a scribe or writer from a region we would currently place just on the southern tip of *langue d'oïl* territory would have perceived the language of his neighbor slightly to the south as another language entirely. Scholars today disagree on where precisely to draw the line between *langue d'oïl* and *langue d'oc* territory because there is no long-standing political frontier or natural barrier to communication between the areas we would now consider two separate regions. Indeed, there is a scholarly consensus that what divided *langue d'oïl* and *langue d'oc* territories was not a firm border but rather an area of linguistic interference known as the Croissant or Crescent. Whether a medieval speaker of *langue d'oïl* would have perceived the *langue d'oc* as a foreign language would, of course, have depended very much on the proximity of the dialects in question. Put another way, one might ask whether the story this book tells relies on the legacy of nineteenth-century philology, with its codified notions of discrete romance languages, cultural traditions associated with those romance languages, and linguistic correctness and fixity. As Simon Gaunt (2013, 79) has recently pointed out, "Our apprehension of medieval languages has [. . .] been refracted through the prism of modern philological traditions." However, despite the greater conceptual fluidity that characterized the medieval linguistic landscape, it is clear that the absence of a widely available label did not preclude some writers and thinkers (discussed above) from perceiving the language we now call Occitan as a distinct language—and one with a distinct cultural tradition associated with it. We know this not just from metalinguistic commentary but from formal praxis; some medieval compositions shore up linguistic boundaries (including that between French and Occitan) by making them coterminous with formal units, suggesting that their composers, like us, viewed the languages involved as discrete. What is more, some theorists, contemporary with several of the compilers and authors discussed in this book, complain of French interference in Occitan morphology, suggesting both a conception of linguistic separation between Occitan and French and some conception of linguistic purity. The Catalan Raimon Vidal, for instance, bemoans the use of French verbs in Occitan poetic composition and advises would-be composers to avoid mixing languages: "Et tut aqill qe dizon *amis* per *amics* et *mei* per *me* an faillit, et *mantenir, contenir, retenir,* tut fallon, qe paraulas son franzezas, et no las deu hom mesclar ab lemosinas, aqestas ni negunas paraulas biaisas" (And all those who say *amis* for *amics* and *mei* for *me* have made a mistake, and likewise *mantenir, contenir, retenir,* they are mistaken, for these are French words, and one should not mix them with Limousin ones, these or other wrong words) (Marshall 1972, 24). Likewise, Terramagnino da Pisa, the author of another Occitan grammatical treatise, the *Doctrina d'acort*, admonishes against linguistic admixture: "E nulls per·l proensal diga / Alcun mot frances, qar eniga / Es aytal parladura dir / Ab lo proensal, ses mentir" (And no one should substitute any French word for Provençal, for it is to say such a word for the Provençal, truly). Redundancy aside, it is clear that Terramagnino, like Raimon Vidal, views French and Occitan (which Raimon calls "Limousin" and Terramagnino "Provençal") as distinct languages that one should avoid mixing with French. The anonymous author of the *Regles de trobar* extends the prohibition to other languages as well:

> Lengatge fay a gardar, car si tu vols far un cantar en frances, no·s tayn que·y mescles proençal ne cicilia ne gallego ne altre lengatge que sia strayn a aquell; ne aytan be, si·l faç proençal, no·s tayn que·y mescles frances ne altre lengatge sino d'aquell.[21]

> Pay attention to language, for if you want to make a song in French, it would not be fitting to mix Provençal or Sicilian or Galician or any other language foreign to that one; similarly, if you make one in Provençal, it would not be fitting to mix French or any other language than that one.

The author goes on, intriguingly, to allow for exceptions based on actual usage of certain "French" words in the territory of Provence:

> Empero, si tu trobes en cantar proençals alcun mot qui sia frances o catalanesch, pus hom aquell mot diga en Proença o en una de aquelles terres qui han lengatge covinent, les quals lor son pres, aquells motz

21. I quote from the *H* version of the text but the passage is nearly identical in *R* (Marshall 1972, 64–65).

> potz pausar o metre en ton trobar o en ton cantar; e si ayso fas, no potz dir per axo que sia fals. (Marshall 1972, 64–65)
>
> However, if you were to find in a Provençal song a word that was French or Catalan, since one says that word in Provence or in one of the lands that are nearby, which has the appropriate language, you can put that word in your composition [*trobar*] or song; and if you do this, it cannot be said that this is wrong for that reason.

Both the notion that there exists a distinct language called either Limousin or Provençal (and that we would today call Occitan) and the notion that that language should not be mixed with French seem widespread, perhaps unsurprisingly, among the authors of grammatical treatises.

That said, there was undoubtedly a multiplicity of perspectives at work on the part of francophone writers and scribes, and, as this book argues, there is no question that medieval thinkers divided up and labeled the linguistic landscape of what is now France differently than we do. Some likely *did* perceive troubadour song as culturally and linguistically foreign but chose to actively assimilate it and occlude this difference for ideological reasons. Others, in the absence of the linguistic label of "Occitan," may have perceived Occitan or Occitanizing sounds not as foreign or strange but as a marker of "poeticity" or else as a coloring associated with love song. The fuzziness of the boundaries between the two languages allowed for a wide variety of perspectives on their precise contours. My claim is not that medieval scribes and authors were *incorrect* in failing to apply a linguistic label ("Occitan") that—at least in that form—was not yet in circulation. This would be an absurd claim. Rather, my point is that a willingness or lack of willingness to perceive linguistic difference is always ideological (in the contemporary context, one could point to the newly conceptualized languages of "Bosnian," "Croatian," and "Serbian" for the formerly conceptually singular lingua franca of Yugoslavia and the employment of translators between what many would view as a single language). The linguistic landscape in any time and place is not an objective reality that can be disinterestedly observed and documented.[22] The central claim of this book is *not* that medieval francophone audiences were wrong

---

22. Many linguistic anthropologists and sociolinguists have studied the influence of ideology in delimiting—or obfuscating—linguistic difference. Susan Gal and Judith T. Irvine's notion of "erasure" is especially apposite here. They argue that "a social group, or a language, may be regarded as homogeneous, its internal variation disregarded. Because a linguistic ideology is a totalizing vision, elements that do not fit its interpretive structure—that cannot be seen to fit—must either be ignored or be transformed" (Gal and Irvine 1995, 974). Gallicization is, arguably, just such a transformation. See also Gal and Irvine (2000); Silverstein (1979); K. Woolard and Schieffelin (1994); K. A. Woolard (1998).

to not apply our own contemporary conceptual framework but rather that their choice (conscious or unconscious) to *not* see troubadour song as a linguistically and culturally distinct body of material (a choice that is not replicated in medieval Italy or Catalonia) is worthy of study.

A Critical History of Franco-Occitan Relations

Scholarly interest in the interaction of the troubadours and their francophone counterparts, the trouvères, reached its heyday, unsurprisingly, in the late nineteenth and early twentieth centuries—the same period in which philology was most caught up in questions of national identity. Critics of this period were often keen to assert the preeminence of their own national literature. Many such critics of French literature thought of troubadour song as a foreign corpus, whose influence on French verse they found lamentable. Typical of this school of thought was Wilhelm Wackernagel, who expressed regret that French poetry "se régla sur des modèles étrangers venus de Provence" ("was formed on foreign models from Provence") (Jeanroy 1889b, xv). As we will see in chapter 5, many nineteenth-century philologists attempted to unearth an "original" (in both senses of the word) French folk poetry—one uninfluenced by the troubadours, whose "courtly" influence they deemed detrimental to the "spontaneous" qualities of this hypothetical French verse. The poems they thought best reflected this hypothetical archaic corpus were paradoxically, as I show in chapter 5, most often drawn from what I call the "Occitanizing" corpus (a corpus that seems to have been produced by francophones but with Occitan linguistic traits). This did not stop the critics in question from appropriating them as remnants of the earliest specimens of *French* literature.

In addition to weighing in on the question of foreign influence, nineteenth-century philologists also traced the contours of the dissemination of troubadour song in French songbooks. The first to do so, in 1872, was Karl Bartsch (1872, 27ff.). Paul Meyer (1890) built on this work, drawing attention to several sources overlooked by Bartsch. Louis Gauchat (1893) was the first to provide a comprehensive survey of Occitan lyrics in French manuscripts, and his study served as the basis for Manfred and Margret Raupach's (1979) more recent survey. As linguists, the Raupachs' focus is on the Frenchified or Gallicized form in which most troubadour song is transmitted in francophone territories (see "Gallicization" below). As we will see, Gallicization often produced songs that sounded and looked like French but failed to make sense as French. Many troubadour songs were in fact transmitted in a form that was only semi-intelligible at best. The Raupachs' study addresses not the *why* of Gallicization but the *how*: their study documents the most frequent linguistic adaptations to which Occitan song was subjected in francophone transmission, showing several fundamental patterns (113–70). *Stolen Song* takes up where the Raupachs' book left off, examining the underlying sociocultural logic behind the linguistic practice of Gallicization. It shows, moreover, that the phenomenon of Gallicization was part of a larger series of assimilative practices that left troubadour song more or less indistinguishable from its francophone surroundings.

Troubadour song's European diffusion—well beyond the contours of what is now France—is the subject of Sarah Kay's *Parrots and Nightingales: Troubadour Quotation and the Development of European Poetry*. Kay's work sheds light on the way in which troubadour songs were generally mined as a source of knowledge in their European dissemination. Alongside this reverence accorded to their songs, individual troubadours were often visually foregrounded, their names underlined in red ink or otherwise distinguished on the manuscript page (Kay 2013, 15). *Stolen Song* shows that the dynamics of the francophone reception of troubadour song were diametrically opposed to the mode of reception that is the focus of Kay's study—a mode that treated troubadour song as a body of knowledge and individual troubadours as worthy of remembrance. In its francophone transmission, troubadour song was, by contrast, often barely comprehensible and almost always anonymous. While Kay shows that some writers who quoted and imitated troubadour song saw their literary practices as akin to those of the parrot and nightingale, respectively, I show that the francophone writers and compilers who interacted with troubadour song typically aligned not themselves but rather the troubadours with the avian.[23] As we will see throughout this book, garbled Occitan song was sometimes framed in its francophone transmission as akin to birdsong.

Birdsong and Unintelligibility

Birdsong occupied a unique place in medieval grammatical theories. It is this theorization, I would argue, that explains, in part, the equivalence between birdsong and language that is only moderately intelligible. Bird vocalizations were often granted a particular status by late antique and medieval theorists as one category of *vox*—itself a subset of the broader category of *sonus*, or sound. A *vox*, according to Boethius, is a sound emitted from the mouth or windpipe of an animal.[24] The concept of *vox* corresponds to what we might

23. See especially chap. 6, "The Parrots' Way: The *Novas del papagai* from Catalonia to Italy," in Kay (2013).

24. Boethius (2010), Book I.1, 15.

call today a vocalization. Some grammarians distinguished between, on the one hand, *vox discreta*—understood either as *vox* capable of being transposed in writing or as *vox* that signified according to semantic conventions, and on the other, *vox confusa*—vox that resisted transcription in writing.[25] Later thinkers, beginning with Priscian, distinguished more systematically between meaningfulness and writability. This led to the categories of *articulata* and *inarticulata*, on the one hand (meaningful or not meaningful), and *litterata* and *illitterata* (writable or unwritable), on the other.[26] As both Elizabeth Leach and Umberto Eco have demonstrated, the placement of the sounds of various species within this grid was susceptible to variation.[27] Most theorists, however, placed bird vocalizations, as opposed to other animal noises, in the category of *vox* that is *inarticulata* but *litterata* (meaningless but writeable).[28] Although some troubadours emphasize birdsong's association with incomprehensibility rather than writability, this categorization makes birdsong most proximate to referential human language among all nonhuman vocal utterances. Because such grammatical treatises were a staple of the medieval curriculum, the association between birdsong and semantic opacity was likely nearly ubiquitous.

The link likely also served to signal the presence of linguistic difference from French, even in the absence of explicit acknowledgment. As anyone who has read troubadour songs knows, birds were often said to sing in their own language ("en lor lati").[29] The same expression is used to describe the dialects of heralds from various distant regions in Jacques Bretel's "Le Tournoi de Chauvency," which elsewhere substitutes *laingaige* (language) for *lati* (literally "Latin") to convey a different idea of language (Fritz 2011, 394). Unlike the relatively neutral phrase *laingaige*, in this text *lati* strongly connotes unintelligibility. The same is true elsewhere. As Christopher Davis (2015, 15) has shown, Guilhem IX uses the term to describe, in addition to birdsong, the Latin of the Church, the babble of a mute pilgrim, and the dialect of two female characters. It seems clear that, for Guilhem IX, at least, the term *lati* was most appropriate as a descriptor for linguistic acts that resist semantic parsing. For the troubadour Peire Cardenal, too, *lati* seems to

25. *Vox discreta* was also sometimes called *articulata*.

26. Priscian (2010), Book I, "De voce."

27. Leach (2007); Eco et al. (1989).

28. Leach (2007), 34. In the category of *vox* that is both *inarticulata* and *illitterata*, theorists often mention the lion's roar and the ox's lowing. Contrary to what I describe above, some thinkers placed birdsong in this same category. Leach thinks this has to do with the discrete pitches (or lack thereof) of the bird vocalizations in question. See Leach (2009, 202).

29. See Christopher Davis's (2015) exploration of this formulation in Guilhem IX's corpus.

have connoted an inscrutable language, one akin to birdsong. He proclaims that his song is as difficult to decipher as the nightingale's: "As little as they understand the nightingale / do the people understand what my song says" (Atretan pauc com fa d'un rossinhol / Entent la gent de mon chant que se di). His language is so opaque, he declares, that only he can understand it: "For no man except me understands my language" (Car homs mas ieu non enten mon lati).[30] That birdsong was understood as semantically obscure (but nevertheless writable) according to (at least some) medieval thinkers is also clear from the instances of "nonsense" syllables that are used to transcribe it, from the trouvère Guillaume le Vinier's "Mout a mon cuer es joi'" (RS 1039) to Chaucer's famous "'Kek kek, cokkou, quek" in the *Parliament of Fowls*.[31] The association between birdsong and semantic opacity persists to this day: while it may be more common to compare something we don't understand to Greek, to call something gobbledygook is, etymologically, to call it turkey talk. In the same vein, according to the OED, the verb "chatter" was initially used to denote all brief bird vocalizations, with the acceptation of the term gradually shrinking to birds whose "sounds approach those of the human voice, e.g., starlings, magpies." When applied to human beings, says the OED, the verb means "to talk rapidly, incessantly, and *with more sound than sense*" ("Chatter, V." n.d.). Thus, to link troubadour song diegetically to birdsong (as Jean Renart's *Rose* and Gerbert de Montreuil's *Violette* do), or to label it as such (as does BnF MS fr. 844), is thus to create on the part of the reader an expectation of linguistic difference and/or unintelligibility. Like the *vox inarticulata sed litterata* of medieval grammatical treatises and the lyric topos of *lati*, troubadour song is proximate enough to referential language to be transcribed using the same tools—writing—but it nevertheless resists decipherment according to normal linguistic codes.

Corpus

A few words are in order about the object of study of this book, which is less straightforward to conceptualize than it might initially seem. One might imagine that it would be easy to count the number of medieval French songbooks or other compilations that transmit Occitan song. But the number one arrives at in this count varies according to the definitions of "French"

30. See "Les amairitz, qui encolpar las vol" (PC 335.30) in Peire Cardenal (1957).

31. In both of these instances, the birds in question seem to be bilingual, capable of speaking both Old French and Middle English, respectively. As Wendy Pfeffer (1985, 134) notes, the nightingale in Guillaume's song speaks both in "bird" ("Fier, fier, oci, oci") and in Old French.

and "Occitan" used. For the sake of this study, I am defining as "French" any territory in which a dialect of *langue d'oïl* was spoken (and not just used as a literary language). This includes England, although only one songbook (Vatican City, Biblioteca Apostolica Vaticana Reg. Lat. MS. 1659) has this provenance.[32] For my purposes, then, "French" does not mean Capetian, and indeed the evidence suggests that some of the relevant manuscripts were compiled within francophone parts of the Holy Roman Empire. The picture is further complicated by the various actors involved in the compilation of a manuscript. Carol Symes (2007, 259) has recently reminded us that the scriptorium in Arras was staffed at least partially with Italian scribes, and a similarly "international" situation likely obtained in other cities. One manuscript often described as French (Copenhagen, Royal Library, Thott 1087) contains a colophon in which the scribe identifies himself as "Coscio da ceçane," a name that would suggest that the scribe—if not the manuscript itself—was in fact Italian. BnF fr. 795, at least partially from Lorraine, also has connections to Italy. Although both songbooks had previously been considered French, I have excluded them for this reason (as I discuss in greater depth below).

The question of what constitutes an "Occitan" song is equally relevant and equally problematic. First of all, the vast majority of troubadour lyric is subjected in its French transmission to a procedure of linguistic Gallicization (on which more below). On occasion, this procedure is so thorough that almost no hint of Occitan remains, but these songs have nevertheless been considered Occitan by critics, usually on the basis of attributions and their linguistic status in other songbooks (usually of Italian or Catalan provenance). Conversely, some of the songs that contain a high degree of Occitan coloring have been excluded from previous studies of Occitan song in France on the grounds that their linguistic patina is not "convincing" enough to allow the songs to pass as real Occitan (a description that assumes an underlying logic of "passing" that may not have been shared by our medieval forebears). Were strict linguistic criteria—and only linguistic criteria—applied in order to establish Occitan status, then, we would end up with a corpus that might exclude songs we know to be "genuine" troubadour compositions from other manuscript witnesses because of their strongly French veneer but also include songs with varying degrees of Occitan coloring—some quite strong—likely composed by the trouvères rather than the troubadours (on the latter corpus, see chapter 5). I have

32. On the provenance of this manuscript, see Catherine Croizy-Naquet's (2014, 188–89) edition of *L'Estoire de la guerre sainte*.

adopted the widest possible definition of "Occitan" for the purposes of this book, including both songs mostly identifiable as Occitan because of their transmission elsewhere and songs previously treated as unconvincing pastiches of Occitan by other critics.[33] Excluding certain pieces that contain Occitan coloring on the grounds that their composers were probably native speakers of French—as the Raupachs do in their study of Occitan song in France—strikes me as somewhat illogical.[34] Although the exactly analogous situation does not arise in francophone space, we consider native speakers of Italian who adopted Occitan as a poetic language—such as Sordello—to be "troubadours," so why shouldn't we do the same for those trouvères, even if the language they deploy does not conform in all respects to the Occitan of the troubadours? Despite the fact that these two bodies of work—Gallicized troubadour song and Occitanizing trouvère song—put similar pressure on the linguistic division between French and Occitan, and despite the fact that they are often transmitted in the same songbooks (sometimes right next to each other), they have never been considered to be two sides of the same coin. Moreover, in the former instance, the blurring of the linguistic divide has often been treated as a result of scribal incompetence, whereas in the latter case it is treated as authorial but "unconvincing," as if the sole plausible purpose of including linguistic coloring from another language were to create the impression of monolingualism.[35] Nevertheless, I feel compelled to state that I find both traditional terms for my core corpus ("troubadour song" and "Occitan song") to be potentially misleading in light of the findings of this book. Because troubadour song was transmitted anonymously with only four exceptions, it is difficult to imagine that it would have been widely associated with troubadours.[36] And because it was almost always transmitted in Gallicized form, it also seems rather inappropriate to describe it as "Occitan." But because formulations such as "the song elsewhere attributed to x troubadour and

33. In the latter category, I have added a few pieces to the Raupachs' list. See chapter 5.

34. For an example of such an exclusion, see the comments on "Al cor ai une alegrance" from Raupach and Raupach (1979, 51–52).

35. Robert Taylor (1993, 463) describes certain Occitanizing endings as failing to "fool" the audience. In another article, Taylor (1986, 190) refers to one of the Occitanizing pieces as "a French work in Occitan disguise." There is, in other words, an underlying assumption that the intent of the composers (or the scribes who Occitanized their material) was one of deceit and that the forms do not actually conform to standard Occitan morphology was a failure. István Frank (1954, 106), for his part, refers to "travestissement."

36. The only named troubadours in francophone transmission are Peire Vidal, Bernart de Ventadorn, Gaucelm Faidit (named in BnF fr. 844), and Folquet de Marselha (named in BnF fr. 844 and Bern 389). See table 0.1 for details.

elsewhere transmitted in a language we today call Occitan" seem unwieldy, I have resorted to the traditional nomenclature of "troubadour song" and "Occitan song." Nevertheless, I invite the reader to keep in mind that one of the main arguments of this book is that the particularities of the francophone transmission of the corpus we call troubadour song so thoroughly divorce that corpus from its identifying features (names of composers, Occitan status, etc.) that it becomes difficult to conceive of the corpus as a meaningful conceptual category.

In addition to including in my corpus songs that are slanted heavily toward French, I have included one piece that is entirely French but is nevertheless associated with the label most commonly used in conjunction with Occitan song: "son poitevin" (poitevin song). As I describe in further depth below, the song bearing this label is a French song found in BnF fr. 12786 by the trouvère Gautier d'Épinal. The label may or may not be intended to call to mind the songs of Occitania, and, consequently, the manuscript is included in this book's corpus. Table 0.1 (at the end of this chapter) outlines my corpus, showing which troubadour song was quoted in which manuscripts, and whether the song was transmitted anonymously or not. Though based on the Raupachs' similar chart, it is both broader and narrower than theirs.[37]

Like the question of what constitutes an Occitan song, the question of what songbooks qualify as francophone turns out to be a thorny one. First, recent and ongoing work on the provenance of various songbooks once thought to be "French" has complicated this picture. I have excluded two songbooks from the Raupachs' corpus for this reason. As we have already seen, the scribe of Copenhagen, Det Kongelige Bibliotek, Thott 1087 (known by the sigla *Kp* and *Y*), names himself as "Coscio de Cezane" in the colophon (Cesana being in the Piemonte region of Italy), and recent work has confirmed the Italian provenance of the codex.[38] The second manuscript in this category is BnF MS fr. 795. At least as concerns its troubadour "songbook" (in fact a series of songs transcribed on the flyleaves of the manuscript), I am

37. I have subtracted from the Raupachs' list those songs that appear only in songbooks whose French provenance seems questionable (those in *Kp* and *Y*). I have also expanded the Raupachs' corpus by considering manuscripts of Richard de Fournival's *Bestiaire d'amour*, whose quotation of troubadour song seems to have been unknown to the Raupachs. I have also added to the Raupachs' list the corpus described in chapter 5. I have also made the following emendation: as Marshall (1982, 84) noted, PC 10.45 is not clearly Gallicized.

38. The colophon is on fol. 103v. While many have read "Ceçane" as a reference to Sézanne in the Marne, I agree with Lino Leonardi that it is more likely a rendering of Cesena in Piedmont. Leonardi (2006, 885) further points to Italianisms in the scribe's *scripta*, and I would note that Coscio is not a common French baptismal name. Zufferey (1987, 281–82) also opts for Italian provenance.

of the opinion that MS fr. 795 is Italian.[39] The count of songbooks also varies depending on whether the consideration of Occitan songs is limited to those transmitting genuine troubadour song or extended to those that include only Occitanizing song, although there is considerable overlap in the two lists.

In sum, then, I have tried to be as inclusive as possible in determining what counts as an Occitan song. Unlike the Raupachs, I have included songs attributed to known troubadours in other songbooks as well as songs likely composed by francophones but with some degree of Occitan phonological coloring (however faint), as long as these songs are transmitted in songbooks or compilations compiled in francophone territories. Despite my inclusivity, I maintain a distinction between these two repertoires, although, as this book argues, the blurring between them in manuscript (where they are often in close proximity) suggests either that medieval compilers perceived no difference between the two repertoires or that they perceived a difference and chose to obfuscate it. Songs attributed to named troubadours in other songbooks, where they are usually transmitted in standard Occitan (i.e., "genuine" troubadour song), are the subject of chapter 1; the Occitanizing corpus is the topic of chapter 5.

Outline

This book begins with the material traces that constitute our main source—and the main medieval written source as well—of knowledge about troubadour song. Chapter 1, "Of Birds and Madmen: Occitan Song in French Songbooks," turns to the first set of sources to transcribe this corpus of (often semi-intelligible) troubadour song: the corpus of francophone songbooks. Although it is possible that the authors discussed in chapters 2–4 encountered troubadour song in live performance, they likely also worked with written sources, including songbooks such as those that have survived. I survey a series of assimilative gestures that obscured the linguistic and cultural alterity of Occitan song. On the other hand, I also demonstrate instances of the

39. Alfred Jeanroy (1916, 18) notes that in the "songbook" of BnF fr. 795, "l'écriture la plus récente paraît italienne." Most scholars accept István Frank's (1952a, 54) argument that, despite the Italian scribal hand used to transcribe the troubadour songs on the flyleaves of the manuscript, it cannot be Italian since the flyleaves are in fact part of the same quire as texts transcribed in a hand that is not markedly Italian. I would point out that this codicological evidence does not rule out the possibility that the manuscript was transported to Italy, where an Italian scribe copied the troubadour songs, or that an Italian scribe came to Lorraine. What is more, the *scripta* contains numerous Italianisms, such as *faglir, meglour, aichel, aychest,* and *che.* Frank, who notes the presence of these Italianisms, has no explanation for them (62).

exoticization and reframing of troubadour song as bestial. Chapter 1 (and the conclusion of this chapter below) thus document the various assimilative gestures (and the less common bestializing ones) that paved the way for the appropriation of troubadour song by the francophone authors whose works form the subjects of chapters 2–4. These chapters turn to the sole three francophone texts that quote troubadour song.

Chapter 2, "Keeping Up with the French: Jean Renart's Francophile Empire in the *Roman de la rose*," draws attention to the way in which francophone lyric and other French artistic objects—the symbolic significance of which has previously been dismissed by critics—are circulated with a peculiar frenzy by the elite of the Holy Roman Empire in Jean Renart's *Roman de la rose* (early thirteenth century). Jean thereby implies, I argue, that instead of taking an interest in the artistic traditions more native to the Empire—such as Minnesang (the German analog of troubadour and trouvère song)—the cultural elite of the Empire are infatuated with French cultural products.

Chapter 3, "Birdsong and the Edges of Empire: Gerbert de Montreuil's *Roman de la violette*," shows how, just like Jean Renart's *Roman de la Rose*, the *Roman de la violette* (ca. 1230) emphasizes the border to the east of Capetian France (the border with the Empire) rather than the border to the south (with Occitania). In the *Violette*, however, the Empire has not been conquered by the "soft power" of francophone artistic traditions. Instead, I contend, it is marked as a dangerous space—a valence conveyed in part through the territory's association with hunting birds, especially the eagle, in recognition of the most commonly deployed imperial symbol. Remapped onto francophone territories through geographical tags that move its provenance farther north, and rewritten to make it look like French, troubadour song has been transformed into part of a francophone tradition in both the *Rose* and the *Violette*. Together, chapters 2 and 3 also show that the cultural and linguistic other in both the *Rose* and the *Violette* is the Germanic Empire rather than Occitania. This suggests a greater interest on the part of thirteenth-century francophone writers in the Battle of Bouvines, which pitted Philip Augustus and his allies against the Holy Roman Emperor Otto IV and his coalition (1214), than in the Albigensian Crusade.

Chapter 4, "From Beak to Quill: Troubadour Lyric in Richard de Fournival's *Bestiaire d'amour*," shows that Richard de Fournival maintains his predecessors' association of troubadour lyric with the avian but decouples it from its association with songbirds. In the *Bestiaire* (ca. 1250), the troubadours are quoted in the passage on the hoopoe—a bird not thought of as a songster in medieval typologies. I argue that this decoupling of the bond between troubadour and avian song is indicative of a broader delyricization of Occitan lyric in the *Bestiaire.* If, as the previous three chapters show, troubadour song was elsewhere hyperlyricized—treated as a sonic event rather than a semantic one—in the *Bestiaire* the troubadours are instead inserted into a writerly genealogy, and their poetry transformed into prose.

While chapters 2–4 show how linguistically assimilated troubadour song was appropriated to various ends by three francophone authors of narrative, chapter 5, "The Rustic Troubadours: Occitanizing Lyrics in France," discusses a corpus, which I call Occitanizing lyric, that might appear to contradict my thesis regarding the assimilation of Occitan lyric in francophone space. The pieces I discuss here are generally thought to have been composed by native French speakers but made to look and sound Occitan through phonological coloring. This coloring gives the impression that Occitan is a palette that can be used within French rather than the distinct and prestigious language that it, historically, was. Although this phenomenon—which makes French pieces look more like Occitan rather than Occitan pieces look more like French—would seem to work against the francophone trend toward assimilation, I show that it occurs primarily in a lower register.[40] Thus, while the prestigious genre of the Occitan *canso* or *grand chant* came to look increasingly French, low-register forms such as the dance song and *pastourelle* came to look increasingly Occitan. While the high-register *cansos* of the troubadours have effectively been transformed into French texts (chapters 1–4), songs of a lower register are passed off as Occitan, so that French is associated with the most refined cultural productions and Occitan with those that are rustic and unsophisticated. The latter repertoire, faux-archaic Occitanizing song, served as a factitious mirage of origins.

The conclusion explores the repercussions of the unusual features of troubadour song in its French transmission (e.g., anonymity, visual assimilation, linguistic assimilation, fictitious provenance), arguing that, on the basis of French songbooks alone, we would not even have sufficient grounds to conceptualize such a thing as "troubadour song," which has been almost universally anonymized, linguistically Gallicized, transmitted with francophone lyrics, and remapped onto the border between French- and Occitan-speaking regions. With only francophone songbooks to use as sources, we would have only a cluster of (mostly) anonymous lyric, in which we would have to include the Occitanizing corpus alongside the songs we know from elsewhere to have been composed by the troubadours. We would, then, see troubadour song not as a distinct repertoire in a foreign language but

40. I use the term "register" not in the musical sense of vocal register, but rather in the sense of a stylistic hierarchy.

instead as one subset of francophone lyric. This appropriation is diametrically opposed to the reception of troubadour song elsewhere in Europe. In Italy, for example, individual troubadours were memorialized through brief biographies or *vidas*, and their songs often accompanied by lavish author portraits. In Catalonia, Occitan was the subject of numerous grammatical treatises for would-be composers. Thus, while elsewhere in Europe troubadour song was represented as a prestigious model to be emulated, in francophone territories it was instead actively transformed to bring it closer to French, rendering it invisible. Remapped to the boundary between France and Occitania, anonymized, and linguistically Gallicized, troubadour lyric became legible as francophone, culturally and linguistically, in most francophone narratives and songbooks.

Assimilating Troubadour Song: Gallicization and Remapping

I want to turn in the final section of this introduction to two of the assimilative strategies that are common to both songbooks (chapter 1) and the lyric-interpolated romances that quote the troubadours (chapters 2–4). These are Gallicization, the linguistic phenomenon already well documented by Manfred and Margret Raupach, and geographical remapping of troubadour song into either francophone or transitional regions between French- and Occitan-speaking territories.

I begin with the former. Gallicization is the term generally used to describe the set of linguistic procedures that brought the Occitan sound system closer to French in the francophone dissemination of Occitan texts.[41] It was applied to almost all Occitan texts disseminated in francophone territories. While the Raupachs, authors of the seminal study on Gallicization, estimate the rate at 80 percent, their corpus includes songs found in songbooks that are likely Italian rather than French in provenance (see chapter 1). Because these songbooks are precisely those that do *not* Gallicize their Occitan songs, the rate is in fact much higher than 80 percent. With only the later additions to BnF MS fr. 844 in standard Occitan, the rate of Gallicization is well into the 90s. Because the phenomenon has already been explored in considerable depth by the Raupachs, I will merely summarize the highlights of their findings. Among the many recurring linguistic transformations they

41. The Raupachs use the term "Französisierung" rather than "Gallisierung" or "Gallifizierung." Although the term "Gallicization" risks creating confusion because of its proximity to "Gallic" (and thus Celtic) languages, I have followed the usage of anglophone critics such as Kay (2013) and Rosenstein (1995).

have documented, the most common phonological substitution that occurs involves that of the unstressed Occitan vowel /a/ for a schwa in Old French (*membra* in Jaufre Rudel's famous "Lanquan li jorn," is, for instance, replaced in BnF MS fr. 20050 and MS fr. 844 with the form *membre*). Final N's were most often replaced with *-nt* (e.g., *commant* for Occitan *coman*), and Occitan words that served a primarily grammatical function (pronouns, articles, etc.) were most often replaced with their French equivalent. Although a certain amount of adaptation was common whenever a text traveled even within various regions of the *langue d'oïl*, such adaptation was typically avoided at the rhyme in order to preserve the rhyme scheme of the original. In the case of Gallicization, however, rhyme sounds were not exempt, leading to an obliteration of the formal structure of many Occitan songs.

And it was not just form that was obliterated. The meaning of the original texts was often obscured by a predilection for the *sound* of the original songs over their sense. The linguistic transformations just outlined were often applied to words, even when there was no discernable equivalent in French resulting from the transformation. Thus, while the Gallicizing transformation of Occitan *bela* into *bele* did in fact produce a meaningful equivalent, many other adaptations instead produce words that are totally meaningless (e.g., Old French *sane* for Occitan *sanha*, or watery meadow).[42] This is true even allowing for the relatively high degree of intercomprehensibility that characterizes romance languages, unless the reader or listener was able to back-translate into Occitan. In the Gallicized version of Daude de Pradas's "Bela m'es la votz" in Vatican, Reg. lat. 1725, the phrase "e ioys auria·m tal mestier" (and I would have such need of joy) is transcribed as "et ioi m'amor tel mestier" (and I hear [and joy?] my love such necessity). In this instance and in others, words were substituted that only vaguely reflect the sound of the original Occitan. In the example just quoted, the conditional and indirect pronoun "auria·m" is replaced with "m'amor" (my love). In another instance, the Old Occitan phrase "sivals del plazers menors" (at least, of the lesser pleasures) is replaced by the Old French "se vos deit plaire m'onors" (if my land/honor should please you) (in Peire d'Alvernha's "Del sieu tort farai esmenda" in BnF fr. 20050). Gallicization thus often falls into the category of homophonic translation—that is, translation more attentive to the sound

42. Here I part ways with critics who argue that Gallicization *facilitated* comprehension for francophones. François Zufferey (1987, 281), for example, comments that "les copistes n'ont pas hésité à franciser [ces textes] pour les rendre plus accessibles au public du Nord" ("scribes didn't hesitate to Frenchify [these texts] to make them more accessible to northern audiences"). Similarly, Fabienne Gégou (1973, 321) has declared of the Gallicized Occitan in Jean Renart's *Rose* that it had "le mérite de pouvoir être mieux comprise des lecteurs du Nord" ("the merit of being able to be better understood by northern readers"). *Pace* Zufferey and Gégou, it also impeded comprehension, as I describe above.

structure of the source than to its meaning. Indeed, some of the "translations" in Gallicized Occitan songs, like the one just cited, are as peculiar as the classic example of homophonic translation: the substitution of "Un petit d'un petit s'étonne aux Halles" for "Humpty Dumpty sat on a wall" (Bellos 2011, 32). That the transfer of meaning was not a priority is also suggested by substitutions that are only tendentiously sonically related to terms in the original Occitan. BnF MS fr. 844, for instance, gives the meaningless word *arsane* for *sanha* in Daude de Pradas's "Belha m'es la votz" (fol. 196) where the sole manuscript of Renart's *Rose* gives the equally nonsensical but more or less homophonic *sane*.[43] Taken globally, Gallicization often produced texts that sounded and looked like French but failed to make sense as French.[44] This by-product of Gallicization, which I refer to throughout this study as semantic opacity, was sometimes fairly localized, in which case the substitution does not have a significant effect on comprehension (if only one Gallicized word has no cognate in French, one can reconstruct the general meaning of a piece well enough). But often Gallicization extended to many words, leaving entire passages in a potentially quasi-indecipherable state. Moreover, this French veneer gives the impression that the text *should* make sense, in the way that an obviously foreign language would not. The texts initially convey a sense of the familiar, via their mostly French linguistic soundscape, but simultaneously offer up a kernel of resistance, in the sense that their domesticated rendering actually forecloses semantic resolution: while they appear to be French, they cannot be understood as French. Scribes and authors acknowledged this indecipherability through comparisons (sometimes direct, sometimes oblique) of troubadour lyric to birdsong (and, in the case of BnF MS fr. 844, also to the ravings of the insane).

If Gallicization did sometimes produce texts that looked thoroughly French (albeit ones that sometimes failed to make sense as French), it did not always thoroughly eradicate all traces of the Occitan language. Hybrid forms such as *auziaus* (formed from Occitan *auzels* and French *oiseaus*; see BnF fr. 20050, fol. 81v) and the verb form *egusse* (from Occitan *agues* and French *eüsse*; see BnF MS fr. 20050, fol. 82) are not uncommon (Gauchat 1893, 376). In short, Gallicization operated on a spectrum. At its most thorough, it left little indication of the original Occitan song it transformed (see, for instance,

---

43. There is only one other manuscript that transmits this song. *C*, generally thought to be of Occitan origin, gives "en la sanha" (Daude de Pradas 2016, 134).

44. This occasional breakdown of sense has also been noted by Christopher Callahan (2012, 36) and by John Marshall (1982, 92), in his review of the Raupachs' study. Marshall notes that when scribes were unable to find an etymological equivalent, they produced total misreadings or meaningless alterations, or else they substituted something that makes less sense.

the version of Pistoleta's *souhait* transmitted in BnF MS fr. 846). At the other end of the spectrum, vestiges of Occitan did remain, most often in hybrid forms, and Occitanisms were sometimes actually introduced into the text, presumably as a way of cuing the soundscape of the Occitan language (just as a profusion of nasal vowels might cue French today).[45]

The varying degrees of "Occitaneity" present in the francophone versions of troubadour songs raise the question of how we are supposed to perceive their language. Are we supposed to see them as "French," and all the remaining Occitan sounds as involuntary? The fact that scribes on occasion introduced rather than eliminated Occitan phonology (by analogy or according to a different logic) suggests that this is not always the case. Are they intended to produce a fictional veneer of "Occitaneity"—that is, to signal a linguistic divide, all the while rendering the texts comprehensible for francophones? Such an effect would be akin to the use of nasal vowels evoked above, or, as David Bellos (2011, 42) describes, to the Hollywood films set during World War II in which German officers speak perfect English except for the occasional "jawohl" or "Gott in Himmel."[46] Although this is possible in instances where Occitan phonology has been maintained or even introduced, it seems quite unlikely in cases where scribes have eliminated almost all Occitan phonology, even in instances where comprehension could hardly have been difficult (e.g., *bele* for *belha*). Alternatively, one could argue that the very breakdown in sense potentially engendered by Gallicization, combined with the occasional Occitanism, aligns with a long-standing strategy for representing linguistic difference: the fusion of gobbledygook with just enough linguistic coloring to signal alterity. This is the strategy used, for instance, in Adriano Celentano's "Prisencolinensinainciusol," in which a professor teaches his class that one does not need to understand any English in order to talk in a language that sounds just like it (Bellos 2011, 43). Similarly, in the Flight of the Conchords' "Foux du fa," a farrago of French 101 vocabulary and nasal vowels magically conjures up a chic Parisian universe. In these scenarios, however, the gobbledygook is in the phonology of the foreign language, whereas in Gallicization the nonsensical passages read

45. In many cases, scribes seem to have overcorrected by analogy. For instance, since Occitan often has an L where Old French has a U (e.g., *altre*), some scribes insert L's where they do not make sense etymologically, e.g., *ioiols* (BnF fr. 20050, fol. 90v) (Gauchat 1893, 377). Similarly, forms such as *aber* are clearly modeled on transpositions of the type seen in Old French *saveir* / Old Occitan *saber*.

46. Many critics have opted for the theory of a veneer of Occitaneity, described by some as an "aura" and by others as a "perfume." Fabienne Gégou (1973, 321) argues that Gallicization left behind a "parfum du Midi." Christopher Callahan (2012, 38) similarly claims that the language represents the efforts of French scribes "to capture the aura of that initiation of the north into the poetry of the more civilized south."

like French rather than like Occitan. This suggests that evoking Occitan was not—or at least not always—the goal. Moreover, unlike these film scenarios, the various framings of troubadour songs in francophone narrative contexts do not suggest a desire to evoke cultural or linguistic alterity: no character in the lyric-interpolated romances ever remarks on their linguistic strangeness, even in close proximity to such metalinguistic commentary concerning other languages.[47] The only clue we are given as to how to interpret them comes in the occasional geographic label such as "and then she heard begin this song from Auvergne" (si oï ele conmencier / iceste chançon auvrignace) (Jean Renart 2008, vv. 4648–49). As we will see in greater depth below, these labels most often take the form of *son x*, where *x* is an adjective designating either a francophone territory or a transitional territory between French- and Occitan-speaking regions. On the whole, then, French compilers and scribes invite us via these labels to view the songs they accompany not as having an Occitan provenance but instead as emanating either from francophone territories or from linguistic border territories. However, such labels are rare, and, in their absence, it is unclear whether the faint trace of Occitan that remained in most Gallicized texts was perceived as the trace of a foreign language or instead as a marking of lyricism. For instance, Dante routinely used the Sicilian form *core* for "heart" in the verse sections of the *Vita nuova* and *Convivio* but the Tuscan form *cuore* in the prose (Usher 1997, 11). It is doubtful that the form *core* was designed to cue an aura of Sicilian. Instead, only Sicilian's association with poetry was maintained, and a similar case could be made for the "poeticity" of Old Occitan.

As this analogy to Italian vernaculars makes apparent, Gallicization was not the only interesting case of contact between medieval vernaculars. Indeed, the mirror image of the corpus I have described thus far, which is to say *French* songs as transmitted in *Occitan*-speaking territories, were subjected to similar linguistic transformations (Ineichen 1969). Quotations of French songs appear in a corpus that is analogous to the corpus outlined in *Stolen Song*: in primarily Occitan songbooks, as well as in narrative texts (Matfre Ermengaud de Béziers's *Breviairi d'amor*, the *Leys d'amors*, and Raimon Vidal's "En aquel temps").[48] Like the Raupachs, Ineichen stresses that this transformation should not be seen as the result of incompetence on the part of scribes. Rather than being haphazard, and like Gallicization, the *scripta*

47. Such comments about linguistic difference appear in relation to Germanic languages in Jean Renart's *Rose* but not in relation to the Occitan quotations in the text. This observation appeared in my doctoral dissertation (Zingesser 2012, 53). See also Kay (2013, 103).

48. Samuel Rosenberg (1998, 2005) has surveyed the presence of French songs in primarily Occitan songbooks.

in which French songs were rendered was governed by its own conventions (Ineichen 1969, 212–18). There are three major differences between Gallicization and what we might call Occitanization, however, and both are germane to the main arguments of *Stolen Song*. First, the "Occitanization" of French songs was much less systematic than the Gallicization of Occitan songs, which, as we have seen, occurs in nearly all francophone sources (only the later additions to BnF MS fr. 844 are not Gallicized, and some may in fact have been composed by francophones in Occitan). As Ineichen (1969, 207–12) has pointed out, the better manuscripts of Matfre's *Breviari* preserve the Occitan of their quotations, suggesting that Occitanization was more often scribal than authorial. The same is true of the better manuscripts of Raimon Vidal's "En aquel temps," which preserve their French quotation without significant linguistic transformation (Kay 2011, 474–75). By contrast, we know, at least in one instance, that the Gallicized version of an Occitan song was—if not authorial in origin—at least sanctioned by its author: in Jean Renart's *Rose*, one Gallicized Occitan song is made to rhyme with the surrounding line of narrative.[49] This suggests either that Jean Gallicized the song himself or else had a Gallicized version on hand. The takeaway here is that Gallicization occurs in a much broader qualitative spread of manuscripts than the "Occitanization" of French songs. A second major difference between Gallicization and Occitanization is the scale of the respective phenomena. While some hundred Occitan songs are Gallicized in francophone transmission, many fewer French songs were transmitted in Occitan sources overall. Rosenberg (1998, 24) counts only twenty-seven French pieces in Occitan songbooks. Finally, the narrative framings of French songs in Occitan sources *do* often acknowledge their foreign provenance. Matfre's *Breviari* attributes its French pieces to Thibaut de Champagne (Kay 2011, 472). Although in some instances this attribution is erroneous, it still suggests a desire to mark trouvère song as foreign, and also as the product of a named author (both traits, by contrast, are absent in the francophone dissemination of Occitan song). Similarly, in Raimon Vidal's short story "En aquel temps," the French quotation, though anonymous, is nevertheless still flagged as French.[50]

A phenomenon somewhat analogous to Occitanization and Gallicization occurred between vernaculars on the Italian peninsula, and especially

49. Jean creates a narrative rhyme pair with the Gallicized form *sane* at the end of Daude de Pradas's "Bela m'es la votz autana" (vv. 4659–60).

50. "Anc non auzis ni aprezes / So que dis us Franses d'amor? /" '*Cosselhetz mi, senhor*' (have you never heard or learned what a Frenchman says about love? '*Advise me, Lord*') (Raimon Vidal de Besalú 1989, vv. 666–68), asks one character. The quoted piece is a *jeu-parti* catalogued as RS 2014. RS numbers refer to Raynaud and Spanke's catalog of Old French lyric (Spanke 1955).

between Sicilian and Tuscan. Tuscan scribes routinely adapted Sicilian poetry to the Tuscan language, sometimes producing changes in the rhyme scheme of the originals. So powerful was the prestige of Sicilian as a poetic language that precisely the forms allowed in the Tuscan adaptations of Sicilian became naturalized in Tuscan. Tuscan poets, for instance, began to rhyme open with closed vowels—a situation that initially arose because of incompatibility between the single forms of certain Sicilian vowels (*e* and *o*) and the open and closed forms of those same vowels in Tuscan (Usher 1997, 10). This phenomenon is commonly known as Sicilian rhyme. The prestige of Sicilian also led to the deployment of Sicilian forms in otherwise Tuscan verse. As we saw above, Dante used the form *core* for heart in the verse sections of the *Vita nuova* and *Convivio* but the Tuscan form *cuore* in the prose (11). Gallicization and Occitanization show the same permeability between vernaculars as do Tuscanization and Sicilianization, and, like Sicilian forms, Occitan phonology must have conveyed a certain "poeticity" in French. Despite these convergences, however, there are significant differences. For the purposes of this book, the most apposite is that the Tuscanization of Sicilian did *not* compromise the intelligibility of the poetry involved. Only authentic Sicilianisms were allowed in "translated" Tuscan versions (11), unlike the situation that obtained in the francophone transmission of Occitan, which saw the creation of hybrid forms and many inauthentic forms.

The above phenomena (and in particular Gallicization) have often been lumped into the broader category of bilingualism. Paul Zumthor (1960, 592), for instance, mentions the procedure of Gallicization (along with Occitanizing French songs) in his seminal article on bilingualism, although both are peripheral to the other types of bilingualism he describes. The limited space he devotes to the two topics seems to correspond to his opinion of their aesthetic significance, which he describes as being "d'intérêt . . . médiocre." And Christopher Callahan (2012, 38), for his part, refers to the phenomenon as "motley bilingualism." This descriptor strikes me as somewhat misleading given how strongly the pieces themselves invite us to view their language as unified. For example, rarely in the corpus is the use of Occitanization or Gallicization confined to the speech of a single character. Even in cases of dialogue poems, linguistic traits specific to French or Occitan are (almost) never deployed exclusively in the speech of one character or another.[51] Rather, the traits infuse the entire text of the song, direct speech and narration alike.

51. The only exception to this is one manuscript witness of the *pastourelle* "L'autrier m'iere levaz," in which Occitanizing traits appear only in the speech of the shepherdess and the narrator but not in that of the interloping knight. On this piece, see chapter 5.

Moreover, formal divisions are not used to shore up the boundaries of languages. Unlike in Raimbaut de Vaqueiras's famous descort, "Eras quan vey verdeyar" (PC 392.4), which cycles through romance languages first on the level of the stanza and then on the level of individual lines, the structures of Gallicized Occitan songs and Occitanizing French songs are never used to delimit the two constitutive languages in question. Although there are, in fact, songs that combine French and Occitan in such a way as to make coterminous formal structure and linguistic division, they are not extant in French transmission.[52] This is decidedly not the case for both Gallicized Occitan songs and Occitanizing French songs, both of which combine these languages in such a way as to mitigate their difference, using one as a kind of coloring within the other. In short, I do not view the term "bilingual" as appropriate in this scenario, given that the effect is one of fusion rather than juxtaposition. The notion of linguistic "hybridity" may be more appropriate, depending on which definition of hybridity one invokes.[53]

Another term that often appears in discussion of Gallicization is that of "translation." Sarah Kay (2013, 11), for instance, describes the process as one of the "translation of Occitan lyrics into [. . .] French." Gallicization is certainly not translation in its colloquial modern sense of the transposition of meaning from one language into another. As we have seen, semantic meaning seems not to have been a priority for francophone scribes and compilers. I used the term "sound translation" above, and this seems like a more apt description on the whole. As David Bellos (2011, 33) puts it with wit, however, sound translation is more or less the opposite of translation as it is habitually understood: "From a conventional point of view the probably universal device of repeating with approximation what you do not properly understand is the opposite of translation—which is to say something else in the place of what you do understand." One could, of course, try to preserve some combination of both sound and meaning. This is precisely the type of translation advocated by Clive Scott (2012, 18), who suggests we put homophonic translation at the center of translation theory and practice. Scott's

52. There is a *cobla* exchange between Raimbaut de Vaqueiras and Conon de Béthune that deploys the two languages separately (PC 392.29) (Harvey and Paterson 2010, 1086–90). Raimbaut de Vaqueiras's descort includes French and Occitan, alongside Italian, Gascon, and Gallego-Portuguese.

53. There are some analogous situations of linguistic hybridity. In addition to the phenomenon of Occitanized francophone lyric, a kind of scribal hybridity akin to Gallicization, there are also instances of authorial hybridity, akin to the Occitanizing corpus described in chapter 5. The most famous of these is "Franco-Italian" and also the Gallicizing Occitan used in some epics (McCormick 2011; Gaunt 2002). I take Gaunt's (2013, 86) point that one risk of the term "hybridity" is that "the categories that are supposedly mixed are presupposed, often unquestioned, and thereby to some extent reified."

phenomenological approach to translation seeks to capture not meaning but instead one's own "listening" to a text with the perceptions and sensations that encounter entails (18, 20). I argue in chapter 2 that Jean Renart suggests just such a phenomenological encounter in order to explain the opacity of his Gallicized source texts. Elsewhere, however, it seems doubtful that the opacity of Gallicized songs was intended to preserve a kernel of foreignness. As described above, no suggestion of cultural alterity (in the way of metalinguistic commentary, for instance) accompanies the songs, and they are almost always transmitted anonymously. Indeed, Gallicization is only one aspect of a broader trend toward domestication in the francophone transmission of troubadour song. I use this term as it is used in recent work in translation theory, such as that of Antoine Berman and Lawrence Venuti, where it alludes to the adaptation of a foreign linguistic object to the norms and expectations of the target culture. A domesticating translation, also called an "ethnocentric" one, sees the highest accomplishment of translation as the appropriation and naturalization of the foreign.[54] This is somewhat paradoxical, because Gallicization would seem, at first glance, to conform to precisely the type of nondomesticating translation *advocated* by Berman and Venuti: one that preserves a trace of the foreign rather than eradicating it. Berman and Venuti have called for a type of translation that seeks to defamiliarize, one that acknowledges the foreign object on which it is based. For Berman (1999, 15), this means embedding in the translation something of the cultural and linguistic alterity of the original. Similarly, Lawrence Venuti, inspired by Deleuze and Guattari, has called for "minoritizing translation," in which the major language is subjected to "constant variation, forcing it to become minor, delegitimizing, deterritorializing." This involves the release of a "remainder" that resists assimilation, making the target language "foreign to itself" (Venuti 1998, 10). In the sense that Gallicization does indeed often make French foreign for *oïl* readers—through words that sound like French but fail to signify as French—it does preserve a kernel of the foreign. And yet it is debatable whether it does this out of an impulse to respect the integrity and identity of Occitan as a foreign language and culture. Gallicized versions of Occitan song are rarely flagged in any way as foreign in origin, and the occasional geographical label that does accompany them situates them not in Occitania but instead farther north, either within or on the edge

54. A good example of this goal is formulated by the eighteenth-century poet Colardeau, as quoted by Berman (1999, 30): "S'il y a quelque mérite à traduire, ce ne peut être que de perfectionner, s'il est possible, son original, de l'embellir, de se l'approprier, de lui donner un air national et de naturaliser, en quelque sorte, cette plante étrangère."

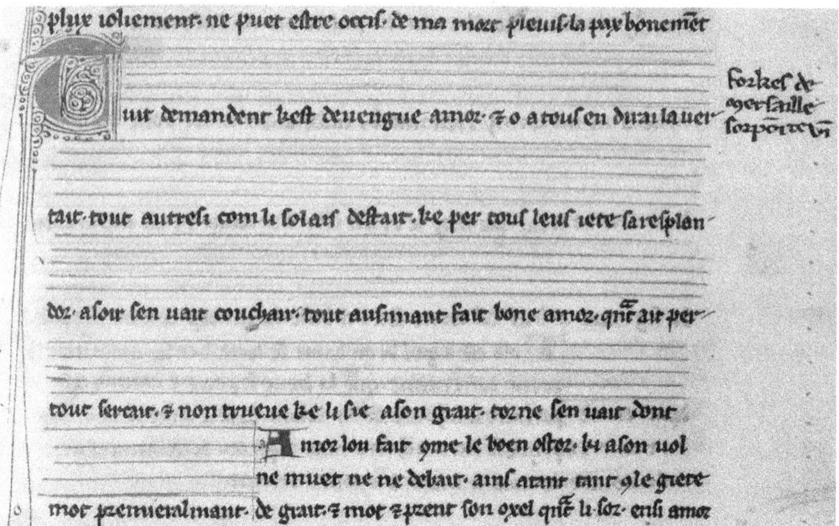

FIGURE 0.1 French-language "Tuit demandent k'est devengue amor" labeled as a "sor [*sic*] poitevin" in the margin of Burgerbibliothek Bern, Cod. 389, fol. 234r. Reproduced with kind permission of the Bern Burgerbibliothek.

of *oïl* territory. They are, moreover, anonymized and transmitted most often in the midst of francophone lyric, both gestures that facilitate a view of these texts *as French*, albeit of a sometimes garbled variety.

These geographic labels are the second assimilative gesture relevant to both the songbooks (chapter 1) and the francophone narratives that transmit troubadour song (chapters 2–4). In the sole songbook that includes such a label, it takes the form of a rubric, as shown in figure 0.1.

In the narratives, the labels are framed as commentary on the part of the narrator of the sort: "and then X began to sing a *son* [geographic adjective]." Table 0.2, at the end of this chapter, is organized according to the approximate chronology of the texts or songbooks, and outlines the labels and the songs they accompany. All of these labels ("poitevin," "gasconois," "limosin," "auvrignace," and "provençal"), with the exception of the last, draw troubadour song into either francophone territory or the linguistic borderlands between *langue d'oïl* and *langue d'oc*.[55] All are applied to songs that

55. R. Anthony Lodge (1993) describes both Poitou and Auvergne as transitional linguistic spaces. On Poitou: "There is indeed a significant blurring of the boundaries between the *langue d'oc* and the *langue d'oïl*. It is widely accepted that during the Middle Ages there existed a mixed transitional zone between Oc and Oïl in Poitou" (75, 77). And on Auvergne: "The dialects of north Aquitania (Limousin and Auvergnat) merge into a broad band of transitional Gallo-Romance varieties known as the 'Croissant' and sharing a number of features with northern French dialects—as one would expect in a situation of dialect continuum" (68).

are, as far as one can tell, *cansos* or *grands chants courtois,* the form most common in the francophone transmission of the troubadours (see chapter 1). The labels span the twelfth century through the fourteenth.[56] What is most striking in this data is the collapse of geography onto Poitou by the second half of the thirteenth century. After this date, territories outside of Poitou are not mentioned. Assuming that all of these labels do refer to Occitan lyric, even those not accompanied by an actual Occitan song, this suggests a remapping on the part of French scribes and authors not just onto border territories between the *langue d'oïl* and the *langue d'oc* but onto Poitou specifically. Poitou is generally considered part of *langue d'oïl* space, although some would put it in an area of interference between the two languages. Although it happens to not be accurate in any of the instances noted above, in the sense that no troubadour whose song is marked as such hailed from Poitou, Poitou was indeed the birthplace of troubadour poetry, and a high number of songs in the late twelfth and early thirteenth centuries came from this region (Paden 2005, 163). The label "poitevin" may thus represent an association of all Occitan songs with the area from which the tradition initially emerged. What is remarkable, however, is the way in which the label seems to have lost its precision over the centuries. Initially applied to songs from the Limousin (Bernart of Ventadorn), just south of Poitou, the label was by the mid-thirteenth century applied to a song that is attributed, right next to the label indicating poitevin provenance, to Folquet de Marselha. Marseille, on the southern coast of France, is at an extreme geographical remove from Poitou. What is more, the label is even applied to a French piece by Gautier d'Épinal (figure 0.2).

All of these labels frame troubadour song as an art form emanating from regions either just north of or on the border between French- and Occitan-speaking territories. As indicated above, this is accurate for some early troubadour song but largely inaccurate for troubadours contemporary with Jean Renart, Gerbert de Montreuil, and Richard de Fournival. From 1220 onward, the main centers for troubadour song were Provence, Languedoc, and Catalonia (Paden 2005, 163). To identify troubadour song with linguistic border territories, and specifically with Poitou, aside from being inaccurate,

56. Paul Meyer was the first to remark on the association between the label "poitevin" and Occitan songs. Meyer (1884, 21) also notes that the label was applied to the works of troubadours from much farther south than Poitou. Even the label *son*, without a geographic qualifier, has been seen as connoting Occitan provenance (Page 1987, 30). I am not wholly convinced by this theory given the high number of songs described as *sons* in the *pastourelle*. These are often quoted and have nothing Occitan about them. Francesco Carapezza (2012) has recently suggested that the label has more to do with form (being associated with the *oda continua*, a form more common in the troubadour repertory) than with language. It remains that Occitan song is remapped onto border territories.

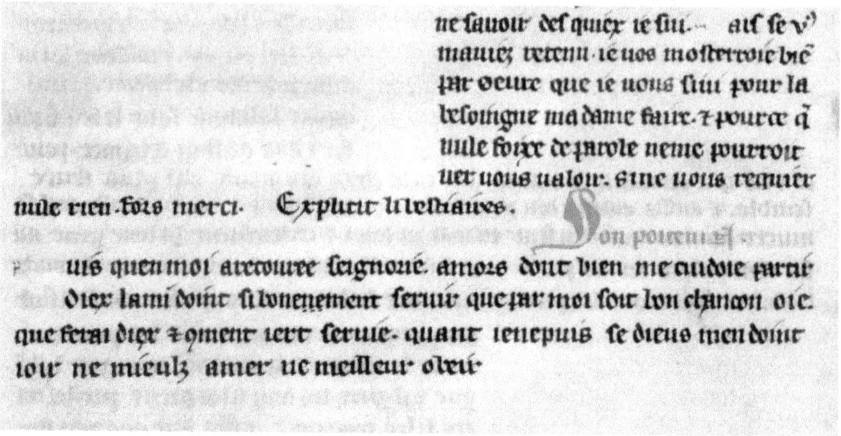

Figure 0.2 Gautier d'Épinal's "Puis qu'en moi" (RS 1208) labeled as a "son poitevin" in BnF fr. 12786, fol. 42v.

dismantles the tradition of troubadour song. Instead of framing the repertoire as a single corpus originating in Occitania, scribes and compilers imagine some (but not all!) troubadour songs as coming from a series of linguistic borderlands. Having progressively lost its regional specificity, the term lost its Occitan connotations entirely, as its application to a francophone piece suggests (figure 0.2). Rather than accurately depicting the spatial divide between themselves and the troubadour songs they quote, then, thirteenth-century authors instead fictitiously positioned these pieces further north in linguistic territories closer to their own.

Table 0.1 Quotations of Occitan and Occitanizing lyrics in songbooks and narratives from francophone territories

	TROUBADOUR	PC	GALLICIZED (G) / OCCITANIZING (O) / ? = OF UNCLEAR PROVENANCE	INCIPIT	LABEL / ATTRIBUTION	SONGBOOKS	ROSE	VIOLETTE	BESTIAIRE	GENRE
1	Aimeric de Peguilhan	10.45	G	Qui la vi, en ditz	Anon.	*W 185* I–II with two added stanzas (Aimeric de Peguilhan 1950, 214)				canso
2	Albertet de Sestaro	16.5	G	A! mi no fai chantar foilla ni flors	Anon.	*W 204* I				canso
3		16.9 / 461.107	G	Destregz d'amor veing denan vos	Modern hand in W: Bernars de Ventadour	*W 192* II			IV, vv. 28–29	canso
					"Li Poitevins"	IV (4-5). See table 4.2.			See also manuscripts of the *Bestiaire d'amour* (chapter 4)	
4		16.14	G	En mon cor ai un'aital encobida	Anon.	*W 203* I				canso
5		16.17a	G	Mos coratges m'es camjatz	Anon.	*X 91* I–III, V				canso
6	Beatriz de Dia	46.2	G	A chantar m'er de so qu'eu no volria	Anon.	*W 204* I				canso
7	Bernart de Ventadorn	70.1	G	Ab joi mou lo vers e·l comens	Anon. in *W*; "son poitevin" in fr. 1553	*W 202* I *X* I, VI, IV, III		fr. 1553 289v IV		canso
8		70.2 / 323.4	G	Amics Bernartz de Ventadorn	Peire Vidal	*W 190* I–II				tenso
9		70.7	G	Ara no vei luzir soleill	Peire Vidal	*W 190* I–V, VII				canso
10		70.10	G	Bel m'es qu'eu chant en aquel mes	Bernart de Ventadorn (table of contents)	*W table of contents*, II				canso
11		70.12	G	Be m'an perdut lai enves Ventadorn	Peire Vidal	*W table of contents*				canso
12		70.13	G	Be·m cugei de chantar sofrir	Bernart de Ventadorn	*W table of contents*				canso

(*Continued*)

Table 0.1 (Continued)

	TROU-BADOUR	PC	GALLICIZED (G) / OCCITANI-ZING (O) / ? = OF UNCLEAR PROVENANCE	INCIPIT	LABEL / ATTRIBUTION	SONGBOOKS	ROSE	VIOLETTE	BESTIAIRE	GENRE
13		70.19	G	Estat ai com hom esperdutz	Anon. (modern hand: Bernars de Ventadour)	*W 195* V–VI, IV				canso
14		70.23	G	La doussa votz ai ausida	Anon.	*X 89* I–III				canso
15		70.24	G	Lanquan foillon bosc e garric	Anon.	*W 202* I				canso
16		70.29	G	Lo rossignols s'esbaudeja	unclear	*W table of contents*				canso
17		70.31	G	Non es meravilla s'eu chan	unclear in table of contents; Bernart de Ventadorn in modern hand on 191	*W 191* I–II, V–VI, III, VII				canso
18		70.33	G	Pel dous chan que·l ros-signols fai	unclear	*W table of contents*				canso
19		70.41	G	Quan per la flors josta·l vert foill	Folq[ue]s de Marselle	*W 188* I, III, VI, II / IV, IV / II				canso
20		70.42	G	Quan vei la flor, l'erba e la foilla	Anon. "Un Poitevin"	*X 88* I–III III (3, 6). See table 4.2			See also transmission in manuscripts of the *Besti-are d'amour* (chapter 4)	canso
21		70.43	G	Quan vei la lauzeta mover	W Pieres Vidaus X Anon *Rose* "son poitevin" *Violette* fr. 1374 "son provençal" *Violette* fr. 1553 "son poitevin"	*W 190* I, II (1–6) *X 148* I–II	*Vatican Reg. lat. 1725 96* I–II	*fr. 1553 311v* I *fr. 1374 158r* I		canso
22		70.45	G	Tuit cil que·m pregon qu'eu chan	unclear	*W 191* I (5–7), III, II, IV–V				canso
23	Blacasset	96.2		Be volgra que venques merces	Anon.	*W 78* I				canso

24	Daude de Pradas	124.5	G	Bela m'es la votz autana	Anon. in W; "chançon auvrignace" in *Rose*	*W 196* I, IV	*Vatican Reg. lat. 1725* *93* I	canso
25	Elias Fonsalada	134.1	G	De bo loc movon mas chansos	Anon.	*W 198* I, III, II, V, IV, ?, VI with modifications		canso
26	Folquet de Marselha	155.8	G	En chantan n'aven a membrar	Folquet de Marseilla in W Table of contents	*W 189* II–III+PC 461.169a, tacked onto PC 155.8		canso
27		155.10	G	Greu feira nuls hom faillensa	Anon.	*W 200* II		canso
28		155.21 / 461.208	G	Si tot me sui a tart apercebutz	Folquet de Marseilla (W table of contents)	*W 188* I (3–8), II, V, III		canso
29		155.22	G	Tan m'abelis l'amoros pensamen	Fouq[ue]s de Marselle	*W 188* I (1–4), III (4–8)		canso
30		155.23	G	Tan mou de corteza razo	Fouq[ue]s de Marselle	*W 188* I–II, V, III (III and V very garbled)		canso
31	Gaucelm Faidit	167.15	G	Chant e deport, joi, domnei e solatz	Anon.	*X 85* I–II		canso
32		167.22	G	Fortz cauza es que tot lo major dan	*W* ? (hole) *X* anon. *η* anon	*W 191* I–II, IV/III *X 87* I–V *η* 89v–90r I–II		*planh*
33		167.30	G	Jamais nul temps no·m pot re far amors	Anon.	*W 200* I–II		canso
34		167.32	G	Lo gens cors onratz	Anon.	*X 90* I–III, VI		canso
35		167.37	G	Mon cor e mi e mas bonas chansos	Anon.	*X 84* I–III		canso
36		167.43	G	No·m alegra chans ni critz	Anon.	*W 202* I		canso
37		167.52	G	Si anc nuls hom per aver fi coratge	Anon.	*X 86* I–III		canso
38		167.53	G	Si tot m'ai tarzat mon chan	Anon.	*X 86* I–III		canso

(*Continued*)

Table 0.1 (Continued)

	TROU-BADOUR	PC	GALLICIZED (G) / OCCITANI-ZING (O) / ? = OF UNCLEAR PROVENANCE	INCIPIT	LABEL / ATTRIBUTION	SONGBOOKS	ROSE	VIOLETTE	BESTIAIRE	GENRE
39		167.56	G	S'om pogues partir son voler	Anon.	*X 89* I–IV, VI				canso
40	Gui d'Uisel	194.7	G	Estat aurai de chantar	Anon.	*W 198* IV				canso
41		194.8	G	Ges de chantar no·m faill cors ni razos	Anon.	*W 196* I				canso
42	Guillem Augier Novella	205.5		Ses alegratge	Anon.	*W 186* I–XI				descort
43	Guillem Magret	223.1	G	Aiga poja contra mon	Anon.	*W 201* I				sirventes
44		223.3	G	Enaissi·m pren com fai al pescador	Anon.	*W 192* I–II			III (10) - *Paris, BnF, MS fr. 25566 95v* - *Paris, BnF, MS fr. 12786 41r* - *Paris, BnF, MS fr. 1444 268v* - *Dijon, Bibliothèque municipale MS 526 29v* - *Arras, Bibliothèque municipale, MS 139 (anc. 657) 113r* - *New York, Pierpont Morgan Library MS 459 19r* - *Oxford, Bodleain Library Douce 308 103v* - *Florence, Biblioteca Mediceo-Laurenziana, Plut. LXXVI, 79 23v*	canso

									- Florence, Biblioteca Mediceo-Laurenziana, Cod. Ashburnhamiani, Fondo Libri 50 4v *- Vienna, Österreichische Nationalbibliothek MS 2609 29v* *- Milan, Biblioteca Ambrosiana l. 78 sup. 140v*	
45	Guiraut d'Espaigna	244.1a			Be volgra, s'esser pogues	Anon.	*W 186* I–VII			dance
46	Jaufre Rudel	262.2	G		Lanquan li jorn	W Gaucelm Faidit X Anon. "cest son" in *Rose*	*W 189* I–III, V (1–2)/IV (4–7) + two added lines *X 81* I, III, V/II, II/V	*Vatican Reg. lat. 1725* I 75		canso
47		262.5	G		Quan lo rius de la fontana	Anon.	*X 149* I–II *ζ 115* I–II, ζ's III has only one Occitan analog, IV = III, V unique to this manuscript			canso
48	Jordan Bonel de Cofolen	273.1	G		S'ira d'amor tengues amic jauzen	Anon.	*W 201* IV/I *X 149* IV/I			canso
49	Marcabru	293.13	G		Bel m'es quan son li frug madur	Anon.	*W 203* I			canso
50		293.35	G		Pax! in nomine Domini	Anon.	*W 194* I–II			crusade song
---	Peire d'Alvernha	323.4 (see 70.2)	G		Amics Bernartz de Ventadorn	Pieres Vidaus	*W 190* I–II			tenso
51		323.15	G		Dejosta·ls breus jorns e·ls loncs sers	Anon.	*X 86* I–III, VII			canso

(Continued)

Table 0.1 (Continued)

	TROUBADOUR	PC	GALLICIZED (G) / OCCITANIZING (O) / ? = OF UNCLEAR PROVENANCE	INCIPIT	LABEL / ATTRIBUTION	SONGBOOKS	ROSE	VIOLETTE	BESTIAIRE	GENRE
52	Peire Vidal	364.4	G	Anc no mori per amor ni per al	Anon.	*X 85* I–II, VI, III–IV				canso
53		364.11	G	Be·m pac d'ivern et d'estiu	Anon.	*X 87* I, IV, III, II, VII				canso
54		364.39	G	Quant hom es en autrui poder	Anon.	*W 204* I				canso
55		364.40	G	Quant hom onratz torna en gran paubreira	Anon.	*W 197* IV (2–7)				canso
56		364.49	G	Tart mi veiran mei amic en Tolza	Anon.	*W 197* I, IV				canso
57	Peirol	366.2	G	Atressi co·l cignes fai	Anon.	*W 197* I				canso
58		366.12	G	Del seu tort farai esmenda	Anon.	*X 88* I–II, IV, III, VI–VII				canso
59	Perdigo	370.14	G	Trop ai estat mon Bon Esper no vi	Anon.	*X 89* I-II, IV				canso
60	Pistoleta	372.3	G	Ar agues eu mil marcs de fin argen	Anon.	*X 82* I–III, (II) *fr. 846 125* I (12) (13) *fr. 12581 88* (18) I–II Douce 308 (19) (14) (15), I, (18) *Montpellier Sec Med. 236, 122* (14), (15), (16), (17), I, (18), II, (19)				souhait
61	Pons de Capdoill	375.14	G	Lejals amics cui amors te jojos	W Anon	*W 202* I				canso
62		375.27	G	Un gais conortz me fai gajamen far	Anon.	*X 90* I–III				canso

63	Raimbaut d'Aurenga	389.36	G	Pos tals sabers mi sors e·m creis	Anon.	*X 88* I–II	canso
64	Raimon Jordan	404.4	G	Lo clar temps vei brunezir	Anon.	*W 192* I	canso
65		404.11	G	Vas vos soplei, domna, premeiramen	Anon.	*W 194* I, V, II–IV	canso
66	Richard de Berbezilh	421.1	G	Atressi cum lo leos	Anon.	*W 195* I	canso
67		421.2	G	Atressi cum l'orifans	Anon.	*W 195* I–II *X 84* I–V *ζ 238* I–IV	canso
68		421.3	G	Atressi cum Persavaus	Anon.	*W 197* I, V *X 85* I, V	canso
69		421.5	G	Be volria saber d'amor	Anon.	*W 194* IV, I	canso
70		421.6	G	Lo nous mes d'abril comensa	Gaucelm Faidit in W Table of contents	*W 189* I–II, III/IV, IV/III, V	canso
71		421.10	G	Tuit demandon qu'es devengu d'amors	Anon. W and X ζ Folquet de Marseilla	*W 200* I *X 150* I–II, IV, III *ζ 234* I–IV	canso
72	Anon.	461.9	G	Aissi com eu sab triar	Anon.	*W 196* I	canso
73		461.12	O	A l'entrade del tens clar - eya	Anon.	*X 82* 5 stanzas	dance song
74		461.13	O?	A l'entrada del tans florit	Anon.	*W 191*, 6 stanzas	canso
75		461.17		Amors, dousors mi assaja	Anon.	*W 199*, 49 verses	descort
76		461.20a		Amors m'art con fuoc ab flama	Anon.	*W 187*, 12 lines	dance

(Continued)

Table 0.1 (Continued)

	TROU-BADOUR	PC	GALLICIZED (G) / OCCITANI-ZING (O) / ? = OF UNCLEAR PROVENANCE	INCIPIT	LABEL / ATTRIBUTION	SONGBOOKS	ROSE	VIOLETTE	BESTIAIRE	GENRE
77		461.35a	G	Belle done, a l'aide de vos	Anon.	*X 149* I				canso
78		461.37		Bella domna cara	Anon.	*W 117*, 74 lines				descort/ acort
79		461.41	G	Bel m'es que chant, quan vei del fau	Anon.	*W 198*, I stanza				canso
---		461.67a		Sill qu'es caps e guitz	Anon.	W 185 2 stanzas tacked onto PC10.45				tacked onto canso
80		461.92		Domna, pos vos ay chausida	Anon.	*W I*, 12 lines				dance
81		461.100	G	D'un deduit	Anon.	*W 193*, 5 lines				canso?
82		461.102	G	Eissamen com la pantera	Anon.	*W 199*, two stanzas				canso
83		461.103a	O?	En aquel temps que vezem verdezir	Anon.			*fr. 1374, 134v–135r* I *Morgan MS 36, 7r* I		canso
84		461.122	O	Finament	Lai Nonpar	*W* 163 lines *BnF fr. 12615* 163 lines				lai
85		461.124	O	Gent me nais	Lai Markiol	*W* 205 lines *BnF fr. 12615* 203 lines				lai
86		461.146	O	L'autrier cuidai aber druda	Anon.	*W 199*, two stanzas				salacious
87		461.148	O	L'altrier m'iere levatz	Anon.	BnF fr. 20050 91v and Bern 389 138v				pastorela
88	see 461.240a	461.148a	O	Li jalous per tout sunt fustat	Anon.	see 461.240a				dance

89	461.150	G	Lo dous chans que l'auzels crida	Anon.	*W 203*, I	genre unclear but includes shepherds
90	461.152	G	Lo premer jor que vi	Anon.	*W 201*, I	canso
---	461.169a (see 155.8)	G	Mout fosson doz mei cossirier	Anon.	*W 189*, 4 lines	lines added to a canso
91	461.170a	O in one source	Molt m'abellist l'amoros pensamen	Anon.	*Montpellier, Bibliothèque Inter-Universitaire, Section Médecine, H196 151* (no Occitan coloring), *Chansonnier de Noailles 181* (with Occitan coloring)	*Onques motet*
92	461.170c	n/a	Molt m'es bel e clar	Anon.	W table of contents	
93	461.192	O	Per vous m'esjau	Anon.	*fr. 24406 151, 5* stanzas	Marian song
94	461.196		Pos qu'ieu vey la fuella	Anon.	*W I,* 12 lines	canso? dance?
95	461.197	G	Pos vezem que l'iverns s'irais	"li sons derues del home sauuage"	*W 190*, 6 stanzas	canso
96	461.206	G	Quan vei les praz verdesir	Anon.	*W 198* 5 stanzas + tornada	song from woman's perspective (canso)

(Continued)

Table 0.1 (Continued)

	TROUBADOUR	PC	GALLICIZED (G) / OCCITANIZING (O) / ? = OF UNCLEAR PROVENANCE	INCIPIT	LABEL / ATTRIBUTION	SONGBOOKS	ROSE	VIOLETTE	BESTIAIRE	GENRE
97		461.230		Tant es gay' es avinentz	Anon.	*W 78*, 12 lines				canso
98	See PC 461.148a	461.240a / vdB 1822	O	Tuit cil qui sunt enamourat	Anon.	Montpellier, Bibl. Interuniversitaire, Section Médecine, MS 196, fol. 219, 1 stanza Refrain in the *Court de paradis* (only two of the three manuscripts have Occitan coloring: BnF MS. fr. 837, fol. 59r and BnF MS. fr. 25532, fol. 334r)				refrain/ motet
99		RS 318	O	Volez vos que je vous chante	Anon.	Paris Arsenal 3198, BnF fr. 845, BnF nouv. acq. fr. 1050				rêverdie
100		Gennrich 319	O	El mois d'avril qu'ivers va departant / Al cor ai une alegrance / Et gaudebit	Anon.	Paris, BnF MS lat 15139 (St. Victor) and Wolfenbüttel, Herzog August Bibliothek, Guelf. 1099 Helmst.				motet

Table 0.2 Geographical labels associated with songs in French texts

LABEL	SONG	MANUSCRIPT	TEXT	DATE OF TEXT
"chançons poitevines"	not quoted	16th-c. copy by Claude Fauchet (Meyer 1884, 21)	*Doon de Nanteuil*	12th c.
"son poitevin"	not quoted	Paris, Bibliothèque de l'Arsenal MS 2983[1]	*Garin le Loherain*, vv. 11377–79 (Vallerie 1947)	12th c.
"gasconois fu li dis et limosin li ton"	not quoted	Paris, Bibliothèque Nationale de France, MS fr. 24387 (Castets 1909, v. 6600)	*Renaut de Montauban*, also known as *Les Quate Fils Aymon*	12th c.
sonnet poitevin	not quoted	see Reinhard's edition	*Amadas et Ydoine* (Reinhard 1926, v. 1652)	1190–1220
"chançon auvrignace"	Daude de Pradas, "Bela m'es la votz autana" (PC 124.5)	Biblioteca Apostolica Vaticana, Reginensi Latini, 1725	Jean Renart, *Le Roman de la rose* (v. 4649)	early 13th c.
"son poitevin"	Bernart de Ventadorn, "Can vei la lauzeta mover" (PC 70.43)	Biblioteca Apostolica Vaticana, Reginensi Latini, 1725	Jean Renart, *Le Roman de la rose* (v. 5211)	early 13th c.
"son poitevin"	Bernart de Ventadorn, "Ab joi mou lo vers e·l commens" (PC 70.1)	BnF MS fr. 1553	Gerbert de Montreuil, *Le Roman de la violette* (v. 322)	ca. 1230
"son poitevin"	"En inqual tans que never dausir" (PC 461.103a)	BnF MS fr. 1374	Gerbert de Montreuil, *Le Roman de la violette* (v. 322)	ca. 1230
"son poitevin"	piece related to PC 461.103a	New York, Pierpont Morgan Library, MS. 36	Gerbert de Montreuil, *Le Roman de la violette* (v. 322)	ca. 1230
"son poitevin"	piece related to PC 461.103a	Saint Petersburg, National Library of Russia, Fr. Q. v. XIV. 3	Gerbert de Montreuil, *Le Roman de la violette* (v. 322)	ca. 1230
"son poitevin"	Bernart de Ventadorn, "Can vei la lauzeta" (PC 70.43)	BnF MS fr. 1553	Gerbert de Montreuil, *Le Roman de la violette* (v. 4186)	ca. 1230
"son provençal"	Bernart de Ventadorn, "Can vei la lauzeta" (PC 70.43)	BnF MS fr. 1374	Gerbert de Montreuil, *Le Roman de la violette* (v. 4186)	ca. 1230
"son provençal"	not quoted	Saint Petersburg, National Library of Russia, Fr. Q. v. XIV. 3	Gerbert de Montreuil, *Le Roman de la violette* (v. 4186)	ca. 1230

(Continued)

Table 0.2 (Continued)

LABEL	SONG	MANUSCRIPT	TEXT	DATE OF TEXT
"sons poitevins" (v. 407, 495), "sons gascoins et auvergnaus" (v. 489)	not quoted	See Wimmer's edition	Huon de Méri, *Tournoiement Antecrist* (vv. 407, 495, 489)	ca. 1234
"un Poitevin" and "li autre"	Poitevin: quotations from Bernart de Ventadorn's "Can vei la flor" (PC 70.42) and "Destregz d'amor veing denan vos" (PC 16.9) [currently attributed to Albertet de Sestaro, but evidence of attribution to Bernart de Ventadorn] Other: quotation from Guilhem Magret's "Enaissi·m pren cum fai al pescador" (PC 223.3)	For the various manuscript readings of this passage, see chapter 4	Richard de Fournival, *Bestiaire d'amour*	ca. 1250
"son poitevin"	Gautier d'Épinal, "Puis qu'en moi a recovrée seignorie" (RS 1208)	BnF fr. 12786, fol. 42v	At the end of Richard de Fournival's *Bestiaire d'amour*	ca. 1250
"sor [sic] poitevin"	Rigaut de Berbezilh, "Tuit demandon qu'es devengu d'amors (PC 421.10) attributed here to "Forkes de Mersaille"	Bern 389, fol. 234r	n/a (songbook)	late 13th c.
"sons poitevinois"	not quoted	BnF MS fr. 24432	Nicole de Margival, *Dit de la panthère*, v. 159	before 1328 (ms. from after 1345)
"sons poitevinois"	not quoted	National Library of Russia, Fr. f°. v. XIV, 3	Nicole de Margival, *Dit de la panthère*, v. 159	before 1328 (ms from 1400 to 1402)

1. I have not studied the dissemination of the label across the manuscript traditions of *Garin, Les Quatre Fils Aymon*, or *Le Tournoiement Antéchrist*.

CHAPTER 1

Of Birds and Madmen

Occitan Songs in French Songbooks

Among familiar (and less familiar) names of composers listed in the table of contents of Paris, Bibliothèque nationale de France, MS fr. 844, a late thirteenth-century songbook containing both French and Occitan lyric, two descriptions stand out: "ioseaus tarduis" and "li son dervé del home salvage."

The first, which has been read as a misconstrued version of the troubadour Gaucelm Faidit's name (Raupach and Raupach 1979, 40) could be rendered as "belated bird," although its precise meaning is unclear, while the second means something like "the deranged sound (or song?) of the wild man."[1] Both of these descriptions, which attribute the songs with which they are paired to a bird and a wild man, respectively, are found in the section of the songbook devoted to troubadour song. Troubadour song is thus reduced to the level of nonsemantic noise, of the sort one would expect from creatures capable of something *akin* but not identical to human language. As we saw in the introduction, birdsong was widely held to be the most proximate to human speech among animal languages, even if it was typically regarded as *vox inarticulata*, or "meaningless voice."

1. In the body of the manuscript, on fol. 189v, the attribution is rendered as "ossiames Faiduis." John Haines (1998, 7) renders the attribution as "Joseaus Tarduis."

In BnF fr. 844 these labels serve to relegate troubadour song to the periphery of the songbook's soundscape, which elsewhere transmits trouvère song. This marginalization is reinforced by the architecture of the manuscript, whose *ordinatio* saves troubadour song for the very end of the codex, in a sequence that reproduces the social hierarchy.[2] In its framing of troubadour song as distinct from—even if less worthy than—francophone song, BnF fr. 844 is unique among the French songbooks that transmit Occitan song.[3] More commonly in this corpus, troubadour song is transmitted anonymously, without any identifying markings, and compiled with *oïl* lyrics. In such cases, only the opaque passages resulting from Gallicization reveal its cultural alterity. After tracing the contours of the corpus of Occitan song in French songbooks, I turn to the various mechanisms that obscure the cultural and linguistic alterity of Occitan song in its francophone transmission in the thirteenth and fourteenth centuries. These include, alongside the mechanisms documented in the introduction (i.e., Gallicization and geographical remapping), anonymization and the compilation of Occitan songs amid francophone songs rather than in a separate section of the manuscript. I also demonstrate a selection bias toward songs in which the lyric "I" is readily appropriable, that is, toward pieces without historical allusions or proper names. And in some instances, proper names were written out of the songs in French transmission. This selection bias is part of a broader trend toward what I call hyperlyricization—a trend that also includes the rewriting of passages in the third person to assign them to the first person, and the inclusion of buzzwords from the love lyric (birdsong, fields, etc.). Throughout this part of the chapter, I draw attention to parallels between the types of translation-induced deformations criticized by Antoine Berman in his seminal *La Traduction et la lettre ou l'auberge du lointain*. Against such translations, which Berman describes as ethnocentric, hypertextual, and Platonist, Berman (1999, 26) advocates a type of translation that acts as the "auberge du lointain," an expression borrowed from the troubadour Jaufre Rudel. By this Berman means translation that preserves the alterity of its source, one that does not assimilate it to cultural and linguistic norms of the target language. The francophone transmission of Occitan song follows precisely the latter pattern, transforming it into something nearly indistinguishable from the francophone lyrics with which it is almost always transmitted. Berman's characterization of ethnocentric translation describes its modalities

2. See my discussion below.

3. It is not unique in its bestialization of the corpus, however; it lays the groundwork for the widespread association of troubadour lyric with birdsong documented throughout this book.

succinctly: "Éthnocentrique signifiera ici: qui ramène tout à sa propre culture, à ses normes et valeurs, et considère ce qui est situé en dehors de celle-ci—l'Étranger—comme négatif ou tout juste bon à être annexé, adapté, pour accroître la richesse de cette culture" (Ethnocentric will mean here: that [type of translation] which brings everything back to its own culture, to its norms and values, and considers everything outside of that culture—the Foreign—as negative or only good for the purposes of annexation, adaptation, in order to increase the richness of its own culture) (29).

As will be clear from the case of BnF MS fr. 844, when troubadour song was demarcated in some way, it was staged not as a foreign cultural artifact but instead as something whose strangeness came from its status as non- or only quasi-human. Cultural and linguistic difference was reimagined on an animal spectrum.[4] We will see this repositioning of troubadour song as avian rather than foreign in all three narratives that quote troubadour song—Jean Renart's *Rose*, Gerbert de Montreuil's *Violette*, and Richard de Fournival's *Bestiaire d'amour*. In short, then, the evidence assembled in this chapter points to a fundamental ambivalence in the reception of Occitan song in francophone territories: on the one hand, and most frequently, it was actively assimilated, allowing for easier appropriation, and, on the other, it was exoticized by being remapped onto an axis not of cultural alterity but of species difference.

I should say at the outset that the type of overview I undertake in this chapter necessarily comes at the expense of extensive consideration of each songbook. My survey of this landscape involves zooming in on particular case studies that are extremely localized and, of necessity, do not fully account for the nuances of each individual songbook. My goal here is to establish broad patterns in the reception of Occitan song in francophone territories rather than attend to the particularities—worthy of study though they obviously are—of individual songbooks.

Corpus

Nine manuscripts from francophone territories transmit troubadour song, almost always as part of a larger compilation of *oïl* lyric.[5] These manuscripts represent a significant percentage of the troubadour manuscript

4. For a similar argument about Chaucer's remapping of difference onto the avian—where the relevant difference is gender and not language—see Lesley Kordecki's (2011) study of birds in Chaucer.

5. The only exception is Vatican City, Biblioteca Apostolica Vaticana Reg. Lat. MS. 1659, which includes Gaucelm Faidit's *planh* for Richard the Lionheart at the end of Ambroise's *Estoire de la guerre sainte*. Although table 1.1 lists ten manuscripts rather than nine, one of these transmits a francophone piece labeled as a "son poitevin."

transmission as a whole (i.e., including all provenances), which numbers some thirty major songbooks (Boorman et al., n.d.). No manuscript from *oïl* territory compiles troubadour song exclusively, without a trace of francophone production, whether lyric or otherwise. This may seem like a banal feature of the French transmission of Occitan song, but it constitutes a significant departure from the pattern established in both Italy and Catalonia, where Occitan songs were often copied in distinct codices with little to no trace of the romance language of the scribes who compiled them or the readers who read them.[6] The transmission of troubadour song *only* within French songbooks (and usually within the same sections of the manuscript as songs in *langue d'oïl*)—as opposed to the compilation of separate codices—suggests a desire to situate troubadour song within the tradition of French lyric. This is true across the whole chronological span of songbooks that include troubadour song, which were compiled between the early thirteenth and the fifteenth centuries, a range that indicates an interest in troubadour song in francophone territories spanning some three hundred years.[7] As far as we can tell from the extant evidence, this fascination dates back to the very earliest stages of songbook compilation in France; both troubadour and trouvère song find their way into writing for the first time in BnF fr. 20050, the Chansonnier de Saint Germain des Prés.[8] These two repertoires continue to be intertwined in their French transmission, as we will see below, to such an extent, in fact, that one argument of *Stolen Song* is that troubadour song was assimilated and compiled in such a way that it was framed not as a separate repertoire but as an integral part of the tradition of songcraft in *langue d'oïl*. Various other features facilitated this vision (some of which are described in

6. There are, of course, exceptions. Some manuscripts show linguistic interference of the scribe's native romance language, and some include snippets in that romance language (e.g., Vatican City, Biblioteca Apostalica Vaticana, Reg. Lat. 5232, which contains a few rubrics in Italian).

7. On the afterlife of troubadour song in the Renaissance and beyond, see John Haines's (2004) survey.

8. Robert Lug (2000, 265) argues that this is the result of an Occitan diaspora in the city of Metz, where the oldest section of the manuscript may have been compiled. In Lug's estimation, the religious refugees created an adequately large audience for troubadour song, leading to the presence of professional Occitan minstrels (266). He suggests that the core of the manuscript was compiled between August and November of 1231 on the occasion of a marriage between a patrician, Perrin Noise, and Helois de Prény-Haussonville (256). Lug's case remains rather speculative, in my view. The same objection can be made to his 2012 article on the songbook. In this piece, he paints a similar picture of Occitan diaspora: "Ce recueil [le cahier occitan] était certainement dû au milieu vivant des exilés, la chanson occitane symbolisait la patrie perdue, assurant leur identité culturelle" (Lug 2012, 476).

the introduction, and some below). These include Gallicization, anonymity, an absence of labels, and manuscript *ordinatio*. All contribute to the impression that Occitan song is not separate from but rather an integral part of the francophone lyric tradition transmitted in these songbooks.

There is no obvious geographical trend in the provenance of these ten codices. Although ongoing work on the songbooks, such as the *Intavulare* series, will undoubtedly shed further light on the philological details of these objects, it is nevertheless safe to say that there was no clear "hub" for the dissemination of troubadour song in francophone territories. The provenances of the relevant songbooks include Lorraine, Burgundy, Artois, and Picardy. There is nevertheless a predominance of regions on the eastern edge of francophone territories—those abutting the Holy Roman Empire, and those within the Empire.[9] As is the case with all French songbooks, Paris was not a center for production.

Anonymization

The cultural and linguistic specificity of troubadour song was either never perceived at all or actively occluded in its transmission in francophone songbooks. It was, first of all, transmitted anonymously almost without exception, even in songbooks such as Bern 389 and BnF MSS fr. 12615, fr. 20050, fr. 846, and fr. 12581, which include author attributions for *oïl* composers. Table 1.1 shows that BnF fr. 844 is almost unique in its author attributions for troubadour song, and, as we saw at the beginning of this chapter, two of its attributions are certainly fictitious and relegate the troubadours to the margins of the human—a fate that is perhaps even worse than anonymization. Its core troubadour corpus is also mostly anonymous: only fourteen of its sixty-one songs are attributed.[10] BnF MS fr. 844's link to the Morea, and possibly to Italy, may explain its anomalous inclusion of author attributions. Bern 389 is the only uncomplicatedly French songbook to include author attributions for troubadour song, and it does so only for one out of the four it transmits (Folquet de Marselha, acknowledged as "forkes de mersaille" on fol. 234r). There is, in short, a strong trend toward anonymity in the French transmission of the troubadours.

9. Songbooks likely compiled within the Empire include Paris, Bibliothèque nationale de France, MS fr. 20050 (if Robert Lug is correct about its provenance in Metz), BnF MS fr. 856, Bern, Burgerbibliothek MS 389, and Oxford, Bodleian Douce 308.

10. The later Occitan additions to BnF MS fr. 844 are an exception, since some are attributed (to the otherwise unknown "Willaumes li Viniers" and "Carasaus").

Table 1.1 Songbooks compiled in francophone territories that include troubadour song, organized by approximate chronology

CALL NUMBER	CALL NUMBER/ OTHER NAMES	PROVENANCE	DATE	NUMBER OF OCCITAN SONGS	SONGS IN SEPARATE SECTION?	AUTHOR ATTRIBUTIONS?	MUSIC NOTATION?	GEOGRAPHICAL TAGS (E.G., "POITEVIN"?)	NOTES
BnF fr. 20050	French *U*; Occitan *X*. "Chansonnier de Saint-Germain-des-Prés"	Metz (?) or elsewhere in Lorraine	1231?	29, including one that is likely pseudo-Occitan	Occitan songs compiled in two areas of the manuscript (fol. 81r–91v, fol. 148v–150r)	Some, but all in a modern hand	23 pieces out of 24 in the first section have notation. No notation in second set of Occitan pieces.	No	Sections not separated in any way from surrounding French pieces. First "Occitan" section includes two French pieces (fol. 82v–83v).
BnF fr. 24406	French *V*; Occitan *n*. "Lavallière"	Northern France	13th c.	1 (pseudo-?) Occitan piece	No, piece transcribed in French section, f. 151v.	No	Yes	No	.
BnF fr. 844	French *M*; Occitan *W*. "Chansonnier du Roi"	Artois	1260s–1270s?	10 scattered throughout folios 1–185 (all in Occitan); series of songs in Gallicized Occitan fol. 188–204 (+ more originally projected, as indicated by table of contents); 2 Occitanizing *lais*, fol. 212–213	some	Yes, some	Mostly	No	
Bern Burgerbibliothek MS. 389	French *C*	Lorraine	end of 13th or early 14th c.	4 (one potentially Occitanizing)	No	One. "Tuit demandent" attributed to Folquet de Marselha, other three pieces anonymous.	No	"Tuit demandent k'est devengue amor" (fol. 234) marked as a "sor [son] poitevin" but other three Occitan pieces are not	

Vatican City, Biblioteca Apostolica Vaticana Reg. Lat. MS. 1659	Occitan *η*	England or northern France	13th or 14th c.	1	No	No	Yes	No	Includes Gaucelm Faidit's *planh* for Richard the Lionheart right at the end of Ambroise's *Estoire de la guerre sainte*
BnF fr. 846	French *O*. "Chansonnier Cangé"	Burgundy	ca. 1280–1290	1	No, Pistoleta's *souhait* is in the anonymous section (f. 125r)	No	Yes	No	
BnF fr. 12786	---	Northern France	early 14th c.	0 (1 French piece labeled as "poitevin")	---	No	No	Lyric by Gautier d'Épinal described as a "son poitevin"	
Oxford, Bodleian Douce 308	French *I*	Lorraine	early 14th c.	1	No, Pistoleta's *souhait* is in *ballette* section (f. 247)	No	No	No	
BnF fr. 12581	French *S*	Northern France	14th c.	1	No, Pistoleta's *souhait* compiled with French songs (f. 88r)	No	No	No	
Montpellier, Bibl. Interuniversitaire, Section Médecine, MS. 236	French *f*	Picardy?	14th-c. ms. with 15th- c. additions, including Occitan piece	1	No, Pistoleta's *souhait* incorporated into a French *souhait*	No	No	No	

This francophone pattern of anonymity diverges from the contours of the overall transmission of troubadour song in songbooks, which, as Francesca Gambino (2000) has shown, includes author attributions more often than not. Her study, which includes a systematic survey of most of the Occitan songbooks, documents such a strong trend toward authorial attribution that she concludes that an absence of such attributions can generally be chalked up to error, or to late additions to a manuscript including pen trials (34).[11] This pattern of anonymity in the *oïl* transmission of troubadour song holds despite the high percentage of *cansos* (on which more below), the genre that is the most commonly attributed (80).

This anonymity facilitates the appropriation of troubadour song as French. A song is obviously more easily assimilated without an appended name of a foreign author—a name that would likely include a toponym in Occitania, such as Raimbaut d'*Aurenga*, and thus an indisputable mark of geographical remove and potentially also of foreignness. (Indeed, it is striking that the sole troubadour whose identity is acknowledged in Bern 389—Folquet de Marselha—is also the one whose piece is accompanied by the label "sor [son] poitevin," as if to counteract the southern geographical pinpoint that Marseille constitutes.) Authorial names also bear the trace of a historical subject behind the lyric "I," and their effacement consequently allows for a dehistoricization and departicularization of the song, phenomena we will see again in the suppression of proper names and *tornadas*. And if the proper name, as Marisa Galvez (2012, 59) argues, provides a "memorial structure for an archive," the effacement of proper names works instead to foreclose this memorial structure. Paul Zumthor (1972, 89) might say that we are in the realm not of an author but of a "sujet de l'énonciation, une instance locutrice intégrée au texte et indissociable de son fonctionnement." Indeed, by suppressing authorial names, French compilers and scribes reduce the voice behind troubadour song to a bare grammatical function—an "I"—into which any male subject can insert himself.

This anonymization is, moreover, all the more significant in light of the predominance of the "author figure" in songbooks. As Sylvia Huot (1987) has documented, the figure of the author assumes a greater importance in lyric material than in romance, in the sense that most French songbooks use authors' names as an organizing principle. Authorship emerges as an organizing principle in lyric collections long before it does for other genres

11. Gambino (2000, 35) does not systematically exclude songbooks based on provenance, but she does exclude those French songbooks that transmit only a few Occitan songs. However, she includes BnF fr. 20050 and BnF fr. 844 because of the number of songs they transmit.

in Old French. Huot points out that while most narrative poems are identified by their protagonist or central image (e.g., "li romans de Cliges"), songs are instead described as belonging to their composers (e.g., "les chansons au Chastelain de Couci") (47–48). Indeed, if we are to believe Gustav Gröber's (1877, 345ff.) theory of *Liederbücher*, authorship was the organizing principle of lyric collections as soon as they were collected in writing. Authorship has also been tied to class nostalgia by certain critics, who argue that many songbooks served to memorialize a disappearing aristocracy. Judith Peraino (2011), for instance, has pointed out that while no French songbooks come from Paris, site of royal government, all come from regions with erstwhile powerful aristocracies, especially Picardy and Artois. As she puts it, "At the time of their compilation these anthologies monumentalized a socioeconomic world no longer operative" (129). To forget the individual troubadours behind each song, then, is also to evacuate them from the social order entirely, leaving their disembodied songs available for revoicing by francophone jongleurs or characters in lyric-interpolated romance.

This trend toward anonymity is diametrically opposed to the trend in contemporaneous Italian songbooks, which amplify rather than suppress the authorial voice behind individual lyrics through the genres of the *vida* and the *razo*—respectively, short biographies and explanatory texts that purport to explain the circumstances behind the composition of a particular song. Even in the absence of *vidas* and *razos*, Italian songbooks are also highly likely to be organized according to the names of individual poets, as the logic of the rubric in songbook *I* (Paris, BnF MS fr. 854) makes unusually explicit: "Aqui son escrig li noms del trobadors qui / son en aq*ue*st livre que ant trobadors laç ca*n* / sos lun apres lautre" (Here are written the names of the troubadours who are in this book who have composed *cansos* one after another) (Galvez 2012, 57).[12] This strange formulation suggests the paramount importance given to the proper name as an index of a historical figure, whose lyric corpus is presented as interchangeable with his physical *corpus* ("trobadors qui son en aquest livre" [the troubadours who are in this book]). As Marisa Galvez has recently argued, here the names of individual poets serve as the node on which an identity can crystallize.[13]

One might object that the compilers of French songbooks simply did not know the names of the troubadours whose work they were transmitting, that they had no means of obtaining this information, and that the anonymization of the troubadour corpus is less the result of a conscious

12. Here and elsewhere, italics indicate realized abbreviations.

13. See chap. 2, "Producing Opaque Coherence: Lyric Presence and Names," in Galvez (2012).

desire to suppress individual poets' identities than of the hazards of material transmission. It is, undoubtedly, the case that many compilers worked with sources lacking author attributions; indeed, many later songbooks in the French tradition are demonstrably indebted to earlier ones, such that the anonymity shrouding the troubadour corpus was likely merely compounded over time. In other instances, however, compilers and authors did actively suppress attributions (this is the case for Richard de Fournival, as I show in chapter 4). Regardless, I am less interested in the *cause* of the anonymous transmission of troubadour song than in its effects: divorced from proper names that would, in many instances, have indicated linguistic and geographical remove from *oïl* territory, and that situate troubadour song within an identifiable, localizable, and historical tradition, troubadour song became a corpus that belonged to no one and was thus more easily imaginable as part of French lyric history.

Architectonics

This fiction was further assisted by a trend toward the compilation of troubadour song not in separate, demarcated sections of the codices in which it was transmitted but in the midst of francophone lyrics. This pattern holds in the vast majority of francophone songbooks. Indeed, the only manuscripts that would seem, at first glance, to be exceptions are Paris BnF fr. 20050 and fr. 844, which have separate sections of troubadour songs. These two songbooks are, however, less exceptional than they might at first appear. In BnF MS fr. 844, the transition from trouvère songs to those of the troubadours is not visually or textually signaled in any way, leaving it impossible for someone without external knowledge of the repertoires to notice the shift (see figure 1.1). Moreover, the later Occitan additions to the manuscript follow the more common pattern of assimilation found in other songbooks; they were interspersed with French songs. The troubadour songs in BnF fr. 20050 are another exception in the sense that they are clustered in two discrete areas of the manuscript (see table 1.1). However, first of all, these sections are not demarcated in any way from the surrounding francophone corpus. One does not have the impression, either from the table of contents or from the *mise-en-page* of the body of the manuscript, that one is dealing with a corpus thought of as distinct, whether linguistically or culturally. The transition from the Old French songs to the Gallicized Occitan ones is visually seamless (figures 1.2 and 1.3).

Moreover, one of the "troubadour sections" (and, again, this label is misleading) includes two Old French pieces in the middle of one of its

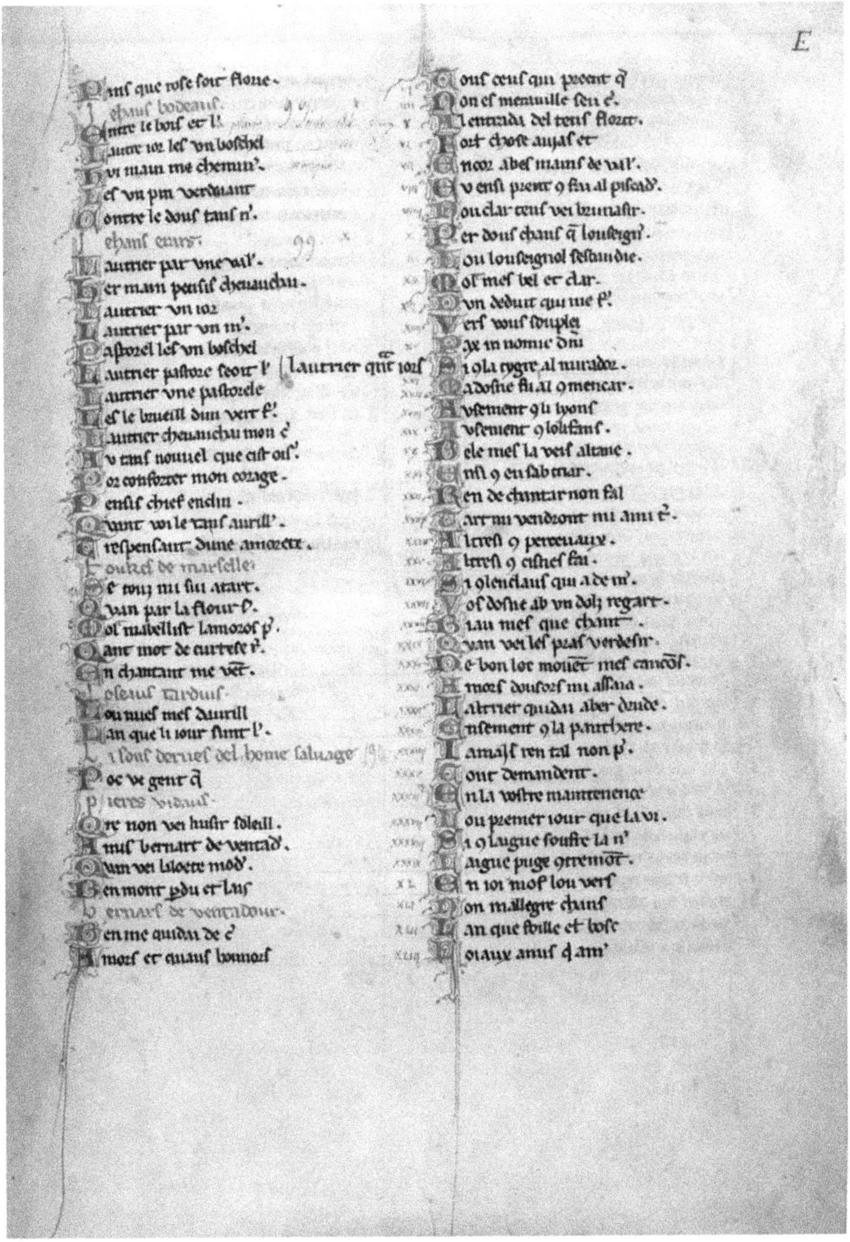

FIGURE 1.1 Table of contents in BnF MS fr. 844 showing the (unmarked) transition from trouvère songs to troubadour songs on fol. Er.

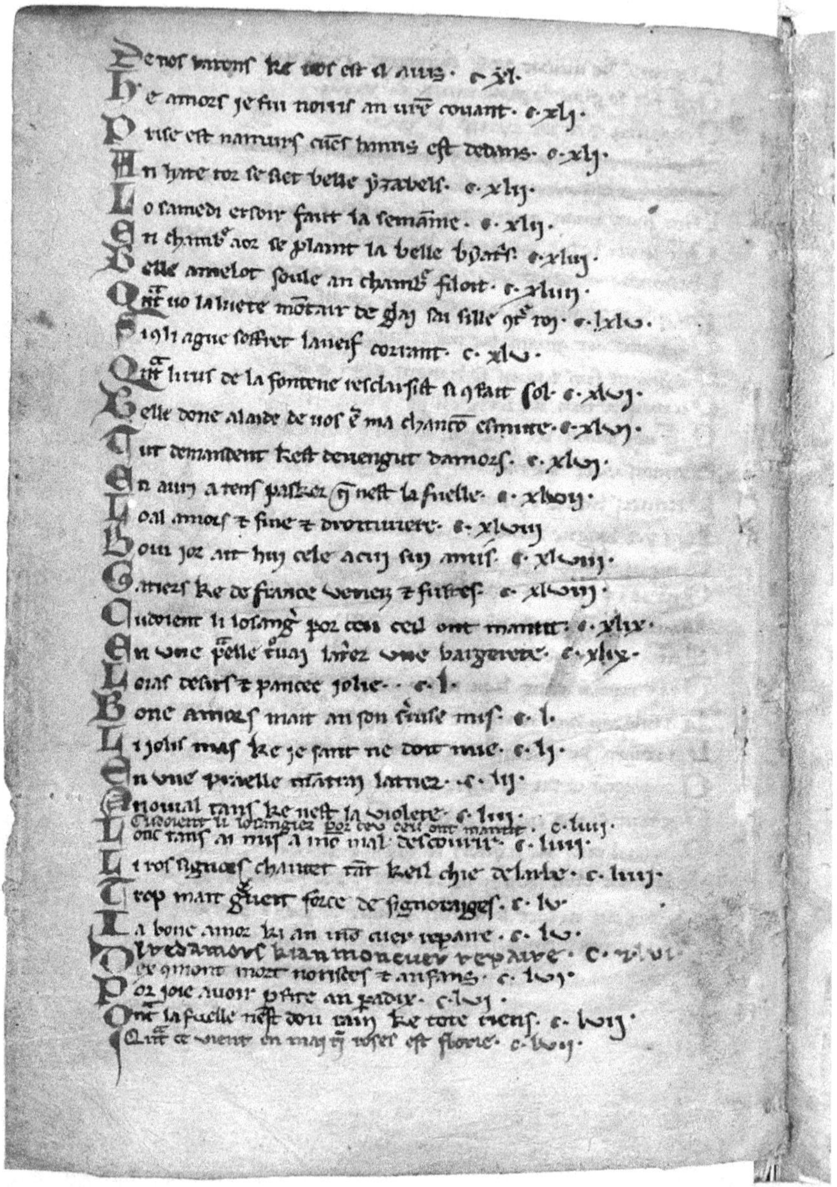

FIGURE 1.2 Table of contents (fol. 2v) in which second Occitan "section" of fr. 20050 appears (Bernart de Ventadorn's "Can vei la lauzeta mover" is the eighth entry).

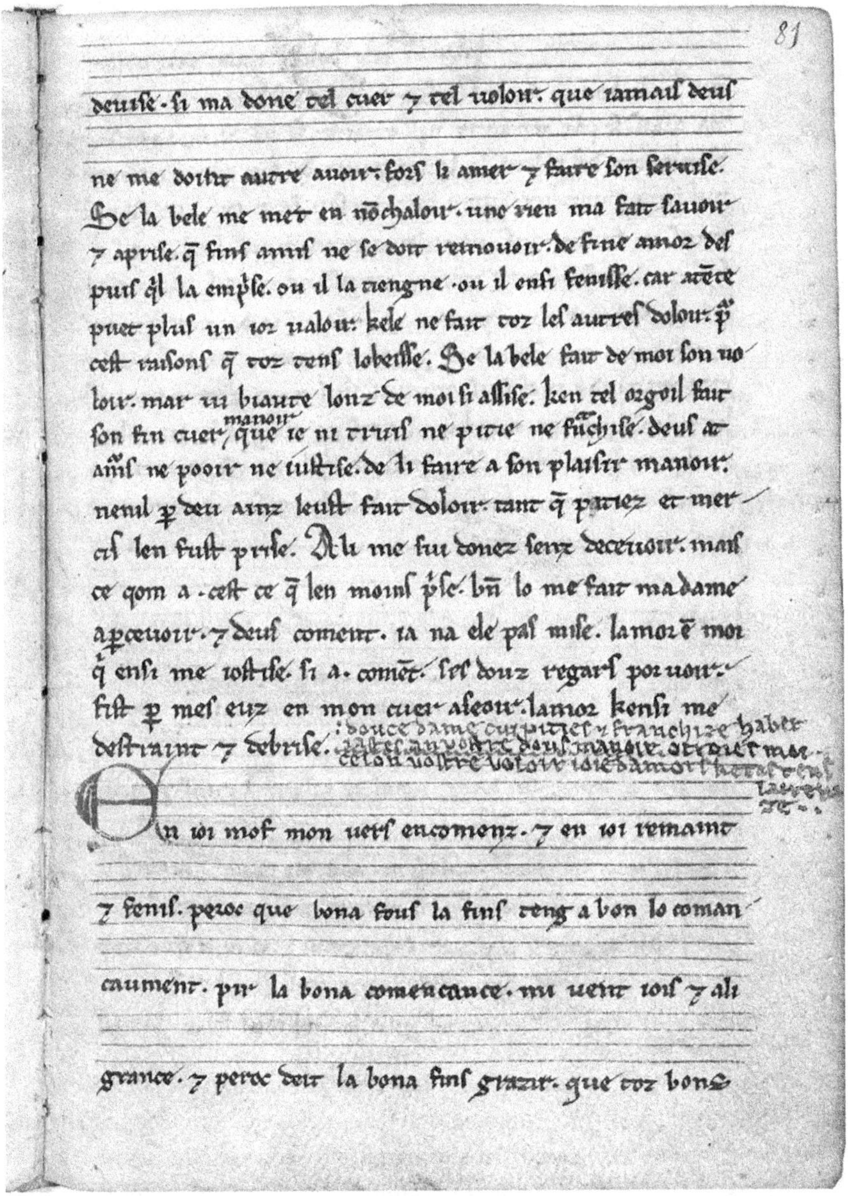

FIGURE 1.3 Transition from *oïl* lyrics to first Occitan "section" in fr. 20050 (fol. 81r). The first troubadour song is Bernart de Ventadorn's "Ab joi mou lo vers," at the bottom of the folio.

troubadour clusters: "Quant voi ces prez florir et verdoier" (RS 1259)—anonymous here but attributed to Moniot d'Arras elsewhere—and the anonymous "Gaite de la tor" (fols. 82v–83r). Many critics have already pointed out the resemblance of "Gaite de la tor" to Occitan *albas*, citing, among other qualities, its mention of a watchman (common in Occitan *albas* but unique in French *aubes*) (Woledge 1965, 388); the fact that its rhymes are *unisonanz*, a trait found only in Occitan *albas* (Bec 1973, 23); an unusual melodic gesture (an octave drop) similar to Peire Vidal's "Pos tornatz sui en Proensa" (Restori 1904, 4); and a general resemblance to the *albas* by Raimbaut de Vaqueiras and Guiraut de Bornelh (Bec 1973, 33). What is more, the cluster also includes songs drawn from the Occitanizing corpus (these are "A l'entrade del tens clar eya" on fol. 82v and "L'autrier m'iere levaz" on fol. 91v). The inclusion of both a French piece that imitates Occitan song formally and two Occitanizing songs undermines the boundary between lyrics in *langue d'oïl* and those in *langue d'oc*. Indeed, because of the heavy Gallicization of the Occitan songs, the Occitanizing songs in BnF MS fr. 20050 look on the whole more Occitan than the originals. The overall effect is the dissolution of both the linguistic divide between French and Occitan (with French phonological traits appearing in the originally Occitan songs and vice versa) and the divide between the troubadour and trouvère repertoires. Thus, both manuscripts that diverge from the general pattern toward interspersing troubadour song rather than separating it turn out to be less exceptional than one might think: although both BnF MS fr. 844 and MS fr. 20050 cluster the Occitan lyrics together (only some in the case of BnF MS fr. 844), they also blur the transition visually from one repertoire to the other. Moreover, MS fr. 844 attributes some Occitan songs to French composers, and MS fr. 20050 includes Occitanizing (but francophone) lyrics in the midst of its Gallicized Occitan songs.

One could productively compare here the Occitan songbook *D* (Modena, Biblioteca nazionale Estense, MS Estero 45), of Italian provenance, which has a separate French section beginning on fol. 217r preceded by the rubric "Iste su*n*t cantiones francigene" (These are French songs) (Bertoni 1917, 317, 320). The compilers of this manuscript treat Occitan and French song as two distinct repertoires, segregating one from the other and labeling the latter.[14] Like anonymization, then, the trend toward the compilation of troubadour songs (mostly heavily Gallicized) amid *oïl* lyrics domesticates them and frames them as unremarkable rather than culturally other.

---

14. There are also, however, Occitan songbooks of Italian provenance that intersperse French songs (Rosenberg 1998, 2005).

Selection

Alongside the above trends, troubadour song was made more readily assimilable through a selection bias toward the *canso* (the love song). *Cansos* are generally unanchored in a particular historical moment, and the beloved remarkably generic; scholars have often remarked on the absence of corporeal descriptions of the troubadour *domna* beyond the most basic clichés, as well as on the occlusion of her identity through the use of *senhals*—code names. Unlike the *sirventes*, songs of praise or blame whose targets are often explicit, the lyric "I" of the *canso* easily allows for identification on the part of readers or the listening public. In performance, the textual "I" of first-person love lyric can easily be appropriated by a new speaker, whereas a song weighed down with historical minutiae cannot easily be ventriloquized without this act of repetition being obvious. The *canso* represents only 40 percent of the troubadour corpus when all extant sources are considered (D. Rieger 1976), but, by the Raupachs' estimate, it represents two-thirds of the Occitan lyric corpus as transmitted in France. I would suggest that this number is actually even higher given that the Raupachs include songbooks whose French provenance has since been questioned—often the ones to transmit other genres (BnF MS fr. 795, for instance, includes a high percentage of moralizing pieces). Discounting the anonymous *unica*, some of which may well be of French rather than Occitan provenance (as I discuss in chapter 5), only eight of seventy-one pieces (11 percent) represent genres other than the *canso*. What is more, as I show below, one of these pieces is in fact made to look like a *canso* (Pistoleta's *souhait*) in one version.

There is, in fact, one part of the *canso* that resists easy assimilation: the *tornada*, frequently a site of proper names or *senhals*, and also of geographic markers ("take my song to x"). *Tornadas* are almost never included in the French transmission of Occitan song.[15] The omission of the vast majority of *tornadas* de facto excludes the portions of the songs that are most likely to anchor its landscape in a particular historical moment and geography—that is, those in which the cultural and linguistic alterity of Occitan song would be most foregrounded. Divorced from their *tornadas*, most *cansos* are rendered totally ahistorical, leaving their subject position readily appropriable.

One could also adduce the fact that many of the troubadours popular elsewhere but not in France are precisely those whose works are either dense with historical references or else fail to conform to the particular type of *canso*

15. There are only two exceptions to this trend: Peirol's "Del seu tort farai esmenda," which is transmitted with one tornada, and Elias Fonsalada's "De bo loc movon mas chansos."

discussed above. Bertran de Born, for instance, whose work often alludes to specific events, was widely quoted in Italian *vidas* (Kay 2013, 216–20) but is totally absent in French transmission. The same absence characterizes Marcabru, whose often-satiric verse is quoted on several occasions in Matfre of Ermengaud's *Breviari d'amor* (240).

Rewriting

Alongside this effacement of the historical through a preference for the *canso* and the omission of *tornadas*, several types of rewriting rendered troubadour song more readily appropriable for francophone audiences. Troubadour songs were rewritten—beyond the rewriting implied in Gallicizing translations—in order to make them both appear more "French" (through the translation of proper names or the substitution of stock characters for proper names) and conform to a certain literary ideal—the first-person, male-voiced, ahistorical love lyric. This ideal, as I have already noted, encourages total identification on the part of the reader, thus providing another form of assimilation. I would propose the term hyperlyricization to describe the aggregate of rewritings discussed here and the selection bias toward the *canso* discussed above. Hyperlyricization is reminiscent of Antoine Berman's (1999, 57) *ennoblissement*, one of the categories of deformation explored in *La Traduction et la lettre* (a mode of translation in which poetry is rendered more poetic and prose more overtly rhetorical, often through the substitution of more elegant phrases). While one does not have the impression that the generation of especially elegant phrases was the goal for French writers and compilers of troubadour song, their predilection for the *canso* and the rewritings discussed below do further poeticize lyrics in no need of such help. Moreover, they transform them into a particular *type* of poetry.

In some cases, proper names have been either Gallicized or omitted entirely. The troubadour "Peire" in the *cobla* exchange between Bernart de Ventadorn and Peire d'Alvernhe, transmitted anonymously in BnF MS fr. 844 (fol. 190), sees his name Gallicized with the diminutive form of "Perrot." An even more dramatic shift away from proper names is evident in the same manuscript's rendering of Peire Vidal's "Tart mi veiran mei amic en Tolza" (PC 364.49), which transforms what the other versions of the song render as the very specific "Na Loba" (Lady Loba) into a generic "bela dosna" (beautiful lady). The same shift away from the proper occurs a few lines later, where "N Barral" (Sir Barral) is rendered as "en baras" (in deceit[?]), and, in the subsequent line, "Mon bell Rainier" as "mos bels regnes" (my beautiful reign).

All of these readings are unique in the transmission of Peire's song, which also appears in five other manuscripts (Peire Vidal 1960, 149). And in BnF MS fr. 20050's version of Rigaut de Berbezilh's "Tuit demandon q'es devengud' amors," the line of stanza IV containing Ovid's name is omitted (this manuscript is, again, unique in its exclusion of stanza IV—the other eighteen manuscripts include it) (Rigaut de Berbezilh 1960, 198–99). These gestures—the linguistic transformation of proper names so as to obscure their cultural and linguistic alterity, and the actual effacement of historic people, sometimes in favor of a quasi-ubiquitous figure of love lyric ("beautiful lady")—enable the appropriation of the Occitan *canso* as "French." Far from being the locus of cultural and linguistic alterity, the proper, and consequently untranslatable, Occitan proper names are omitted (in the case of troubadours), Gallicized (in the case of Peire, above, and also in the table of contents of BnF MS fr. 844), replaced by stock figures from the love lyric ("beautiful lady") or bestialized (as we saw above, Gaucelm Faidit's name was rendered as "belated bird" in the table of contents of BnF MS fr. 844).

The same impulse lies behind the regendering of the female voice of Beatriz de Dia's "A chantar m'er de so qu'eu no volria" as male in French transmission, the male lyric "I," as feminists have long pointed out, being more readily perceived as universal.[16] Here is how the stanza reads in BnF MS fr. 844 (fol. 204r–v), with line breaks added and abbreviations (indicated in italics) realized:

A chantar mer al cor que n*on* deurie
tant mi rancun cele a qui sui amigs.
et si lam mais que nule ren qui sie.
non mi val ren beltat ni curtesie.
ne ma bontaz ne mon pres me mon sen.
altresi sui enganade et tragide.
queusse fait vers lui desavinence.

The second line here rewrites the predominant reading of line 2 ("tant me rancur de lui cui sui amia" [I am so upset about him whose (female) beloved I am]), transforming it into "She so upsets me, whose [male] friend I am."[17] The male-voiced love lyric is, of course, the more predominant form by an enormous margin. To show the deviation from this pattern evident in

16. Monique Wittig (1992, 80), for instance, has pointed out the widespread perception of the masculine as universal and the feminine as particular.

17. Quoted from Bruckner, Shepard, and White (1995, 6–7). Rieger's (1991, 595) list of variants would suggest that this change is unique to fr. 844.

Beatriz de Dia's song would be to draw attention to the historical female composer behind the text, an attention that would detract from the transparent identification enabled by Gallicization and the other assimilative gestures documented in this chapter. Indeed, Sarah Kay's observation that the *trobairitz* are never quoted outside of the *razos* suggests just such a resistance to assimilation of their female subject position elsewhere in the transmission of their songs, too (Kay 2013, 60).

Beyond the effacement of proper names and the regendering documented above, some songs have been otherwise rewritten to make them conform to the "ideal," ahistorical, first-person *canso*, either through the insertion of a first-person speaker where there was none, or through inventive sound translations that insert keywords, themes, or scenarios typical of the love song. Folquet de Marselha's "En chantan n'aven a membrar," for example, has been rewritten in BnF MS fr. 844 such that a third-person statement is transformed into the first person. Instead of "Qu'el guarda vos e us ten tan car / que l Cors en fai nesci semblar" (For it [my heart] keeps you and holds you so dearly that [your] body seems inconsequential), fr. 844 supplies: "Et vos am et ten tant car / quel cor mi fai nice semblar" (And I love you and hold you so dearly that the body seems inconsequential to me).[18] We will see the inverse of this type of transformation in Richard de Fournival's *Bestiaire* in chapter 4, which transforms first-person declarations into third-person ones, in a pattern I describe as delyricization.

Turning to the category of hyperlyricization (the insertion of keywords or other elements from an erotic lexicon), perhaps the most striking example is Pistoleta's *souhait* as transmitted in Montpellier, Bibliothèque de la Faculté de médecine, MS 236, where only two stanzas—of what the piece's most recent editor imagines to be the original five (Meyer 1890, 47–48)—remain, and they have been relegated to the middle of the piece (stanzas V and VII). I would argue that the initial two (added) stanzas hyperlyricize Pistoleta's song, echoing the ubiquitous vernal exordium and even inserting some *médisants*, the usual suspects of the love lyric who attempt to thwart the lovers' union with their malicious speech. Here are the first two stanzas, as edited by Meyer:

Et je souhaide tous tamps avril et mai,
Et cascun mois tous fruis renouvelast,
Et tous jours fuissent flours de lis et de glay
Et violetes, roses, u c'on alast,

18. I quote from Stroński's edition of Folquet de Marselha (Folquet de Marseille 1910, 28).

Et bos fuelly et verdes praeries,
Et tout ami eüssent leur amies,
Et si s'amaissent de cuer certain et vrai,
Cascuns eüst son plaisir et cuer gay.

Et je souhaide le mort as mesdisans,
Si ke jamais nuls naistre ne peüst;
Et s'il naissoit, qu'il fust si meskeans
Que iex ne bouche ne orelle n'euyst,
C'a vrais amans il ne peüst rien nuire;
As bons loisist a lor voloir deduire,
Partout fust pais, concorde et loiautés,
Et de tous biens abondance et plentés.

And I wish for April and May all the time,
And every month for each fruit to be renewed
And that each day there were lilies and gladioli
And violets, roses, wherever one went,
And flowering woods and green fields,
And that all [male] lovers had their [female] beloveds,
And that they loved each other with a certain and true heart,
And that each had his pleasure and a joyful heart.

And I wish death to the *médisants*,
Such that not one of them could be born;
And if he were born, may he be so unfortunate
That he not have an eye, mouth or ear,
Such that he would not be able to hurt true lovers;
And may it be permitted to the good to enjoy themselves as much as
 they wish,
And may there be peace everywhere, concord and loyalty,
And of all good things abundance and plenty.

These stanzas are a far cry from what Meyer proposes as Pistoleta's original opening, which presents a plea for money, a castle, wisdom, and the protection of one hundred valiant knights, among other things. In lieu of more material desires, these two initial French stanzas foreground lyric themes: the renewal of love in a springtime cadre and the omnipresent *lauzengiers* or *médisants*, who threaten the lovers. In so doing, they draw Pistoleta's *souhait* into line with the *canso*, a genre whose initial two stanzas often feature precisely these themes, albeit in an affirmative rather than an optative mode. Though versions of Pistoleta's *souhait* vary greatly across manuscripts, only this rendering hyperlyricizes the motifs of what Meyer (and Pistoleta's other editors) imagine to be the authorial version.

Hyperlyricization also occurs on a more local level. The last line of Gaucelm Faidit's *planh* for Richard the Lionheart has been altered in Vatican City, Biblioteca Apostolica Vaticana MS Reg. lat. 1659 to include the verb *amar* (fol. 90r). Rather than "as us doptar et als autres grazir" ([Richard knew how to] make himself feared by some and please others), it reads "as uns amar *et* as autres grazir" (to make himself loved by some and please others) (v. 18).[19] This pleonastic parallelism introduces the courtly verb *amar* into the totally incongruous setting of a *planh*. And if love is typical of lyric, the same is true of the vernal landscape, which is introduced in a rather strange fashion in BnF MS fr. 20050's rendering of Peire d'Alvernha's "Dejosta·ls breus jorns e·ls loncs sers" (fol. 86r). The *pretz* ("worth," VII) that Peire's most recent editor (Peire d'Alvernhe 1996, 97) hypothesizes in the authorial version of the song has been transformed—solely in BnF MS fr. 20050—into *praz*, a common Occitanizing form denoting "meadow" in other texts. This leads to the incomprehensible "*et* al praz tortre en gran poder" (and in the meadow turtledove in great power) instead of Aniello Fratta's hypothesized original "e sos pretz mont'a grans poders" (and its worth augments to great power).[20] Another song in the same songbook is transformed to align it more closely with the typical lexicon of the *canso*, this time through subtle eroticism. In BnF MS fr. 20050's version of Peire Vidal's "Anc no mori per amor ni per al" (fol. 85v), Avalle's hypothesized original "anc mais no vi plag tan descomunal" (never have I seen such an extraordinary thing) has been replaced by the only vaguely comprehensible but suggestively erotic "e re ne*n* vol plait tendre co*m*munal" (and a tender and communal agreement [?] wants nothing of this).[21] What is more, in the same piece, Avalle's hypothesized authorial "No·i puesc trobar ab lei nulh chauzimen" (I cannot find in her any indulgence) has become "Ne poc en li trobar nul iauzimant" (I cannot find any *jouissance* in her) (fol. 85v).[22] These rewritings complement Maria Carla Battelli's

19. I quote from Mouzat's edition (Gaucelm Faidit 1965, 416). There are no similar readings in Mouzat's variants. Transcription of the Vatican manuscript is my own.

20. Fratta reads this line in BnF MS fr. 20050 as "et al praz torna en gran poder." I agree with Peire's earlier editor, Alberto del Monte, on the reading *tortre* (Peire d'Alvernhe 1955, 71) (compare with the initial word of stanza II, *contre*). Although it is of course impossible to know what the scribe's source looked like, his own *n* and *tr* are fairly similar visually, and this may explain the mistake. Turtledoves also appear in the song at I.7.

21. This reading bears no resemblance to any other version of the text in other songbooks. Avalle reads "ne*n*" as "no*n*." I do not see how the vowel could be an *O* (Peire Vidal 1960, 333).

22. This manuscript is, once again, unlike the rest of the manuscript tradition in its substitution of "iauzimant."

(2001, 168) observation that the troubadours' courtly lexicon was often the most resistant to adaptation in the French transmission of troubadour song; she points, for instance, to the word *amors*, which is invariant in the vast majority of songs. Through both gestures—actual rewriting to include lyric tropes and the preservation of a courtly vocabulary—troubadour song was made to conform to a very particular notional love lyric: one with very little content beyond its springtime setting and declaration of love, but nevertheless replete with common keywords from the lexicon of *fin'amor* (we will see this trend taken to an extreme in one song in the *Violette*). Indeed, that the semantic content of Gallicized troubadour song was not its primary appeal for French readers is clear from the fact that Gallicization—and the insertion of the keywords just discussed—often comes at the expense of intelligibility. Though often only semicomprehensible, the parts of troubadour songs that were preserved or rewritten mark them as participants in a particular type of erotic discourse.

The garbled nature of troubadour song is "explained" by a final category of rewriting, which inserts the suggestion of insanity via direct allusion or performatively via nonsense syllables. The former strategy is evident in Peirol's "Del seu tort farai esmenda" as transmitted in BnF MS fr. 20050. There, the line all other manuscripts give as "lieys que·m fetz partir de se" (she who made me leave her) has been rendered as "li que fist partir del sen" (she who made [me?] leave my senses) (Peirol 1953, 81). The possibility of the loss of sanity is also evoked in the French rendering of Perdigo's "Trop ai estat mon Bon Esper no vi" in BnF MS fr. 20050, where the speaker warns that one might "perdre son seignor e sen" (lose one's lord and sanity) rather than the original "senhor e se" (lord and self).[23] Both strategies are present in the versions of Bernart de Ventadorn's famous lark song in BnF MS fr. 844 and BnF MS fr. 20050, respectively. In the former (fol. 190v), what Appel proposes as Bernart's authorial version, "meravilhas ai, car desse / lo cor de dezirer no·m fon" (it is a miracle that suddenly my heart does not melt from desire), has been replaced with "miravill me qeu nies del sen et cor de desirrier non fon" (it is a miracle that I do not lose my mind and that my heart does not melt from desire) (Bernart de Ventadorn 1915, 250).[24] The subsequent stanza renders more concrete this notion of loss of sanity, substituting for Bernart's "tout m'a mo cor, e tout m'a me" (she has taken away my body from me and my whole being), "tol me lou cor et tol lou sen" (she has taken away my body

23. The only manuscript to transmit a similar variant is *P*, which gives "e sen perd" (Perdigon 1926, 60).

24. According to Appel's variants, *N* gives "desen" (Bernart de Ventadorn 1915, 250).

from me and my sanity).[25] If these rewritings introduce insanity explicitly, BnF MS fr. 20050 instead suggestively performs a loss of sanity. Alongside its nonsensical renderings of Bernart's song, which include "de gai sa sille contre roi" (of gay *sa sille* [?] against the king) for Appel's proposed authorial "de joi sas alas contral ral" (because of joy its wings against the ray [of the sun]), and "da cor ke uoi ke ioe gent mer la ui mer" (of the body I see that I *oe* [?] nobly [?] the sea [?] woe that I saw her [?]) for "da cui qu'eu veya jauzion" (of he whom I see rejoicing), the manuscript includes a series of nonsense syllables, which seem to be appended to the fourth line of the first stanza: "per la dousour ca cor li va .e.e.e" (fol. 148v).[26] Though common in certain genres such as the *pastourelle*, nonsense syllables are very rarely found in the *canso* or *grand chant*.[27]

All of the above phenomena—Gallicization, anonymization, compilation with *oïl* lyrics, and a selection bias for the *canso*, with its easily appropriable lyric "I"—facilitate a view of Occitan and Old French lyric as part of the same cultural tradition. They also enable identification between readers and/or audience members and the speaking subject of troubadour song, an identification facilitated by the omission of proper names and historical references. The same phenomena also constitute a homogenization of an originally heterogeneous corpus of songs, both in their foregrounding of a particular genre—the *canso*, the omission of *tornadas*, a preference for initial stanzas, and the rewriting of certain passages to include lyric buzzwords. Such homogenization constitutes another parallel between the modalities of the francophone reception of troubadour song and the deformations typical of the type of translation Antoine Berman calls ethnocentric and domesticating.[28]

---

25. I quote directly from the manuscript, although I have realized abbreviations and added punctuation. I quote Bernart's song from Appel's edition (Bernart de Ventadorn 1915, 250). Other manuscripts mention sanity, too. *N* gives "e tot mon sen," *O* gives "e tol mon sen."

26. "Sa sille" preserves the possessive adjective *sas* (albeit it with a space before the final *S* in the manuscript). No other manuscript gives anything resembling BnF MS fr. 20050's "da cor ke uoi ke ioe gent mer la ui mer." A series of the letter *E*—which seem to be unique in the manuscript—are part of the stanza that appears to have been destined for notation (there is space between lines but no staves or notation). This may indicate that the scribe's source included notation and he was attempting to supply the appropriate amount of text per note.

27. The only exceptions that come to mind are Jaufre Rudel's "Non sap chantar qui so non di" (PC 262.4), which uses nonsense syllables at the rhyme (v. 6), and Guilhem IX's "Farai un vers de dreit nien" (PC 183.7), where the expression "barbariol" is used to convey a foreign language.

28. According to Berman (1999, 60), homogenization "consiste à unifier sur tous les plans le tissu de l'original, alors que celui-ci est originairement hétérogène."

Of Birds and Madmen: Troubadour Song in BnF MS fr. 844

It has often been noted in studies of the troubadours that French songbooks preserve, by a significant margin, the largest number of melodies for their songs (Battelli 1992, 596; Raupach and Raupach 1979, 59). That French audiences were interested in the musical aspect of troubadour song seems clear enough, then. This interest in the musical aspect of troubadour song can be fruitfully thought of as part of a broader interest in its *sound*. Indeed, the procedure of Gallicization is, as we saw in the last section of the introduction, a type of translation that prioritizes sound over sense. The two labels with which this chapter began—"belated bird" and "crazy song/sound of the wild man" ("i oseaus tarduis" and "Li sons derves del home salvage")—further associate troubadour song with nonsemantic or barely semantic sound. We will see below that the label "belated bird" responds to the content of the songs associated with it, but the label would nevertheless have cued for medieval readers an expectation of the unintelligible. As already discussed, birdsong had a special status in medieval theories of voice as capable of being transcribed in writing but meaningless; other animal vocalizations were typically categorized as *both* unwritable and meaningless.[29] The second label arguably had the same effect, given a long-standing tradition of the madman's speech as incomprehensible.

In the sense that BnF MS fr. 844 exoticizes these troubadour songs, it arguably departs from the pattern of assimilation documented in the songbooks described in the rest of this chapter. In other respects, however, it resembles them: this particular section of troubadour songs is transcribed in Gallicized (and sometimes incomprehensible) Occitan, and although the core section of Occitan song is segregated in the sense that no *oïl* lyrics are interspersed, as we have seen, it is nevertheless not clearly labeled or physically separated, thus facilitating the vision of Occitan song as part of the *oïl* lyric tradition (see figure 1.1).

The strange labels described in the opening pages of this chapter appear in a section of forty-nine troubadour songs.[30] The manuscript also includes a set of Occitan songs—these transcribed in non-Gallicized Occitan—added at

29. I have elsewhere argued for lyric evocations of birdsong as a locus of sonic experimentation blurring the divide between meaningful and meaningless *vox*, and thus between the human and the avian (Zingesser 2017).

30. Haines (2013, 62) notes that this is the same number of songs as the number of French songs in the Modena manuscript, which he thinks is because it is the number of pieces that fit on a quaternion.

a much later date (Peraino 2011, 156–85).[31] My focus here will be only a small subset of the core group of Gallicized Occitan songs: those that include the two exoticizing labels. The manuscript's provenance may be either Arras or the Morea, or perhaps both.[32] John Haines has recently proposed Prince William of Villehardouin, ruler of Morea from 1245 to 1278, as the major artistic force behind the manuscript, more specifically putting forth the theory that the songbook was compiled to honor Prince William's marriage to Anna Doukaina of Epiros in 1258 or 1259 (Haines 1998; 2013, 100).[33] This theory builds on a hypothesis first proposed by Jean Longnon, who noticed that a certain "Prince de la Morée" was given pride of place at the beginning of the manuscript, even coming before Charles of Anjou, whom the Becks thought had commissioned the manuscript, positing Provence, northern France, or Naples as the provenance (Longnon 1939; Beck and Beck 1970, 1: ix).

The troubadours in BnF MS fr. 844 are relegated to its peripheries, both in terms of an animal-human axis and in terms of its architectonics. Many critics have noted that the songbook moves roughly from those at the top of the social ladder—kings and princes, and so on—down to those who have no noteworthy rank and are designated only by their names (Beck and Beck 1970, 1:ix, 2:12; Battelli 1993, 277).[34] As Sylvia Huot (1987, 57) has described, this social hierarchy is reinforced through the iconographic program of the manuscript, which depicts aristocratic trouvères such as the count of Anjou and the count of Bar on horseback (fols. 4r and 5r), even including their heraldic emblems. Compounding the marginalized position of the troubadour cluster as a whole is the fact that two "poets," as we have seen, are transformed into a bird and a madman.[35]

As already described, these attributions, "i oseaus tarduis" and "Li sons derves del home salvage," could be translated as "one belated bird" and "the

31. Many of the later additions have been edited by Radaelli (2004).

32. Haines (2013, 73) suggests an overall focus on Arrageois composers in the manuscript. He ultimately suggests that the songbook was compiled either in Arras shortly after 1253 or by Arrageois scribes in the Morea using exemplars from France (93, 95).

33. This theory would explain the attribution of the very first song in the manuscript to the "Prince de la Moree" (Haines 1998, 12). Haines also suggests that the later musical additions, which refer to Charles of Anjou, correspond with Charles's position as successor to Guillaume as prince of Morea (16).

34. Battelli (1993, 277) suggests that the projected manuscript was more strictly hierarchical in its organization, to judge from the table of contents, than the actual manuscript. Longnon (1939, 98) had already pointed out that the organization is not as hierarchical as the Becks made out.

35. It is difficult to say whether there is some kind of hierarchy at work in the troubadour section, given how few named composers there are. The two attributions I have discussed follow "Foukes de Marselle," who comes first, but precede "Pieres Vidaus" and "Bernars de Ventadour" (fol. Er).

crazy song/sound of the wild man." Although the word *tarduis* is meaningless in French, it may be intended to conjure up the Occitan adjective *tardiu* (late, slow). I want to turn here to the logic of these attributions. Why, of all the pieces transmitted in fr. 844, are these three singled out? The two pieces attributed to "i oseaus tarduis" in the manuscript's table of contents are "Lo nous mes d'abril" and "Lanquan li jorn" (PC 421.6 and PC 262.2); these pieces are generally attributed not to a bird but to Rigaut de Berbezilh and Jaufre Rudel, respectively. The piece described as the "crazy sound of the wild man" is "Poc ve gent" (a *unicum* catalogued as PC 461.197).

I turn first to the pieces attributed to the "belated bird." Both concern birdsong—delayed in the first instance and spatially distant in the second. It is impossible to say how closely the version of the piece transcribed in fr. 844 resembles Varvaro's edition (quoted below), because the part of folio 189 that transmitted this stanza of the piece has been excised. Of the first stanza, only the last few words of line 9 remain. If, however, fr. 844's version bore some resemblance to Varvaro's edition, we can assume the allusion to birdsong. The speaker of "Lo nous mes d'abril" declares at the start of the song that, just as birds have suffered through winter to begin their song in spring, so does he patiently await reward from his beloved:

> Lo nous mes d'abril
> apres la freidor
> e l'ausel son chantador,
> qu'atendut an en parvensa
> lo pascor.
> Miels-de-dompna, atretal atendensa
> aten de vos ab joi et ab temensa,
> c'apres los mals, c'ai traitz durs e cosenz,
> m'en veingna bes amoros e jauzenz.
> (Rigaut de Berbezilh 1960, 171)

> The new month of April begins after the cold, and the birds, who seem to have waited for Easter, begin their song. Better-than-Lady, with similar patience, from you I hope—with joy and with fear—that after the hard and burning pains I have endured, rewards of love and joy may come to me.

The rubricator of the table of contents of fr. 844 (or whoever was responsible for its content) follows up on a threefold identification already latent in the lyric—between its speaker (whose song testifies to his patience in love service), his beloved (whose erotic rewards—or so the speaker hopes—are merely deferred rather than permanently withheld), and finally the birds whose song belatedly bursts forth in vernal splendor. In a manner similar to *vida* authors, the rubricator literalizes the metaphoric in the song at hand, taking *au pied de la lettre* the poet's implied comparison of himself to songbirds.

The second song attributed to the "oseaus tarduis" in MS fr. 844's table of contents, PC 262.2, Jaufre Rudel's famous song about *amour de loin*, also features birdsong prominently.[36] Here, famously, the speaker observes how sweet birdsong is to him in the long days of May, since it reminds him of his distant love. I quote here from the piece as it is transcribed in fr. 844:

[. . .] an que li ior sunt lonc en mai.
[. . .] mest bel dolz chanz doisel de
[. . .] an me sui partis de lai. membre
[. . .] amor de loig. vais de talens bru*ns*
et enclins. si que chanz ne flors daubespins
non val maiz que livers gelatz.

[when] the days are long in May
the song of birds is beautiful to me
[. . .] I have left there, I remember
[. . .] love from afar. I go with desire, brown [?]
and bent over, such that song or the flower of hawthorn
is not worth more to me than frozen winter.[37]

This piece, like PC 421.6, foregrounds distant birdsong: the speaker rejoices in the birdsong he overhears from migratory birds (presumably coming from the same distant place as his absent beloved). A similar identification between the lyric "I" and the birds described is implied; they have followed the same trajectory away from the object of the speaker's affections, and both engage in the act of song. Both pieces, then, are plausibly attributable to a "belated bird," in the sense that the label builds on an identification already present in both pieces between the lyric "I" and songbirds. We will see throughout this book the same association between birdsong and troubadour lyric in many of the francophone narratives that quote Occitan song.

The next attribution within this section—"li sons derues del home saluage" (fol. Er, "derue" on fol. 190r)—further situates troubadour song on the margins of the human. This is how the attribution appears just before the song with which it is associated, "Poc ve gent" (PC 461.197) (figure 1.4). Unlike

36. As we have seen, the attribution is "corrected" to "ossiames faiduis" in fol. 189v.

37. BnF MS fr. 844's reading of "bru*ns* et enclis" echoes that of fr. 20050 and also, more distantly, "broncs etendis" of Chiarini's manuscript *e* (Jaufre Rudel 1985, 89).

FIGURE 1.4 The beginning of "Poc ve gent," described as "li sons derue del home sauuage" in BnF MS fr. 844, fol. 190r.

the label of "oseaus tarduis" discussed above, this attribution is impossible to explain away as a misreading of an actual troubadour name. The label may respond primarily to the acoustic fabric of the piece—both to its unusual rhymes, which are approximative rather than exactly identical, with some bordering on assonance, and to its quasi-incomprehensibility in the Gallicized form in which it is presented here. While many of the Gallicized troubadour songs in the manuscript have moments of semantic opacity, this one actually defies decipherment in many places. Like birdsong, this song might be considered *vox literata* but *inarticulata* (scriptable but meaningless voice). Table 1.2 shows how the song appears on folio 190r of the manuscript.

As the number of question marks in my translation should make clear, this piece as transcribed in fr. 844—which is in fact the only source for it—contains passages that border on incomprehensibility. It is by far the most incomprehensible of the Gallicized troubadour songs in BnF MS fr. 844. Its most recent editor, Francesca Gambino (2003), has done a remarkable job of cleaning it up, but as actually transcribed in fr. 844, it is highly opaque in several places.[38] That the critical apparatus justifying Gambino's editorial decisions spans thirteen pages is a testament to the difficulty of making it intelligible (97–109).

38. I do not intend at all to cast aspersions on Gambino's proposed interpretations of these opaque moments, many of which I find convincing. Rather, I wish here to draw attention to the garbled nature of the piece in manuscript.

Table 1.2 "li sons derues del home saluage" (fol. Er, "derue" on fol. 190r)

I.	Poc ve gent que liuer sirais. et part se del tanz amoros. que non auges notes ni lais. des auselz per ver- gers foilloz. per lou freit del brun tempo- rau. non leisserai un vers a far. et dirai al ques mon talant.
II.	Lonc desirrier et griu pantais. nai agut al cor cubitos. vers cele qui soaf mi trais. maiz ainc vers li non fui greignos. ainz la portaue el cor leial. mol fui legiers aen- ganar. mes peccas naie deus amans.
III.	No gins per autre orgueill non lais. de samor dont tant sui corcous. et *co*nneis ben *con* ben mi pais. et sui galias aestrous. las re masus sui del chabau. quant per autre non vol poignar. per me ni per mon dru- ghemant.
IV.	Tot mes chauat car agran fais. me tieg dosne quan pens de vos. et quant noi parlar mes esglais. et ia ior non serai iauzos. queu sui irais de vostre lau. et ab ioi de vostre blasmar. et plaisen me tuit vostre dan.
V.	Non pos mudar que non biais. vers a quen ioi tant orgueilloz. quainc non vi or- gueill non abais, quan pluz en poie meuz caous. et est folz qui ve et qui au. et si non sab son meuz triar. et na el siegle da- ques tans.
VI.	H vi mais sen faignent druc et lais. cel q*ui* non estat enuios. qua toz les fenis et le lais. per oc que non si poderos. pos poder ni sab ben ni mau. ben es dreis *com* la desampar. et ai me perdu mes enfans.
I.	I see few people whom winter makes sad [?] and who take leave of the amorous season, who do not hear notes or *lais* from the birds in the leafy orchards, because of the cold of the brown season, I will not renounce composing a song, and I will speak a little about my desire.
II.	Long-lasting desire and serious anguish I have had in my desirous heart toward she who sweetly pulls me close but never toward her was I deceitful, rather I held her in my loyal heart. It was very easy to deceive but she had pity on her lovers [?].

III.	Not at all [?] through another pride do I leave her love of which I am so [?] and I know well how much it nourishes me and I am completely deceived. Alas, I have remained [*del chabau*?] since for another I do not wish to exert myself, Either through myself or through an intermediary.
IV.	Everything [*m'es chauat*?] me, for a great burden weighs on me, lady, when I think of you, and when I hear speak of you, I am dismayed [?]. And never will I be joyful, for I am angered to hear praise of you, and joyous to hear you blamed, and all of your misadventures please me.
V.	I cannot change if not through [?] toward that joy so proud. For I have never seen pride that does not debase itself, for the more it climbs, the better it falls. And he is crazy who sees and hears and yet does not know how to choose the best. And there are so many of these in the world.
VI.	From now on friends and vile people [?] occupy themselves with this, he who has not become [?] jealous, for I completely abandon it [her?] and leave it [her?] because I do not possess it [her?]. Since of [?] possession [?] she does not know pleasure or displeasure, it is fitting that I leave her. and I have lost my children [?].

Note: "et" has been added in III, above the line.

Various explanations have been proposed to account for the strange label attached to the song. Giulio Bertoni (1913, 35–36) linked—unconvincingly, in my estimation—the "mad song" to the seminonsensical songs sung by young men on the first Sunday in May in Switzerland. Alfred Jeanroy subsequently, but with no reference to Bertoni's claim, proposed first of all that the piece was by Peire Vidal, on the sole grounds that it evokes a certain "drughement" (stanza III), a *senhal* used in another of Peire's songs, and then suggested that the label alluded to Peire Vidal's insanity as reported in his *vida* (Jeanroy 1891, 86).[39] Joseph Anglade subsequently subscribed to this theory (Peire Vidal 1913, 178, 155–59). I would object, first of all, that the term is not clearly used as a *senhal* here. Second, Peire Vidal appears in the table of contents of fr. 844 as a distinct entry just beneath this piece. Had the rubricator thought him its composer, he might easily have merged the two entries. Third, this theory assumes a knowledge of the *vida* tradition in France and/or the Morea (although the French and Italian songbook traditions seem mostly

39. Mouzat (1958) proposed Eble de Ventadorn as the composer of the piece, as well as a handful of other anonymous lyrics, all on vague stylistic grounds. He makes no mention of the "son dervé" label.

independent, this is certainly possible, but it has yet to be demonstrated). Gambino (2003, 94), for her part, suggests that the rubricator was aware of the tradition according to which the wild man sings happily in storms and cries in good weather. She proposes further that the lover has been reduced to a semiferal state because he is faced with the "excessively proud hostility" of the lover. In her reading, the speaker's mental state actually devolves over the course of the poem (95). Gambino's suggestions certainly all constitute plausible explanations, in my opinion, but the most obvious explanation—one not mentioned by Gambino—is that the rubricator is responding both to the formal strangeness and to the semantic opacity of the song in the version he had on hand.

This may, in fact, explain the label *son*, which refers not just to "melody" but also to "sound" more broadly.[40] The semantic breakdown in the song means that we have no choice but to listen to it as sheer *sound*, given that the piece both solicits and frustrates any attempt to parse it semantically beyond brief blips of sense. This mode of listening—for sound beyond sense—is further encouraged by the use of graphically heterogeneous rhyme sounds, an unusual feature remarked on by Gambino (2003, 91). Even Gambino's cleaned-up version of the piece contains such irregularities. In her edition, the *b* rhyme conjoins *-os*, *-oz*, and *-ous*, the *c* rhyme *-al* and *-au,* and the *e* rhyme *-ant, -ans,* and *-an*. Although the use of graphic variation at the rhyme is certainly not unprecedented in troubadour lyric, PC 461.97 contains an unusual amount of variation, even in Gambino's highly sanitized hypothetical original. Indeed, the *b* and *e* "rhymes" are so capacious that they might be better accounted for through assonance than strict rhyme. These approximative rhymes force the listener to listen differently: whereas generally the rhyme scheme of a poem might well fade from the foreground as its semantic content develops, here the slant rhymes draw attention to the sonic fabric of language through their failure to conform (or rather to conform exactly) to the expected pattern. This distinction is akin to the one Michel Chion (2012) theorizes between semantic listening (listening in order to interpret a code such as language) and reduced listening (listening to the sound itself, independent of its cause and meaning). It would seem, then, that the "crazy sound" of this "wild man" is crazy both in its unusual sonic components—highly approximative rhymes or even assonance—and in its resistance to decipherment as referential language, despite its proximity to such referential language.

40. Godefroy (2002) glosses the term as follows: "sensation produite sur l'organe par des mouvements vibratoires rythmiques."

This hypothesis is supported by Emma Dillon's recent work on the figure of the *dervé* in Adam de la Halle and his sonic free association.[41] Building on Sylvia Huot's (2003, 1) observation that the mad in Old French texts are characterized by either a dearth or an overabundance of speech, Dillon (2012, 138) explains, "[the *dervé*] experiences words phonetically—grammatically, even—rather than semantically." This is certainly the case for the *dervé* in Adam de la Halle's *Jeu de la feuillée*, who, as both Huot and Dillon have demonstrated, tunes in to rhyme sounds and free associates with them at the expense of meaning. For example, the verb *aourer* ("adore") conjures up in the *dervé*'s mind *tuer*, "to kill," leading him into a fit of vituperative paranoia (Dillon 2012, 138–39; Huot 2003, 59; Adam de la Halle 1995, vv. 392–95). Adam's *dervé*, like BnF MS fr. 844's madman, veers into nonsensicality, choosing words for their phonetic properties rather than for their semantic content. The same acoustic disregulation defines Guillaume in the *Farce du maître Pathelin*, causing Guillemette to remark: "Il s'en va si fort grumelant / Qu'il semble qu'il doive desver" (he goes around grumbling so much that it seems he must be mad) (cited in Godefroy 2002). Recognition of madness also hinges on the acoustic in many of Godefroy's attestations of the word: "li rois l'oï, le sens cuide derver," a recurring formula in *Hervis de Metz*, and "Fromons l'entent, le sens cuide dever" (P. Taylor 1952, v. 13071). The label in PC 461.97 thus arguably builds on a lengthy tradition in which madness is registered acoustically. While his speech is not free-associative in the manner of Adam's *dervé*, MS fr. 844's madman's speech is also nonsensical (perhaps only as the result of garbled transmission). And his rhymes, like those of Adam's *dervé*, encourage attentiveness to the signifier over (or at least in addition to) the signified.

Both rubrics, "belated bird" and "the crazy sound / song of the wild man," invite us to see troubadour song not as a high art form but as non- or only semilinguistic noise. Although both labels reflect an intelligent and playful reading of the poems with which they are associated, they still have the effect of transforming two troubadours into a bird and a madman, respectively. If all of the troubadours in fr. 844 are positioned at the bottom of the manuscript's social hierarchy, coming last within a stratified organizational structure, only these two have been relegated to the periphery of the human. These designations also arrogate from the troubadours their humanity and sanity, respectively, and efface the rational composer who lay behind each

41. On the madman and sound, see chap. 4, "Madness and the Eloquence of Nonsense," in Dillon (2012). Huot (2003, 59–64) also discusses the figure of the *dervé*, but not primarily from the perspective of his language.

song (and, in this sense, they only build on the trend toward anonymization established in the other songbooks discussed earlier in this chapter).

We will see in the subsequent chapters in this book that the authors of the French narratives that quote troubadour song echo BnF MS fr. 844's framing of this tradition as primarily a sonic event (rather than a semantic one), a sonic event that was only marginally human and certainly anonymous. All the francophone narratives that quote Occitan lyric do so anonymously, even those that acknowledge authorship of other lyrics. Jean Renart's *Rose* stages troubadour song as a sonic rather than a semantic event, "explaining" its referential breakdown through various diegetic performance scenarios. Gerbert de Montreuil's *Violette*, meanwhile, associates it with birdsong, and Richard de Fournival, humorously, with birds but *not* with birdsong. The three narratives also build on the pattern established in this chapter in the sense that they frame the troubadour corpus not as a linguistically or culturally foreign body, but rather as one that is part and parcel of a francophone lyric tradition, even if one sometimes on the nonrational and nonhuman margins of this tradition.

Chapter 2

Keeping Up with the French

Jean Renart's Francophile Empire in the Roman de la rose

At the court of the Holy Roman Empire in Jean Renart's *Roman de la rose* (early thirteenth century), the latest hits of francophone music ring from all corners. The oddity of this linguistic feature in the imperial soundscape has either been overlooked by critics or instead dismissed as a feature of the text lacking any symbolic significance. Gaston Paris's (non)explanation is typical of the latter approach:

> Il faut encore noter qu'il [Jean] fait chanter à la cour d'Allemagne et par l'empereur lui-même non seulement des chansons françaises, mais les chansons les plus nouvellement en faveur. Il ne faut sans doute pas voir là une preuve de la diffusion de notre poésie lyrique à l'étranger: le poète a fait simplement abstraction de la différence des lieux comme il a fait abstraction de celle des temps, puisqu'il nous dit que son empereur Conrad régnait "jadis" en Allemagne, ce qui ne l'empêche pas de chanter les chansons de Gace Brulé et du châtelain de Couci. (Jean Renart 1893, cxiii)

> It must further be noted that he [Jean] has sung at the court of Germany—and by the emperor himself—not only French songs, but those that had most recently come into favor. One must surely not see there proof of the diffusion of our lyric poetry abroad: the poet has discounted difference of space as he has difference of time, since

> he tells us that his emperor Conrad reigned "long ago" in Germany, which does not prevent him from singing songs by Gace Brulé and the Châtelain de Couci.

William Paden (1993, 46, 47), meanwhile, merely raises the question of why "this court of the German emperor rings with songs in French," noting that the German court as depicted in the French romance seems to be "agog over French as a lyric language" and to resound "with French poetry and song." Paden seems to imply that this is merely part of the fictional framework of the narrative, and that we are supposed to assume that the Germanic languages occasionally mentioned are in fact intended to indicate the ambient linguistic landscape of the text—that is, we should read these francophone pieces as German.[1] Like Gaston Paris, then, Paden concludes that the French slant of the musical landscape of the Holy Roman Empire is symbolically insignificant.

In addition to the two trouvères mentioned by Gaston Paris (Gace Brulé and the Châtelain de Couci), the francophone soundtrack to the text includes songs attributed to Renaut de Beaujeu, Renaut de Sabloeil, the Vidame de Chartres, and Gontier de Soignies, along with numerous anonymous pieces.[2] In total within the text there are forty-eight insertions that span several genres.[3] These are quoted, usually only partially, in such a way as to suggest diegetic performance. All the songs date from between the mid-twelfth century and the years directly preceding the composition of the romance (Ibos-Augé 2006, 263).[4] Included in the lyric portfolio of the *Rose* are selected

1. The analogy Paden proposes is with films featuring Native Americans such as *Dances with Wolves*, where the few passages involving characters speaking Sioux are enough to suggest that the English the characters actually speak in the film is supposed to stand in for Sioux. In his estimation, "the French language becomes intrinsically ambivalent, representing either itself, in contrast to German, or language in general—both French and German" (1993, 47).

2. Isabelle Arseneau (2010) points out that some of these attributions may well be fanciful, given how rarely they match up with attributions in extant songbooks, and that Jean may have composed many of the pieces himself.

3. See table 2.1 for a chart of these insertions.

4. Most critics place the composition of the romance in the early thirteenth century. Rita Lejeune (1935, 105) argues that the work was written between 1212, when Savaric de Mauléon entered the service of the king of France (Savaric appears on the "French" side of the tournament), and the end of May 1213, when Renaut de Dammartin revolted against Philip Augustus. Félix Lecoy, for his part, proposed that Jean intended to evoke the period between 1210 and 1215 but actually wrote the text between 1227 and 1228 (Jean Renart 2008, xi). Gustave Servois, by contrast, suggested that the text was written before Bouvines. In his assessment: "un poème où l'on voit Allemands, Flamands et Français se rencontrer dans des luttes courtoises d'un tournoi et dans les fêtes qui s'y joignent, ne peut dater ni du lendemain ni de la veille de la bataille de Bouvines" (a poem in which one sees Germans, Flemings, and French come together in courtly battles at a tournament and at the associated parties cannot date from the day after or the eve of the Battle of Bouvines) (Jean Renart 1893, l). He opted more precisely for the period between October 1199 and May 1201 (lxxxvi).

stanzas of three troubadour compositions. In the sole manuscript that transmits the *Rose*, all three songs are heavily Gallicized, unattributed, and, in two out of three cases, fictively relocated to border regions between *langue d'oïl* and *langue d'oc* through the labels "son auvrignace" (auvergnat song, v. 4649) and "son poitevin" (poitevin song, v. 5211).[5] These are Jaufre Rudel's "Lanquan li jorn" (PC 262.2), Daude de Pradas's "Belha m'es la voiz altana" (PC 124.5), and Bernart de Ventadorn's famous "Can vei la lauzeta mover" (PC 70.43).[6] As established in the introduction and chapter 1, Jean Renart likely encountered these songs in Gallicized form. Beyond the statistical prevalence of Gallicized forms, we know from the fact that Jean rhymes his narrative to the Gallicized form *sane* (vv. 4659–60) at the end of one of the three included Occitan songs that he was either working with a Gallicized version of the song, or else that he sought to "naturalize" his own Gallicized version through the rhyme sounds of the narrative.

The francophone soundtrack of the *Rose*'s Empire should not be rationalized away or dismissed as symbolically insignificant. It is, in fact, part of a broader cultural current in the romance in which French art objects, including French song, are fetishized as glamorous and desirable by imperial audiences. The three formerly Occitan songs quoted in the narrative are either staged or transformed in such a way as to blend thoroughly into this alluring francophone musical tradition, which has, at least in a cultural sense, subjugated the Empire. The second part of this chapter documents the processes through which Occitan is assimilated into the broader francophone lyric landscape, one of which is linguistic Gallicization. This process has resulted in this text, as elsewhere in the French reception of the troubadours, in occasional moments of nonsensicality—and this chapter documents the various ways in which this nonsensicality is accounted for within the narrative. Finally, I turn to the ramifications of this staging of French culture (including Gallicized Occitan) within the narrative, arguing that it exerts such a strong ideological hold over the Germanic emperor Conrad that he begins to see himself as French and views Germanic languages, which are in fact much more native to his Empire, as foreign. We might expect this abundance of "French" cultural exports to spark in Conrad a very particular *amour de loin*—love of a relative of the French monarch. This is, after all, the

5. The sole manuscript of the *Rose* is Vatican City, Biblioteca Apostolica Vaticana, Reg. Lat. 1725, fols. 68v–98v.

6. Jean's self-proclaimed innovation of lyric insertion has been the focus of much secondary literature on the romance (Jean Renart 1893; Arseneau 2010; Baumgartner 1981; Boulton 1993; Butterfield 2002; Callahan 1990; Coldwell 1981; Duport 1993; Huot 1987; Jewers 1996; Lejeune 1935; Lacy 1980; van der Werf 1997; Zink 1979). The bibliography is too extensive to cite in its entirety here.

choice for which his barons have been rooting all along, and one that would create an actual political sphere of the sort Conrad fantasizes about. But the emperor's fetish for all things French stops short of precisely this mark. In choosing Lienor, who hails from imperial territory, Conrad fails to follow the path set out for him by the French songs that circulate at his court.

But first, to briefly summarize the plot of the *Rose*: As Conrad, leader of Jean Renart's Holy Roman Empire, gets on in age, his barons begin to fear that he will leave no heir on the throne upon his death unless he quickly identifies a suitable spouse. Their favored candidates are relatives of the king of France, and thus part of the Capetian bloodline. While they are out riding one day, one of Conrad's jongleurs, a certain Jouglet, tells him a tale of a beautiful French maiden and her valiant suitor, an accomplished knight from Champagne. So enraptured is Conrad by Jouglet's story that he sets out to find two real people who compare to those of Jouglet's tale. He is put onto the trail of Lienor and her brother Guillaume, who reside near Dole, within the borders of the Empire.[7] After having them vetted by a messenger, Conrad gives his approval, and a marriage is arranged between him and Lienor. One of the emperor's seneschals, however, throws a wrench into the plan by making the false claim that he has taken Lienor virginity. His "proof" of this sexual act is his knowledge of a rose-shaped birthmark on Lienor's thigh, the existence of which Lienor's chatty mother has inadvertently revealed. Conrad is distraught, Guillaume furious, and Lienor outraged. She decides to exact revenge through an ingenious scheme of her own: coming to court disguised, she convinces the seneschal—via the medium of a messenger—to wear several intimate objects (including a piece of fabric worn next to his skin). In order to persuade him to accept them, she has her intermediary claim that they are from the Châtelaine de Dijon, one of the seneschal's failed conquests. She then accuses the seneschal of rape, using as "proof" his possession of these symbols of their intimacy. The seneschal must defend himself and, in so doing, admit that he has had no carnal knowledge of the woman who accuses him, thus allowing Lienor to exculpate herself.

Jean Renart's Francophile Empire

I am not the first critic of the *Roman de la rose* to note the conspicuous presence of French cultural products—including song—in Conrad's Empire.[8] In John Baldwin's (1997, 53) estimation, France is upheld as the standard of

7. Baldwin (1997, 54) has commented on the location of Dole.

8. That this Empire is inspired by the historic Holy Roman Empire and can in some sense be said to be "Germanic"—despite the fact that everyone seems to speak French there—is evident both

chivalric life, with clothing, wine, and armor all judged by French quality. Indeed, French products are not just the standard against which quality is measured; a connection to France is precisely what distinguishes the most opulent objects in the Empire, which are described as being of either French manufacture or French style. Conrad's lavish ermine robe, which exudes a delicate odor, is, as Jouglet recognizes, "de la taille de France" (cut in the French manner, v. 1535). In addition to his French-style robe, Conrad has at his disposal what he maintains is the best helmet in all of Germany ("le mellor de tote Alemaigne," v. 1662), but the narrator emphasizes the fact that this helmet was manufactured in France at Senlis (v. 1664). Its aesthetic qualities are inextricable from its foreign French provenance, since "Senlis" is rhymed with "fetiz" (v. 1663), the latter meaning "beautiful" or "elegant." Jean Renart's evocation of Senlis was likely quite calculated; Senlis had long been associated with the Capetian monarchy. The site of one of Hugh Capet's royal castles, and possibly also of his coronation, it was also the location of Philip Augustus's victory chapel after his defeat of imperial forces at Bouvines (Baldwin 1986, 389). As if to highlight the paradox in Conrad's assertion that the best helmet in the Empire is in fact French, Guillaume responds to this remark in such a way as to draw attention to the origin of the object: "Il n'a si bel en .ii. roiaumes" (There is none as beautiful in two kingdoms, v. 1680), he declares.[9] That the provenance of Conrad's favorite piece of military equipment is a long-standing Capetian stronghold suggests a certain jejune Francophilia on the part of the emperor.

---

in the landscape of the text, which is routinely anchored in imperial toponyms, and in Jean Renart's comment that the current occupants of the Empire are German: "En l'Empire, ou li Alemant / ont esté maint jor et maint an, / si com li contes dit, segnor, / ot jadis un empereor" (in the Empire, where the Germans have had power for many days and years, as the story says, there once was an emperor, vv. 31–34). As I describe later, this initial framework intriguingly raises the possibility that the Germans are not the rightful inhabitants of the Empire, in Jean's view. Conrad's name, which he is said to have inherited from his father (vv. 35–36), also links him to historic Germanic leaders (Conrad I lived from approximately 890 to 918, Conrad II from the end of the tenth century to 1039, and Conrad III from 1093 to 1152).

9. Guillaume seems acutely attuned to the commodity pathway of the object. Having drawn attention to its production in France, he subsequently points to its next function. In Guillaume's assessment, Conrad is attempting to buy loyalty by distributing such gifts: "[. . .] est dons d'empereor / qui por tels joiauls doit aquerre / les haus bachelers de sa terre" ([this] is the gift of an emperor, who through such jewels acquires the young nobles of his land, vv. 1682–84). This is one of many situations where Guillaume appears especially adroit at economically navigating the social sphere. As a nonlandowner, he uses the name of the nearby Dole to confer additional status on himself. As Jouglet explains to Conrad: "Guillaume de Dole l'apelent / tuit cil qui el païs reperent, / non pas por ce qu'ele soit soe. /—Di moi dont par qoi s'en avoue?—Qu'il en maint pres, a un plessié; / s'a par Dole plus essaucié / son surnon que par une vile: / ce vient plus de sens que de guile" (They call him Guillaume de Dole, all those who live in his region, not because it belongs to him.—Tell me why he uses it?—Because he lives nearby, in a fortified house; he has enhanced his reputation more through [the name of] Dole than through [that of] a village. It comes more from good sense than from trickery,

These Francophilic trends in the imperial court's conspicuous consumption are not limited to the sartorial.[10] They also extend to song, which, as Caroline Jewers (1996, 110) and Emma Dillon (2016) have shown, is circulated as a kind of luxury good in the romance. Before turning to the francocentric quality of the lyric insertions, I would like to expand on Dillon's and Jewers's observations on song's association with opulence. This association is evident as early as the prologue, which uses much-discussed metaphors of embroidery and dyeing for the procedure of lyric insertion. Jean further presents the inset lyrics as precisely that which makes the text as a whole inaccessible to peasants. In other words, they are the status goods that are supposed to distinguish the nobility within Jean's readership:

> cestui *Romans de la rose*
> [. . .] est une novele chose
> et s'est des autres si divers
> et brodez, par lieus, de biaus vers
> que vilains nel porroit savoir.
>
> this *Roman de la rose*
> [. . .] is a new thing
> and is so different from the others,
> and [is] embroidered, in places, with beautiful songs
> such that the peasant cannot understand it.
>
> (vv. 11–15)

This declaration is ambiguous: Is it the novelty of the romance that makes it difficult to understand for the "vilain," or do the "embroidered" songs act like a sumptuary marker, distinguishing the "vilain" from the good aristocratic reader? Along with these metaphors in the prologue, later scenes link songs with luxury goods.[11] In some instances, this link is based on contiguity, as

vv. 780–87). Later, Guillaume has to borrow the money to cover the cost of his equipment for the tournament (v. 1955), thereby increasing his family's debts, but this additional debt ultimately "pays off"; Guillaume and his equipment are widely admired at the tournament. Although Jean Renart's text has generally been read as aristocratic and anti-bourgeois (Lejeune 1935, 60–61), I would point out that Guillaume's social maneuvering is ultimately rewarded: his sister becomes an empress and Conrad fails to make a politically strategic marriage.

10. There are, of course, exceptions to this predilection for French or French-style goods. To cite a few, the *destriers* used by Guillaume and his companions are Spanish (v. 1551), Jouglet's palfrey Norwegian (v. 2176), and the *orfroi* decorating Guillaume's tunic English (v. 2197). For a discussion of *orfroi*, see E. Jane Burns (2009, 48–51).

11. Emma Dillon (2016) has recently explored the link between song and luxury in Renart's *Rose*.

when songs are performed by characters whose lavish clothing is described shortly before or after they begin to sing, as is the case with the lady dressed in a kermes-dyed tunic ("vestue d'une cote en graine," v. 512) or the emperor and his companions whose silk blanket ("coute de soie," v. 1777) is sewn in homonymy to the last word of the song they have just sung ("en quel lieu que onques *soie*," v. 1776). In other instances, it is the songs themselves that depict opulent garments (table 2.1, nos. 4, 5, 9, 10, 13, 14, etc.).

Table 2.1 Chart of all the lyrics insertions in the *Roman de la rose*[1]

NO. IN ROMANCE	LINE NUMBER IN NARRATIVE	INCIPIT	NUMBER OF STANZAS QUOTED AND PLACE WITHIN LYRIC	AUTHOR ATTRIBUTION/ GEOGRAPHICAL TAG	STANDARD CATALOG NUMBER	RHYME PAIR CONSTRUCTED WITH NARRATIVE?
1	291–292	E non Deu, sire se ne l'ai	n/a		VdB (Ref.) 676	No
2 = 28	294–297	La jus, deoz la raime	n/a		VdB (Rond.) 1	No
3	304–305	Se mes amis m'a guerpie	n/a		VdB (Ref.) 1703	No, but echo in *-ie*
4	310–315	Main se leva bele Aeliz	n/a		VdB (Rond.) 2	No
5	318–322	Main se leva bele Aeliz	n/a		VdB (Rond.) 3	No
6	329–333	C'est tot la gieus, el glaioloi	n/a		VdB (Rond.) 4	No, but quasi-echo in *-er/-ere*
7	514–519	C'est tot la gieus, enmi les prez	n/a		VdB (Rond.) 5	No
8	522–527	C'est la jus desoz l'olive	n/a		VdB (Rond. 6)	No
9	532–537	Main se levoit Aaliz	n/a		VdB (Rond.) 7	No
10	542–547	Main se leva la bien fete Aeliz	n/a		VdB (Rond.) 8	No
11	846–852	Quant flors et glais et verdure s'esloigne	1 (I)	Song is sung "en l'onor monsegnor Gasçon" (v. 845) [= Gace Brulé]	RS 1779=2119	No
12	923–930	Li noviaus tens et mais	1 (I)	[Châtelain de Couci]	RS 985=986	No

(Continued)

Table 2.1 (Continued)

NO. IN ROMANCE	LINE NUMBER IN NARRATIVE	INCIPIT	NUMBER OF STANZAS QUOTED AND PLACE WITHIN LYRIC	AUTHOR ATTRIBUTION/ GEOGRAPHICAL TAG	STANDARD CATALOG NUMBER	RHYME PAIR CONSTRUCTED WITH NARRATIVE?
13	1158–1162	Fille et la mere se sieent a l'orfrois	2 (I–II)		RS 1834	No
14	1183–1187	Siet soi bele Aye as piez sa male maistre	2 (I–II)		RS 202	No
15	1203–1216	La bele Doe siet au vent	3? (I–III)		RS 744	No
16	1301–1308	Lors que li jor sont lonc en mai	1 (I)	"cest son" (v. 1300) [Jaufre Rudel]	PC 262.2	Yes
17	1335–1367	Des que Fromonz au Veneor tença	n/a	"cest vers de Gerbert"	not extant elsewhere	No
18	1456–1469	Loial amor qui en fin cuer s'est mise	1 (I)	"la chançon Renaut de Baujieu, / De Rencien" (1451–1452) [= Renaut de Beaujeu]	RS 1635	Yes
19	1579–1584	Aaliz main se leva	n/a		VdB (Rond.) 9	No
20	1769–1776	Mout me demeure	1 (I)		RS 420	Yes
21	1846–1851	C'est la jus en la praele	n/a		VdB (Rond.) 10	Yes
22	2027–2035	Contrel tens que voi frimer	1 (I)		RS 857=2027	Yes
23	2235–2294	Bele Aiglentine en roial chamberine	selections from whole piece		RS 1379	No
24	2369–2374	La jus desouz l'olive	n/a		VdB (Rond.) 11	No
25	2379–2385	Mauberjon s'est main levee	n/a		VdB (Rond.) 12	No
26	2389–2391	Renaus et s'amie chevauche	n/a		---	Yes
27	2398–2404	De Renaut de Mousson	1 (I)		RS 1871a	No

NO. IN ROMANCE	LINE NUMBER IN NARRATIVE	INCIPIT	NUMBER OF STANZAS QUOTED AND PLACE WITHIN LYRIC	AUTHOR ATTRIBUTION/ GEOGRAPHICAL TAG	STANDARD CATALOG NUMBER	RHYME PAIR CONSTRUCTED WITH NARRATIVE?
28 = 2	2514–2518	La gieus desoz la raime	n/a		VdB (Rond.) 1	Yes
29	2523–2527	Sor la rive de la mer	n/a		VdB (Rond.) 13	Yes
30	3107–3114	Mout est fouls, que que nus die	1 (I)		RS 1132	Yes
31	3179–3195	Quant de la foelle espoissent li vergier	2 (I–II)		RS 1319	Yes
32	3403–3406	Quant ge li donai le blanc peliçon	1 (I)		RS 1877a	No, but echo
33	3419–3430	Cele d'Oisseri	1 (I)		---	No
34	3625–3631	Je di que c'est granz folie	1 (II)	"Des bons vers mon segnor Gasson" (v. 3620) [Gace Brulé]	RS 1232	Yes
35	3751–3759	Por quel forfet ne por quel ochoison	1 (I)		RS 1872 = 1876a = 1884	Yes
36	3883–3899	Ja de chanter en ma vie	2 (I–II)	"Des bons vers celui de Sabloeil / Mon segnor Renaut" (vv. 3878–3879)	RS 1229	No
37	4127–4140	Quant la sesons del douz tens s'asseüre	1 (I–II)	"la bone chançon le Vidame / de Chartres" (vv. 4123–4124)	RS 2086	Yes
38	4164–4169	Tout la gieus, sor rive mer	n/a		VdB (Rond.) 14	No, but echo in *-é/-ez*
39	4568–4583	Quant revient la sesons	1 (I)		RS 1914b	Yes
40	4587–4593	Amours a non ciz maus qui me tormente	1 (I)		RS 754	Yes
41	4653–4659	Bele m'est la voiz altane (see Appendix 3)	1 (I)	"chançon auvrignace" (v. 4649) [Daude de Pradas?]	PC 124.5	Yes

(Continued)

Table 2.1 (Continued)

NO. IN ROMANCE	LINE NUMBER IN NARRATIVE	INCIPIT	NUMBER OF STANZAS QUOTED AND PLACE WITHIN LYRIC	AUTHOR ATTRIBUTION/ GEOGRAPHICAL TAG	STANDARD CATALOG NUMBER	RHYME PAIR CONSTRUCTED WITH NARRATIVE?
42	5106–5111	Que demandez vos	n/a		VdB (Ref.) 1561	Yes
43	5113–5115	Tendez tuit vos mains a la flor d'esté	n/a		VdB (Ref.) 1773	Yes
44	5188–5207	Or vienent Pasques les beles en avril	n/a		---	No
45	5212–5227	Quant voi l'aloete moder (see Appendix 4)	2 (I–II)	"son poitevin" (v. 5211)	PC 70.43	No
46	5232–5252	Lors que florist la bruiere	2 (I–II)	"des bons vers Gautier de Sagnies" (v. 5229) [= Gautier/Gontier de Soignies]	RS 1322a	No
47	5427–5434	C'est la gieus, la gieus, q'en dit en ces prez	n/a		VdB (Rond.) 15	Yes
48	5440–5445	C'est la gieus, en mi les prez	n/a		VdB (Rond.) 16	No, but echo in *-é/-ez*

1. As elsewhere in this book, RS numbers refer to Raynaud and Spanke's catalog of French lyrics (Spanke 1955), and PC numbers to Pillet and Carstens's catalog of Occitan lyric (Pillet and Carstens 1933). VdB numbers refer to van den Boogaard's catalog of rondeaux and refrains, *Rondeaux et refrains du XIIe siècle au début du XIVe* (Paris: Klincksieck, 1969).

And on one occasion, the lavishness evoked referentially in a song is sonically reduplicated. "Fille et la mere se sieent a l'orfrois" embroiders the gold thread evoked in its second line into the rest of the piece acoustically through the effect of assonance on *or* (vv. 1159–66):

Fille et la mere se sieent a l'*or*frois,
a un fil d'*or* i font *or*ïeuls croiz.
Parla la mere qui le cuer ot c*or*tois.
Tant bon'am*or* fist bele Aude en Doon!

"Aprenez, fille, a coudre et a filer,
et en l'*or*frois *or*ïex crois lever.
L'am*or* Doon vos convient oublier."
Tant bon'am*or* fist bele Aude en Doon!

Daughter and mother are seated at the *orfrois*,
with a thread of gold they make golden crosses.
The mother, who had a courtly heart, spoke.
Beautiful Aude felt such love for Doon!

"Learn, daughter, to sew and embroider,
and to make golden crosses in the *orfrois*.
You must forget love for Doon."
Beautiful Aude felt such love for Doon!

(vv. 1159–66)

Here the golden thread of the crosses ("*croix*") is supposed to reverse—as it does visually—Aude's love ("am*or*") for Doon. The connection of the songs in the text to luxury thus exceeds the actual imagery within and around the pieces to encompass their very acoustic materiality.

In the economy of the *Rose*, the provenance of the luxury commodities that songs constitute is, quite often, explicitly French. When the minstrel Hugues comes to the emperor's court, Conrad implores him to teach him a particular French dance performed by young women near Tremeilli (Trumilly in modern French, a town in Picardy near Senlis):

L'empereres le tint mout cort
que li apreïst une dance
que firent puceles de France
a l'ormel devant Tremeilli,
ou l'en a maint bon plet basti.

The emperor beseeched him
to teach him a dance
that the maidens of France performed
near the elm tree in front of Trumilly
where many good resolutions were made.

(vv. 3410–14)[12]

Hugues goes on to sing a couplet about "belle Marguerite"—perhaps one of the "puceles de France" in question—and Conrad remarks that imperial

12. "[. . .] ou l'en a maint bon plet basti" (v. 3414) has usually been translated as "where many good parties have been had." Dufournet, for example, translates as "où l'on a organisé plus d'une joyeuse partie" (Lecoy 1962, 278), while Psaki proposes "where many a celebration had been held" (Jean Renart 1995, 157). All instances of *plet* used with the verb *bastir* in Godefroy refer to a resolution or decision. Given this more frequent denotation of *plet* in conjunction with the verb *bastir*, it seems possible that Jean Renart is alluding to a particular decision made at Trumilly.

maidens pale in comparison to the French ones: "Celes ne l'en doivent de rien, fet li rois" (These ones here [in the Empire] do not surpass her in anything, said the king, vv. 3431–32). Here it is not just French art but also its origin in a performance context in France that interest Conrad.[13] He presses the jongleur not just to sing the piece but also to inform him of all of the details surrounding its performance in France. We learn, first of all, that the lyric is usually sung under a tree ("a l'ormel," v. 3413), probably the very same "ormel" mentioned in the song itself (v. 3424). Hugues is well placed to inform Conrad about the latest French fashions, having just come from "Braie Selve vers Oignon" (v. 3408); Ognon, just to the northeast of Senlis, was in the royal domain. What is more, Hugues is not the only person at Conrad's court to circulate music of French provenance. A young man from Normandy, part of the Capetian domain since 1204, sings a piece starring "Bele Aiglentine en roial chamberine" (v. 2231). This piece, which evokes the same French royal circles as Hugues's, is a *unicum* and may have been composed by Jean Renart expressly for the *Rose.* The same is true of the epic *laisse* about a certain Gerbert, which features the king of France (v. 1357).[14]

Sometimes it is not the content of the pieces but the provenance or composer with which Jean Renart associates them that anchors the lyrics in French or French-allied territory. For example, Renaut de Beaujeu, an otherwise unknown composer whom Jean presents as hailing from Champagne ("La chançon Renaut de Baujieu / De Rencien le bon chevalier," vv. 1451–52), infuses into the Empire the region associated with French royal coronations from Philip Augustus onward.[15] Gace Brulé, mentioned twice in the *Rose*, worked for the Plantagenets but also for the Capetians. For example, historical evidence shows he received a gift from the future Louis VIII (Karp, n.d.). Chartres—mentioned via the reference to the Vidame de Chartres—was a regalian bishopric, although the king appears to have had little direct power there in the early thirteenth century (Power 2004, 99). Of the named composers, only Gontier de Soignies (v. 5229) hails from imperial territory. Thus, the provenance of most of the lyrics, at least as Jean Renart presents them, is strikingly at odds with the geography of the narrative, which, as Baldwin (1997, 54) has noted, centers on traditional imperial cities along

13. Conrad is not alone in his fascination with French art. Even the evil seneschal wears the blazon of that Arthurian *bête noire*, Kay: "cil qui portoit un escucel / des armes Keu le seneschal" (he wore a small shield / with the arms of Kay the seneschal, vv. 3159–60). Indeed, the churlish seneschal of Jean Renart's *Rose*, who is responsible for defaming Lienor, and whose main vice is thus calumny, is likely modeled after the Arthurian Kay in more than just his emblem.

14. Arseneau (2010, 113–21) argues that this is a pastiche of *Gerbert de Metz*.

15. Jean may be mistaken about Renaut's origins. There is no Beaujeu in Champagne.

the Rhine and Meuse such as Mainz, Cologne, Kaiserwerth, and Maastricht. In all these instances in the text, imperial audiences are entranced by songs whose composers or characters are—explicitly or implicitly—French.

Against this backdrop of pieces that feature a French cast or are of explicitly French provenance, many of the other artistic works circulated at the imperial court take on a similar hue. For example, what are we to make of the fact that Conrad's imperial courtiers, including a young man in the service of the count of Speyer (v. 520), the son of the count of Dagsburg (v. 529) and the duchess of Austria (v. 538), sing obsessively about Robin, Marion, and Aélis?[16] As if to suggest a disjunction between the cultural sphere of those who sing the songs and the world evoked within them, Jean Renart emphasizes both the topics of the compositions and the fascination they exert on Conrad's courtiers: "Que de Robin que d'Aaliz / tant ont chanté que jusq'as liz / ont fetes durer les caroles" (About Robin and Aélis they sang so much that the *caroles* lasted until bedtime, vv. 548–50). The same question is invited by Conrad's choice of prandial entertainment, which features stories of Perceval and Roland (vv. 1747–48). Although the Empire did have its own flourishing literary and musical traditions, such as the songs of the Minnesänger, Jean Renart completely elides these actual cultural products of the Empire in favor of French pieces. At least in Conrad's world, Jean suggests, real culture must be francophone, of French style and, ideally, imported from France.[17]

Occitan Song in Jean's Francophile Empire

Rather than supplying a source of foreign geographical and linguistic material within the lyric portfolio of the romance, the three troubadour songs quoted in the narrative are mostly subsumed into this francophone and French cultural sphere through a variety of authorial sleights of hand. The first of these is the fictive provenance assigned to two of the three pieces. Daude de Pradas's "Bela m'es la votz autana" is described as a "chançon auvrignace" (v. 4649) and Bernart de Ventadorn's "Can vei la lauzeta mover" as a "son poitevin" (v. 5211), while Jaufre Rudel's "Lanquan li jorn" goes

16. The pieces in question are "Maint se leva bele Aeliz" (vv. 310–15), "Main se leva bele Aeliz" (vv. 318–22), "C'est la jus desoz l'olive" (vv. 522–28), and "Maint se levoit Aaliz" (vv. 532–37).

17. It is possible that Jean Renart is poking fun at the quite real Francophilia of contemporary imperial audiences, much of whose literature was an adaptation from or an imitation of French models. The bibliography on medieval Franco-Germanic literary relations is abundant, but see, *inter alia*, Bumke's (1967) overview. Ingrid Kasten and others have examined the relationship between Minnesang and the troubadour and trouvère repertoires (Kasten 1986; Kasten, Paravicini, and Pérennec 1998; Frank 1952b; Gennrich 1926; Ranawake 1976).

without any geographical label. Pradas (Prades-Salars) is due south of Auvergne, while Ventadorn, in the Limousin, lay to the south of Poitou. Both troubadour lyrics are thus remapped in such a way as to suggest provenance not in Occitan-speaking territory but farther north on the linguistic frontier between *langue d'oïl* and *langue d'oc.*[18] The Gallicized Occitan of the insertions may constitute an attempt to reflect the linguistic patterns of these border regions, but, regardless of their logic, the fake provenances are used to demarcate the southern boundary of Jean Renart's French lyric tradition. This tradition, as we have seen, is associated elsewhere with places such as Champagne (v. 1452) and Chartres (v. 4124). As Sarah Kay (2013, 100) notes, the toponyms associated with the composers of these pieces "form a line that crosses France from the southwest to the northeast, from the Auvergne and Poitou up to Sablé-sur-Sarthe (near Le Mans), then Chartres, Reims, and its most northern point, Soignies in Hainaut. Most of the places along this line fall in the heartland of the French kingdom in the Île-de-France and Champagne, while its two most extreme lie on contested frontiers: the northeastern one with the Empire, the southwestern one with Occitania."[19] Although Auvergne is not mentioned elsewhere in the romance, Poitou is represented on the French side of the tournament and is explicitly described, along with Perche and Maine, as a constitutive French space.[20] This remapping allows Jean to suggest cultural continuity between the trouvère pieces he cites elsewhere in the text and the three Gallicized troubadour lyrics, the anonymity of which aids in this act of appropriation or assimilation.

This relocation of troubadour song to the southern edge of a French geographical space in the romance constitutes one way of accounting for the Gallicized language in which the pieces are transmitted. Table 2.2 shows the pieces as edited in their hypothetical original Occitan form, along with the Gallicized versions supplied in the *Rose*, with translations of both.

---

18. R. Anthony Lodge (1993) describes both Poitou and Auvergne as transitional linguistic spaces. On Poitou, he writes, "There is indeed a significant blurring of the boundaries between *langue d'oc* and the *langue d'oïl*. It is widely accepted that during the Middle Ages there existed a mixed transitional zone between Oc and Oïl in Poitou" (Lodge 1993, 75, 77). And on Auvergne: "The dialects of north Aquitania (Limousin and Auvergnat) merge into a broad band of transitional Gallo-Romance varieties known as the 'Croissant' and sharing a number of features with northern French dialects—as one would expect in a situation of dialect continuum" (68).

19. On the remapping of Occitan song in the *Rose*, see also Zingesser (2012, chapter 1).

20. It is described as part of the *là-bas* (*la*, v. 2083) that makes up the opposing side of the tournament. This space is not described as a kingdom explicitly here, as Lecoy's translation would suggest. Lejeune (1935, 88–89) notes that this French mapping of Poitou and Maine reflects Philip Augustus's early thirteenth-century conquest of these formerly Plantagenet territories.

Table 2.2 Occitan songs in the *Roman de la rose*

JAUFRE RUDEL, "LANQUAN LI JORN"	
Edition of Occitan version by Chiarini (Jaufre Rudel 1985, 89)	**Gallicized version in the *Roman de la rose* (Reg. Lat. 1725, fol. 75r–v)**[1]
Lanquan li jorn son lonc en mai m'es belhs dous chans d'auzelhs de lonh e quan me sui partitz de lai remembra·m d'un amor de lonh vau de talan embroncx e clis, si que chans ni flors d'albespis no·m platz que l'iverns gelatz.	**L** ors queli ior sont lonc en mai mes biaus doz chant doisel.de lonc & q[ua]nt me sui p[ar]tiz de la. m enbre mi dune amor delonc vois de ci gens bruns & enduis si que chans ne flors daubes [75v] pin ne mi val ni cuivers gelas
Translation	**Translation**
When the days are long in May, the sweet song of birds from afar is beautiful to me, and when I have departed from there, I am reminded of a distant love. I am burdened and bowed down with desire, such that neither song nor hawthorn flower pleases me more than frozen winter.	When the days are long in May, the sweet song of birds from afar is beautiful to me, and when I have departed from there, I am reminded of a distant love. *I go* [or: *a voice?*] *from here noble, dark and led (?),* such that neither song nor hawthorn flower is worth anything to me, *or a frozen wretch* (?).
DAUDE DE PRADAS, "BELHA M'ES LA VOTZ AUTANA"	
Edition of Occitan version by Appel (Daude de Pradas 1933, 87)	**Gallicized version in *Rose* (Reg. Lat. 1725, fol. 93r)**
Belha m'es la votz autana del rossinhol em pascor quan fuelh' es vertz e blanca flor nays et l'erbet' en la sanha e retendeysson li vergier e ioys auria·m tal mestier que tot mi reve e·m sana.	Bele mest la voiz altane. del roissillol el pascor. q[ue] foelle est verz blanche flor & lerbe nest en la sane. dont rav[er]dissent cil vergier. & ioi mamor tel mestier que cors me garist & sane.
Translation	**Translation**
Beautiful to me is the high voice of the nightingale in the spring, when leaf is green and the white flower is born and the grass is in the watery meadow, and the orchards resound. And I would have such need of joy which revives and heals me completely.	Beautiful to me is the high voice of the nightingale in the spring, for leaf is green, flower white and the grass is born [or: *is not*] in the *sane,* as a result of which these orchards become green. And joy [or: *I hear*] *my love such necessity* [?] that [my] body protects and heals me.

(Continued)

Table 2.2 (Continued)

BERNART DE VENTADORN, "CAN VEI LA LAUZETA MOVER"	
Edition of Occitan version by Lazar (Bernart de Ventadorn 1966, 180)	**Gallicized version in *Rose* (Reg. Lat. 1725, fol. 96r)**
Can vei la lauzeta mover de joi sas alas contral rai que s'oblid e·s laissa chazer per la doussor c'al cor li vai ai! tan grans enveya m'en ve de cui qu'eu veya jauzion meravilhas ai, car desse lo cor de dezirer no·m fon. Ai, las! tan cuidava saber d'amor, e tan petit en sai, car eu d'amar no·m posc tener celeis don ja pro non aurai Tout m'a mo cor, et tout m'a me e se mezeis e tot lo mon e can se·m tolc, no·m laisset re mas dezirer e cor volon.	Quant voi laloete moder de goi.ses ales contre el rai. que sobete lesse cader. par la doucor qel cors li vai. ensi grant en- vie mest pris de ce que voi. a ma grant miravile est que vis del sens ne coir[2] do[n]t desier non fou. ha las tant cuidoie savoir donor & point nen sai. pas on damar non pou tenir celi dont ia prou nen au[ra]i tol mei lor cor et tol meismes. & soi mees me & tol le mon. & pos tantel ne moste rent fors desier & cor volon. ----oooo---
Translation	**Translation**
When I see the lark move with joy its wings against the rays, [and] that it forgets itself and lets itself fall because of the sweetness that moves in its heart, alas! such great jealousy overcomes me, of those whom I see rejoicing. It is a miracle to me that my heart does not immediately melt from desire.	When I see the lark move with joy its wings against the rays, [and that] *often* [?] [Old French = *soubitainement*] it lets fall because of the sweetness that goes through its body. In this way a great jealousy of what I see *has taken me* [?]. *To my great miracle* it is that *a face of the sense/that I do not leave my senses*[3] *does not have sex* [?], as a result of which desire *I do not burn* [?].
Alas! I thought I knew so much about love, and I know so little, since I cannot stop myself from loving The one from whom I will never have profit. She took my heart and she took me And herself and the whole world And when she took herself away, she left me nothing Except for desire and a longing heart.	Alas, I thought I knew so much about honor and I don't know anything. [*pas on?*] I cannot keep from loving the one from whom I will never have profit. She takes my heart and she takes the same and herself and she takes the world. And since then she [*they*?] did not show anything except for desire and a longing heart.

1. Transcriptions of the Occitan songs in Reg. Lat. 1725 are my own. Line numbers on the right are those of the manuscript, not those that would be dictated by rhyme. Realized abbreviations are indicated in square brackets.

2. Godefroy glosses *coir* as "faire le coït."

3. I am grateful to one of Cornell's anonymous readers for pointing out that this reading of leaving sanity echoes that of *O*, which gives "car neis desse" according to Appel's variants.

In Fabienne Gégou's estimation, this Gallicization is intended to facilitate comprehension on the part of northern speakers, while maintaining a "parfum du midi."[21]

This perfume is faintest in "Bela m'es la votz autana" (vv. 4653–59), which looks thoroughly French, although it does not make a great deal of sense in its Gallicized version (an issue to which I will return later). "Lanquan li jorn" (vv. 1301–7) has kept a faint hint of its original Occitan composition, mostly through intermediary forms such as *lonc* for Occitan *lonh* and *aubespin* for Occitan *albespis* (cf. French *aubépine*).[22] Although one might argue that the piece ends on a strongly Occitan note, with the form *gelas* (Occitan *gelatz*; French *gelé*), the form is retrospectively cast as a form of French by its echo of the subsequent line of narrative ("Fet Nicole, ou mout a *solas*," v. 1308). That the Occitan (?) form *gelas* is made to rhyme with the French term *solas* suggests an imagined linguistic continuity between the language of the insertion and the language of the narrative. As is the case for "Bela m'es," the occasional moments of semantic opacity in this piece convey a sense of strangeness more than any linguistic coloring. Bernart's lark song (vv. 5212–27) is the most recognizably Occitan, despite Gallicization. The Occitan verb *vai* has been preserved, perhaps as a way of maintaining the rhyme with *rai*, and the Occitan verb *amar* is also intact.[23] The same is true of the final word of the insertion, *volon*, also in a rhyme position. On the whole, the piece demonstrates the same preference for intermediary forms as "Lanquan li jorn." The verbs *moder* and *cader*, for instance, are neither French nor Occitan (Fr. *movoir*, Occ. *mover*; Fr. *cheoir*, Occ. *chazer* or *cazer*). We have already seen how the final word of "Lanquan li jorn" was sonically bound to the narrative, and this is also the case for "Bela m'es": here the final lexeme *sane* is made to rhyme with *forsane* in the narrative ("A poi que li rois ne forsane," v. 4660). In two out of three instances, then, the language of these pieces is made to ring retrospectively as French through a rhyme pair in the narrative.

---

21. Fabienne Gégou (1973, 321) comments: "si, de l'avis des puristes, cette langue est corrompue en de nombreux endroits, elle a le mérite de pouvoir être mieux comprise des lecteurs du Nord, *tout en gardant un parfum du midi*; elle représente une adaptation qu'il faut louer, à notre sens, plutôt que blâmer."

22. The form *lonc* is attested in French. Godefroy gives several examples, including "De son ceval lonc le trebuce" and "Sa besague a lonc jetee," both from *Partonopeu de Blois*, and "Lonc de sa gent aloit pensant," from Wace's *Roman de Rou*. As Gégou (1973, 321) suggests, Jean Renart may have chosen it over alternative forms because it most approximated the Occitan. In Occitan, the form *long* (if not *lonc*) is attested in the *Doctrine des Vaudois*, the last example in Raynouard's (1836) *Lexique roman*. Godefroy lists a variety of forms for the word corresponding to modern French *aubépine*, including *aubepine*, *aubespine*, and *aube espine*. Raynouard lists *albespi* and *albespina*.

23. Psaki's transcription is incorrect here; the manuscript reads "amar."

Although the linguistic palette of the pieces is quite effectively slanted away from Occitan and toward French, the French of these songs is on occasion completely opaque (and, for this reason, I find it difficult to accept Gégou's assertion that Gallicization *facilitated* comprehension for a French audience). What appears to be mostly homophonic translation from the original Occitan—the approximate repetition of the sounds of the original Occitan in French—often makes the text more difficult to understand, while at the same time giving the impression that the text *should* be comprehensible (since it fully resembles French). For instance, the substitution of French *sane* for Occitan *sana* (watery meadow) produces a moment of untranslatability, since *sane*, with this definition, only had meaning as a masculine noun ("assembly," from the Latin *synodum*). After this moment of semantic irresolvability, the poem returns to the more expected idea of orchards turning green ("as a result of which these orchards become green"). In light of these green orchards, one should presumably opt for the first possible translation of "l'erbe nest en la sane"—"the grass is born in the assembly"—since *dont* suggests a causal relationship between the grass and the green orchards. But what is this assembly described in the poem? Taken collectively, then, these fragments make little sense. Similar moments of opacity dot the other Gallicized troubadour lyrics in the text, which, although they (mostly) sound and look French, do not actually make a great deal of semantic sense as French (see table 2.2 for examples).

The breakdown of semantic meaning resulting from Gallicization is subtly accounted for within the romance in a variety of ways. In other words, Jean lays the groundwork for his audience to "make sense" (albeit of a nonsemantic variety) of the insertions' nonsensicality. All of the text's strategies for preparing the audience for the insertions' opacity begin by shifting attention toward the acoustic dimension of language and away from the semantic, especially in the narrative lead-up to the three troubadour lyrics. Before turning to this shift from the semantic to the acoustic in the case of the three troubadour songs, however, I will explore how the seeds for this acoustic mode of listening to lyric are sown over the course of the narrative.[24] Some

---

24. The distinction between a mode of listening that is more attentive to sense and a mode of listening that is more attentive to sound has been theorized recently by Mladen Dolar. His preferred examples for the latter category, unsurprisingly, revolve around song. In his account: "Singing [. . .] brings the voice energetically to the forefront, on purpose, at the expense of meaning. Indeed, singing is bad communication; it prevents a clear understanding of the text (we need supertitles at the opera [. . .])." He notes further that "singing blurs the word and makes it difficult to understand—in polyphony to the point of incomprehensibility" (Dolar 2006, 30). One need not turn to contemporary theory for the distinction, of course. As Emma Dillon has recently pointed out, Johannes

critics of the *Rose* have remarked that Jean sometimes sonically binds his insertions to the narrative by placing within the narrative the rhyme pair to either the initial or final line of a lyric insertion.[25] We have already seen this strategy used in the case of two of the three troubadour songs, in which, in one instance, the Occitan term *gelas* is made to rhyme with *solas* in the subsequent line of narrative (vv. 1307–8) and, in the other, the term *sane* finds a rhyme pair in the narrative's *forsane* (vv. 4659–60). This technique, which is not confined to the troubadour songs in the text (although it does occur for the first time in conjunction with them), constitutes an extreme instance of prioritizing sound over sense. While typically the lyric portions of the romance and their narrative frame are formally self-sufficient, here the narrative is made to sound, retrospectively, like the last line of the lyric poem that precedes it (admittedly, one might also construe instead the last line of the poem as part of the narrative). Except in these instances of suturing through rhyme pairs, someone who encounters the *Rose* aurally—even someone who does not speak French—can generally rely on her ear to reconstruct the formal structure of the text. Elsewhere, one can distinguish the lyric insertions from the surrounding narrative based only on the various metrical and rhyme schemes of the former (even assuming the songs were not sung) and the octosyllabic couplets of the latter. But in these instances of suturing, the reader is forced to listen more closely to the *sound*—the acoustic sound, in addition to the referential sound—of Jean's narrative in order to orient herself within its formal landscape.[26] Although this sound ultimately deceives—by creating the impression that the last line of a lyric insertion and

---

de Grocheio's description of the motet makes clear that he conceives of motet texts as comprising both numerous words ("plura dictamina") and multifarious syllables ("multimodam discretionem syllabarum"). As Dillon observes, "these are not two different kinds of texts, but rather two different conceptions of the same thing: words as poetry, and words as a pattern of syllables and sounds" (Dillon 2012, 169). Here is Grocheio's text: "Motetus vero est cantus ex pluribus compositus, habens plura dictamina vel multimodam discretionem syllabarum [. . .]. Dico [. . .] *plura* autem *dictamina* quia quilibet debet habere discretionem syllabarum" (The motet is a music assembled from numerous elements, having numerous poetic texts or a multifarious structure of syllables [. . .]. I say [. . .] having 'numerous poetic texts' because each [part] must have its structure of syllables) (Johannes de Grocheio 1993, 36). Even if we imagine that Grocheio's initial "vel" flags up an opposition (a motet can have "numerous poetic texts" *or* "a multifarious structure of syllables"—perhaps nonsense syllables?), his subsequent causal link between the "numerous poetic texts" and the "structure of syllables" in each part makes clear that these are not mutually exclusive categories.

25. See, on table 2.1, nos. 16, 21, 22, 26, 28, 29, 30, 31, 25, 27, 39, 40, 41, 42, 43, 47.

26. I use the term "reader" advisedly; because the lyric insertions are not always transcribed on a line-by-line basis, their rhyme schemes are not always immediately apparent. Even someone who encountered the text in manuscript might well have voiced it aloud in order to reconstruct the rhyme scheme.

the first line of the narrative are formally united, the reader is nevertheless forced to listen acoustically in order to verify that she has reconstructed the boundary between lyric and narrative correctly.

This sonic stitching of insertion and narrative—and the acoustic mode of listening it cultivates—is just one of many ways in which such a mode of listening is encouraged by the text. We saw above how the syllable *or* reverberates throughout "Fille et mere se sieent a l'orfrois," thus sonically doubling the gold thread woven by the characters in the song. Similar echo effects occur in the passages surrounding several of the romance's lyric insertions. These effects, like the actual suturing via rhyme of insertion and narrative we have just seen, draw the ear toward the acoustic dimension of language. The procedure occurs as early as the third insertion in the *Rose*. Here is the narrative lead-up to and quotation of the piece:

> une pucele secorcie
> d'un trop biau chainze,
> a un blont chief,
> en reconmence de rechief:
>
> *Se mes amis m'a guerpie,*
> *por ce ne morrai ge mie.*
>
> Ainz que ceste fust bien fen*ie*,
> une dame sanz vilon*ie*,
> qui ert suer au duc de Maience . . .
>
> A maiden who had rolled up
> her beautiful tunic and (who had)
> a blonde head of hair
> begins again:
>
> *"If my beloved has abandoned me*
> *I will not die as a result."*
>
> Before this one was over,
> a lady without fault,
> who was the sister of the duke of Mainz . . .
>
> (vv. 301–8)

The rhyme sound of the lyric insertion, *-ie*, is echoed in the subsequent lines of narrative ("fenie" / "vilonie"); in other words, the insertion and narrative are formally blurred together, even though strictly speaking both the lyric and the narrative are self-sufficient. Moreover, the lyric insertion—a heptasyllabic couplet—comes close to formally doubling the narrative's octosyllabic couplets, forcing readers or audience members to listen even more closely for the passage from one discursive mode to the other. An echo effect that is even more intense—in that it both precedes and follows the lyric insertion—is used before "C'est la jus en la praele" where the *-ele* rhyme is prepared in the two preceding lines of narrative (vv. 1844–5) and the piece's only other rhyme sound, *oir*, is doubled in the subsequent line of narrative ("Fet Boidins: 'Bien dit Jouglés *voir*,'" v. 1852).[27] This echo phenomenon, which obscures the line between song and narrative, is the sonic double of the thematic "hall of mirrors" effect noted by Limentani (1980, 312), in which characters in the narrative are named after and seem to emerge from the world of lyric. In all of these cases, the repetition of sound is used not only to formally constitute song but to invite a mode of listening that prioritizes the identification of these repeated sounds instead of (or at least along with) attributing semantic meaning to them.[28]

I have already indicated that the three troubadour songs in the romance push this cognitive shift toward an acoustic mode of listening to an extreme. In the case of "Lanquan li jorn," this reorientation toward the acoustic pivots on an allusion to Guillaume's and his companions' overhearing of birdsong: "Cel jor qu'il dut venir a cort, / entre lui et ses compegnons, / por le deduit des oisellons / que chascuns fet en son buisson, / de joie ont commencié cest son" (The day he had to come to court, he and his companions, because of the joy of the birds, which each one displayed in its bush, out of joy they began this song, vv. 1296–1300). If we take this reference as a guide,

27. I would also note that the visual presentation of the text in manuscript is complicit in the blurring of narrative and lyric. Lyric insertions are sometimes transcribed line by line, as is the surrounding narrative, and sometimes as prose. And in one instance, a lyric insertion is visually subsumed into the octosyllabic couplets of the narrative ("Lors que florist la bruiere," RS 1322a; see Psaki's transcription, p. 240). Each line of the lyric insertion (with one exception) is given a line in the manuscript, with an offset initial letter. In the subsequent song, the opposite is true: the narrative is visually annexed to the lyric insertion ("C'est la gieus, la gieus, q'en dit en ces prez," van den Boogaard [Rond.] 15, see Psaki's transcription, p. 248). Here the lyric insertion is transcribed as prose, but the two octosyllabic couplets of the narrative that follow the insertion are transcribed as if they were part of the song. This may be a response to the rhyme pair formed by the last line of the insertion and the following line of narrative: "*car j'ai bele amie.* / Fet uns quens: 'Or ne voi ge mie'" (vv. 5434–35).

28. In addition to these instances, see "Quant ge li donai le blanc peliçon" (RS 1877a) and the subsequent lines of narrative, where the *on* rhyme of the piece is made to resound (vv. 3406–7); "Por quel forfet ne por quel ochoison" (RS 1872), in which the same rhyme sound (*-on*) is echoed in both the preceding and subsequent lines of narrative (vv. 3750ff.); "Tout la gieus, sor rive de mer" (van den Boogaard, Rond. 14), where the *-ez* / *-ai* rhyme of the lyric is echoed in the subsequent *é* rhyme in the narrative (vv. 4169–70); and "C'est la gieus, en mi les prez" (van den Boogaard, Rond. 14), whose *-ez* / *é* rhyme, in addition to echoing the thematically related piece above, also echoes the two lines of narrative that introduce it (which have a rhyme in *-és*).

en abyme, to the broader hermeneutic framework operating at this moment in the romance, we are instructed to make sense of the sounds of "Lanquan li jorn" not as referential language but as the sort of sheer, nonsemantic sound we associate with birdsong. First of all, the repetition of a homophone for "son" (sound, melody), initially as a possessive adjective and then in the word "buis*son*," lays the ground for listening beyond the referential. Second, the proximity of the birdsong and "Lanquan li jorn" is not just temporal. Guillaume and his companions are inspired to sing by the birds, with whom they explicitly identify. They are akin to them in their emotion, and also in their plurality. The songs are also alike in their seminonsensicality. That both birdsong and the performance of "Lanquan" are communal events is highlighted acoustically, through the rhyme on "compegnons"/"oisellons." Although "Lanquan li jorn" is not the only lyric in the romance to be preceded by a narrative evocation of birdsong (the same is true of "Quant de la foelle espoissent li vergier," RS 1319, vv. 3180ff.), the identification between performers is unique (in the case of Conrad and the trouvère lyric, the narrative does not imply a causal relationship or an emotional identification between the character's motivation to sing and the birds he has just heard).

Like "Lanquan li jorn," the quotation of "Belha m'es" in the *Rose* is associated with a sonic encounter, although here "Belha m'es" itself, rather than birdsong, constitutes the object of said encounter. Lienor, we are told, overhears unnamed singers at Conrad's court performing the piece but is unable to sing it herself:

> . . . oï ele commencier
> iceste chançon auvrignace.
> Se ne fust cil, cui Diex mal face,
> qui la cuida desloiauter,
> mout seüst bien cest vers chanter.
>
> She heard [them] begin
> this Auvergnat song.
> If it were not for the one—may God curse him—
> who desired to dishonor her,
> she would have been very capable of singing this song.
>
> (vv. 4648–52)

Our perspective as readers is limited to Lienor's—like her, we catch only the initial snatches of the piece. Although Jean rarely quotes more than one or two stanzas, here our fragmentary encounter with the piece is aligned with Lienor's perception ("oï ele *commencier*"). We might even imagine that the piece's garbled transmission reflects Lienor's imperfect auditory faculties—that we are listening through her listening. In any case, in the narrative's inclusion of this piece, the emphasis is resolutely on Lienor's auditory encounter with the song, rather than on its production; Jean emphasizes the fact that Lienor's does *not* sing the piece herself.

The presentation of the third troubadour song likewise shifts attention away from the semantic and toward the acoustic, this time by framing the performance of the piece as simultaneous with the performance of another (French) song. The nephew of the bishop of Liège begins to sing "Or vienent Pasques" (v. 5188), but before this piece is over, someone else begins to sing Bernart's lark song:

> Ceste n'est pas tote chantee,
> uns chevaliers de la contree
> dou parage de Danmartin
> conmença cest son poitevin.
>
> This one was not totally sung
> [when] a knight from the region
> from the family of Dammartin,
> began this poitevin song.
>
> (vv. 5208–5211)

Is "Can vei" drowned out by this simultaneous song? This moment of the narrative is, in any case, polyphonic in the broadest sense of the term: multiple voices conjoin at this moment in the narrative, in which two songs compete with one another. Jean's narrative staging, then, accounts for the garbled transmission of "Can vei."

In sum, in all three instances Jean prepares his audience to hear the acoustic dimension of the quoted troubadour songs such that their garbled nature can be rationalized. By framing these pieces as phenomenological auditory encounters of the sort where the construction of semantic meaning would either be difficult or unexpected (the overhearing of birdsong, the overhearing of a performance at a distance, and the parsing of polyphony), Jean lays the groundwork for rationalizing their semantic breakdown.

This phenomenological slant is almost unique to the three troubadour songs in the *Rose*. Jean's emphasis, generally speaking, is not on the way in which the pieces are perceived (although many are, of course, performed in situations where this is implied) but instead on the way in which the pieces are performed (singers' voices are singled out, as in vv. 1193, 1202, 3624, etc.). In instances where the pieces' reception is foregrounded, outside of the three troubadour lyrics, Jean makes it clear that the referential capacity of language is functioning properly. For instance, the mention of someone named "Jordains" in "De Renaut de Mousson" (v. 2398–2404) leads to a discussion of said Jordain, and the evocation of the beautiful woman at Oisseri in France sparks a discussion of which women—French or imperial—are superior (vv. 3431–32). In the case of the three troubadour lyrics, however, the narrative draws attention to the process of auditory perception. It does so, respectively, through Guillaume's overhearing of birdsong (doubled in the overhearing of birdsong in the actual insertion), through its emphasis on Lienor's overhearing of "Bela m'es" rather than on its performance by the courtiers, and finally by making "Can vei" part of a broader sonic spectacle, a moment of polyphony.[29] In shifting our attention to the sonic dimension of language precisely at these three moments, Jean allows us to begin to make sense (of a nonsemantic variety) of the opaque language of the troubadour songs in the romance; one would not, after all, expect birdsong, a song overheard at a distance, or a song sung simultaneously with others to be perfectly decipherable within the referential code of language.

Another means the text proposes of rationalizing this nonsensicality is to view it as a constitutive feature of the medium in which it occurs: song. Sarah Kay has noted how the stanzas selected by Jean Renart are often metadiscursive ones, in which the act of singing or the object of song is foregrounded thematically. As she puts it, "The exordia overwhelmingly chosen in *Guillaume de Dole* are those most likely to highlight songs' status as song" (Kay 2013, 94). Two of the three troubadour songs explicitly present themselves as such—via implied analogy with birdsong: "Lanquan li jorn" evokes the "chant d'oisel" (song of birds) and "Bela m'es" the "voiz altane del roissillol" (high voice of the nightingale). The pieces are thus self-conscious specimens of song; they are songs that contain within them *mises-en-abyme* of the act of singing. We have already seen how Jean sows the seeds for a view of song as inscrutable in the prologue, and how the act of comprehending the lyric insertions in the romance is precisely the sorting mechanism that is supposed to distinguish the societal wheat from the chaff ("cestui *Romans de la rose* / [. . .] est une novele chose / et s'est des autres si divers / et brodez, par lieus, de biaus vers / que vilains nel porroit savoir" (this *Romance of the Rose* is a new thing and is so different from the others and [is] embroidered, in places, with

29. To be clear, I do not intend to suggest that Jean frames "Can vei" as part of an already-composed polyphonic piece, but rather that he stages it diegetically as part of a "polyphonic" moment—one in which multiple singing voices are competing with one another.

beautiful songs, such that the peasant cannot not understand it, vv. 11–15). Having promised in the first lines of the romance that the inset songs resist easy interpretation, Jean delivers on that promise here: Gallicization results in a movement toward hermeticism, inaugurating a kind of French *trobar clus*, the Occitan poetic style associated precisely with opaque language and social exclusion.[30] The sorts of abstruse turns of phrase produced through Gallicization—for example, "for grass is born in the *sane*" ("Bela m'es"), "a face of the sense does not?" ("Can vei")—are strange intruders in the overall poetic landscape of the *Rose*, but they are not unlike the types of recondite metaphors found in *clus* compositions. Indeed, both the semantic obscurity and the self-conscious, metadiscursive nature of the songs are two of the hallmarks of *trobar clus* style. By preparing his audience to associate lyric insertions with incomprehensibility in the prologue, Jean Renart allows us to register these moments of opacity within the troubadour lyrics as a mark of their poeticity and, if we are able to make sense of them, as a mark of our own superiority. What is remarkable here, of course, is that this *clus* style within French is a linguistic mirage: it is Gallicized Occitan that is made to function as a hermetic register within Jean's French poetic soundscape. Jean develops his fiction that Occitan is not foreign but rather an obscure variety of French, both through Gallicization, which brings the original Occitan closer to French acoustically, and through the labels attached to two of the three Occitan songs, which locate them on the border between *langue d'oïl* and *langue d'oc*.

Two of the Gallicized pieces hint slyly at a different explanation for their own opacity. As we have seen, the last word of Daude's stanza, *sane* (from the verb "to heal"), is rhymed in the subsequent line of narrative with *forsane* (from *forsaner*—"to go insane," v. 4660). Although this insanity is not said to characterize the performer of the piece, sonically the rhyme *sane/forsane* forges a link between the Gallicized Occitan poem and madness. The

30. Hermeticism had, of course, long-standing associations with lyricism that antedate *trobar clus*. Daniel Heller-Roazen's discussion of the many varieties of *cant*—obscure languages that serve precisely to exclude linguistically and thus forge a selective community—is especially apposite here (Heller-Roazen 2013). On *trobar clus*, see the work of Ulrich Mölk (1968) and Aurelio Roncaglia (1969). Many contemporary theorists of poetry would argue that this sonic strangeness—which can itself be productive of opacity—is its defining feature. Perloff, for example, has commented that "poetic language is language made strange, made somehow extraordinary by the use of verbal and sound repetition, visual configuration and syntactic deformation" (Perloff and Dworkin 2009, 7). Craig Dworkin similarly offers the following summary of a certain critical position: "Poetry is understood as a kind of text that deviates from conventionally utile language by self-reflexively foregrounding elements other than the referentially communicative. Poetry, in these accounts, calls attention to structures such as sound while damping the banausic, denotative impetus of language" (10).

Gallicized version of Bernart's famous lark song, for its part, also hints at madness. It renders Bernart's "meravilhas ai, car desse" (it is a miracle that immediately) as "miravile est que vis del sens," which might mean something like "it is a miracle *a face of the sense* [?]" or "it is a miracle that [v?] I leave my senses." In either interpretation, the poem thematizes precisely what begins to evaporate at this moment: sense.

At the same time as Jean prepares his audience to listen differently to the troubadour lyrics—to listen for their sound, rather than their sense, and to associate them with madness—he also frames them in such a way that what *can* be understood of their semantic content blends in thoroughly with the rest of the romance. The three pieces are incorporated into their narrative surroundings through thematic and lexical resonances. The most striking of these is the way the allusions to birdsong constitute a thread that links the troubadour stanzas to the surrounding *grands chants courtois* in the narrative. Of the sixteen pieces of this genre quoted in the romance, nine feature birds, including the three Gallicized Occitan *cansos*.[31] This feature serves here to camouflage Occitan song within the surrounding (francophone) lyric tradition. Birds appear in the piece preceding Bernart's lark song, "Or vienent Pasques les beles en avril" (at v. 5191), but also in the piece following it, Gautier de Soignies's "Lors que florist la bruiere" (at v. 5235). Even the narrative evocation of birdsong *before* a lyric insertion, as is the case for "Lanquan li jorn" (v. 1298), which obviously doubles the "biaus doz chant d'oisel de lonc" (v. 1302) evoked *within* the lyric, is not a distinguishing feature of the troubadour *cansos*. As we have seen, this echoing device is used again before "Quant de la foelle espoissent li vergier" (RS 1319), a piece featuring the nightingale's song ("le chant [. . .] dou roissignol," vv. 3182–83), which is performed by the emperor shortly after he and Guillaume have overheard, from the orchard below, "des oisillons les chans divers" (v. 3178). It is as if these *grands chants* collectively usher in a bevy of birds, in which the birds mentioned in the songs are only three individuals.

This link to birds anchors the Gallicized Occitan songs not just in the francophone lyric tradition that circulates in the text but also in the romance's broader construction of eroticism.[32] Birds appear not just in and around the songs in which the characters express their desire but also on garments

31. These are, on table 2.1, nos. 11, 12, 20, 31, 44, 46, and all three originally Occitan songs. Beretta (1998, 748–57) has also noted this predilection for seasonal *exordia* in Jean Renart's selection of troubadour songs.

32. This link between the avian and the erotic is, of course, also present in Jean Renart's *L'Escoufle*. As Marion Vuagnoux-Uhlig (2009, 360) has demonstrated, sexual conquest is described in terms of avian hunting (Guillaume "paist et enoisele" his beloved, v. 4513).

described in moments of sexual intimacy. The women in the opening scene of the sexually charged idling of Conrad's courtiers wear garlands decorated with birds and flowers ("et ces puceles en cendez / a chapelez entrelardez / de biax oisiaux et de floretes," vv. 203–5), and their golden brocades are decorated with bird motifs (v. 235). In the same scene, birds are said to have replaced chaplains (v. 227), serving as secular priests who presumably bless the carnality they witness. The association between birds and sexual pleasure is, moreover, reinforced here through the rhyme pair *oiseaus* and *aveaus*: "si n'i ont [. . .] chapelains, fors les oiseaus; / Mout orent tuit de lor aveaus" (they did not have chaplains except for the birds; they all had their pleasure, vv. 225–28).[33] Birds also decorate the belt that the seneschal wears against his skin, and with which Lienor "proves" the seneschal's guilt (v. 4826). And they also appear on the garments of the church procession that takes place after she has been exculpated (v. 5368). Birds thus populate not just the lyric landscape of the romance—both Gallicized Occitan and genuinely francophone—but also the other erotically charged spaces of the text.

Although birds are the most striking link between the troubadour songs and the genuine French *grands chants courtois* in the romance, there are other lexical echoes. Hawthorn flower, for instance, makes an appearance both in "La bele Doe siet au vent" (v. 1204) and in the insertion that follows it directly, "Lanquan li jorn" (v. 1306). Similarly, a broader reflection on love appears in the second stanza both of Bernart's lark song and in the subsequent piece, Gautier de Soignies's "Lors que florist la bruiere." The rhetorical contour of both pieces is the same—at least as far as can be discerned from the excerpts in the romance. Both move from a springtime exordium that begins with external observation of the landscape (the lark against the sun in Bernart's poem and the flowering of heather and birdsong in Gautier's piece) to the speaker's emotional turmoil (the speaker's envy in "Can vei" and his sighing and pain in "Lanquan"). Both pieces then turn to quasi-philosophical ruminations on love, preceded by the interjection "alas!" (v. 5220 in "Can vei" and v. 5242 in "Lanquan"): the speaker in Bernart's poem laments his inability to refrain from loving a woman who refuses to return his affection while the speaker of "Lanquan," who suffers from the same affliction, declares that it is folly to love without fear and to make one's love public. Thus, the broader rhetorical contours of the two songs, their shared imagery and even their

33. The term *avel* (as in "Mout orent tuit de lor aveaus") often had sexual undertones in medieval French. It is, for example, used to describe Fauvel and Vaine Gloire's exploits in the night of their marriage during the charivari, where he is more interested in the "aviaus" he has with his wife than the noise outside (Strubel 2012, vv. 4937–40).

incipit—which both begin with a temporal adverb—conspire to give the reader the impression of similarity. These thematic and rhetorical echoes constitute yet another way in which the specificity of the Occitan songs is effaced in their francophone surroundings.

Conrad, *imperator Francorum*?

Given this dense network of (pseudo-)francophone and French song in the Empire—into which the originally Occitan pieces have been woven—we might well expect Conrad's perspective—whether cultural or political—to explicitly include France. And indeed, on several occasions, Conrad actually identifies with the French monarch. The most striking instance of this identification, in a much-discussed passage, occurs when Conrad refers to the king of France as "noz rois" (our king, v. 1629). That Conrad seems to view himself as a subject of the French monarch is bizarre, to say the least, and critics have come up with a variety of ways to dismiss this passage.[34] But what if Conrad does—at least temporarily—imagine himself as a subject of the French monarch? This would suggest that the Empire has been symbolically conquered, perhaps as a result of the French art that circulates there. And indeed, this unusual identification on Conrad's part with French royalty is not unique in the romance, although elsewhere the emperor's identification with the French monarch is expressed more speculatively. For instance, Conrad is so completely delighted by Lienor's name that he declares that if he were king of France, he would make the priest who baptized Lienor archbishop of Reims (vv. 799–800). Neither Lienor nor Conrad is French, politically speaking, and Conrad seems again to be living out a fantasy. Later on, Conrad exhibits unusual familiarity with and fondness for the French king Louis (probably Louis VII) referring to him as the "bon roi Loeïs" (v. 3138). He also possesses an intimate knowledge of court life under Louis, complaining about a certain Brocart Viautre (v. 3137) who dawdled when

34. Félix Lecoy explains this remark as coming from Jean Renart's perspective, rather than reflecting Conrad's or Guillaume's. The full passage reads as follows: "Il li a demandé s'il ere / point privez dou roi d'Engleterre. / Mout a eü longuement guerre / encontre lui noz rois de France" (vv. 1626–29). In Dufournet's assessment: "Comme le roi de France n'est le roi ni de l'empereur ni de Guillaume (qui est chevalier d'empire), la formule *noz rois de France* ne peut être placée dans la bouche ni de l'un ni de l'autre. Si étrange que cela puisse paraître, il faut voir, sans doute dans les vers 1628–1629, une réflexion de l'auteur lui-même" (Jean Renart 2008, 169, 171). I find Lecoy's explanation unconvincing, given that the romance is entirely devoid of such parenthetical asides to the audience. I believe it should be read as part of Conrad's self-positioning with respect to the French monarchy.

called to court.[35] Taken collectively, these moments of identification with the French monarchy suggest either that we are supposed to read the explicitly imperial Conrad as a stand-in for an actual historical figure associated with French royalty or else that we are supposed to read these "lapses" on Conrad's part not as a reflection of his actual sphere of influence but instead as indications of his political fantasy. Given that the text does clearly distinguish elsewhere between French and imperial space, the latter hypothesis is the more compelling of the two.

It is unclear whether Conrad's fantasized Empire—which clearly includes France—is a throwback to an undivided Francia or instead a political space with no historical analog. In support of the former hypothesis, one could adduce Conrad's name, which harks back to actual eleventh- and twelfth-century leaders of the Holy Roman Empire (although this still puts us a few hundred years from an undivided Francia). One could also point to the fact that Conrad's imagined political sphere which includes not just the kingdom of France but also Lotharingia and the Empire—is consistent with the older definition of the *regnum Francorum* evoked by chroniclers. Rigord, for instance, recognized two interpretations of the *regnum Francorum*: (1) a smaller, restricted one that encompassed the territory of the French king, that is, the land between the Rhine, Mosel (called "Francia" by the "moderni," he acknowledges), and (2) a larger one shaped by the former Francia—one that included German lands (Baldwin 1986, 360). The political space imagined by Jean Renart in the *Rose* may be intended to conjure up this broader Francia. But Conrad's political sphere also reflects the one Otto IV and his allies attempted to forge at the Battle of Bouvines, where the imperial forces were widely reputed to have mentally divided up France in anticipation of their victory. The Minstrel of Reims reports the following:

> And the Emperor Otto and the Count of Flanders and Count Renaud and Count William Longsword who was the brother of the King of England—who had sent him as he himself was in Poitou at La Ruche fighting against My Lord Louis who was giving him a very hard time—these aforementioned great lords were parceling France out and were each reserving part for themselves. Count Ferrand wanted Paris, Count Renaud wanted Normandy, and the Emperor wanted Orleans

35. Servois identified this historical figure as Bouchart le Veautre, accused of misappropriating the king's revenues. Bouchart's name appears in a certain number of royal charters (Jean Renart 1893, xlix). It is this allusion to Bouchart that makes most critics think the king is Louis VII.

> and Chartres and Estampes, and Hugh of Boves wanted Amiens, and, in this way, they each picked their share.[36]

In other words, Conrad's imagined Empire fictively produces the remapping that might have resulted from the Battle of Bouvines, had the historical Otto IV and his allies won the war.

This territorial imaginary would explain why Conrad's coat of arms exhibits emblems of the Empire and the Plantagenets: "Et si portoit l'escu demi / au gentil conte de Clermont, / au lïon rampant contremont / d'or et d'azur. Et, d'autre part, / plus estoit hardiz d'un liepart, / quant il ert armez, l'escu pris" (And he wore a bipartite shield with the [arms] of the noble count of Clermont, and a gold lion rampant on an azure field on the other side. And, moreover, he was braver than a leopard, when he was armed, and his shield taken up, vv. 68–73).[37] Antoine Fourrier (1969) has noted that the arms of the family of Clermont-sur-Meuse included an eagle with its wings spread. But how to account for this combination of eagle and lion? Some critics have searched for a particular historical figure whose coat of arms replicates Conrad's exactly. This is, for example, what led Rita Lejeune (1974, 5) and other critics to read Conrad as a figure for Otto IV of Brunswick (1198–1218), the Welf claimant to the Empire. *Pace* Lejeune, I would suggest that the shield need not be read as historically accurate. Philippe Walter (1989) has already proposed such a reading, although he identifies the lion with the royal kingdom, despite noting its more frequent use in Plantagenet heraldry. Depending on how one glosses the lion, Conrad's eagle and lion symbolize either the imperial-Plantagenet coalition at Bouvines (lion as Plantagenet), or the possible world foreclosed by Bouvines—one in which France and the Empire were united (lion as Capetian).[38]

---

36. The original reads as follows: "Et l'empereres Otes, et li cuens Ferranz, et li cuens Renauz, et li cuens Guillaumes Longue Espée (qui estoit freres le roi d'Engleterre; et l'i avoit envoié en lieu de lui pour ce qu'il n'i povoit estre, ains estoit en Poiteu à la Roche contre mon seigneur Loueys qui mout le contrelioit): cil grant seigneur que je vous ai ci nommeiz departoient France entre'eus, et en prenoient en rost et en essiau. Li cuens Ferranz vouloit Paris; et li cuens Renauz vouloit Normandie; et l'empereres vouloit Orliens et Chartres et Estempes; et Hues de Boves vouloit Amiens: ainsi en prenoit chascuns sa piece" (Wailly 1876, 146).

37. Although the leopard evoked here is not discursively part of the heraldic description, this may be a joke on Jean Renart's part. A "leopard" in heraldic language is habitually a lion *passant guardant*—that is, a lion walking with its head toward the viewer and one paw raised.

38. Philippe Walter notes that one of the oldest heraldic attestations of the lion is attached to Geoffroi Plantagenet in Jean de Marmoutier's chronicle. The same emblem is preserved on an enameled plaque representing Geoffroi. The lion "se trouvera pour ainsi dire fixé politiquement par la région française ou l'influence Plantagenêt a été la plus sensible: l'Ouest de la France par opposition à l'aigle qui se trouve attachée à l'Est, en terre d'Empire." In support of his association of the lion with

But if Conrad's ambitions align with those of the Plantagenet-imperial coalition at Bouvines, the art that circulates in the Empire inverts the power dynamic of the emperor's fantasy. While Conrad seeks to conquer France politically, Jean Renart suggests that it is the Empire that has been conquered artistically via the "soft power" of French artistic objects. Indeed, the French songs performed at the imperial court—which feature French royalty and other suspiciously French figures, and which spark discussions about the historical realm of France (in the case of Trumilly lyric discussed above)—exert a remarkable hold on the imperial elite. This French artistic conquest is so successful, I would argue, that it creates a cultural sphere in which—even within the Empire—Germanic languages are registered as foreign. Rather than being treated as if its presence were self-evident, the speech of the Flemish participants in the tournament is framed as a linguistic anomaly. They scream their friends' exotic-sounding names ("Boidin! Boidin! ou Wautre! Wautre!" v. 2168). Their linguistic acts are, in fact, depicted as quasi diabolical; they move throughout the streets "tïeschant comme maufé" (speaking Flemish like devils, v. 2169).[39] Even to Conrad, the Holy Roman Emperor, German seems a foreign enough language that it is worthy of comment (v. 4664). Jouglet's description of the Germans as painfully boring ("Alemanz [. . .] m'ont mort d'anui," v. 2211) only confirms that it is German—and not French—that is the foreign linguistic and cultural presence in Jean's Holy Roman Empire.

The political ambitions of Jean Renart's fictional leader of the Empire are thus comically at odds with the composition of this monolingual francophone imperial court, in which French products—including Gallicized troubadour song—are circulated as a gold standard, and in which Germanic languages are treated as barbaric. Indeed, Jean goes so far as to suggest that the Germans are mere *occupiers* in the Empire in the first lines of the *Rose*, which is set "en l'Empire, ou li Alemant / ont esté maint jor et maint an" (in the Empire, where the Germans have lived for many days and many years, vv. 31–32). The French cultural trends of the Empire make it clear who Jean

French royalty, he cites Philip I's throne with two lion-shaped legs, Pseudo-Fredegar's comparison of Clovis to a king, and the *Chevalier au lion*. Although he notes that there is much wider attestation of the lion as a Plantagenet symbol, Walter nevertheless reads the lion on Conrad's shield as a royal symbol: "L'aigle renvoie bien dans le cas de Conrad à l'Empire dont Conrad est l'héritier; quant au lion, il désigne le royaume. Ainsi, l'empereur Conrad rêve d'une souveraineté exemplaire qui combine l'Aigle et le Lion, *l'imperium* et le *regnum*" (Walter 1989, 727).

39. The verb *tïeschier* is not included in Godefroy's dictionary (Godefroy 2002), and the only attestation is from the *Rose* in the *Altfranzösisches Wörterbuch* (Tobler 1925) and in the *Dictionnaire étymologique de l'ancien français* (DEAF). It is formed on the adjective *tiois*, which Godefroy glosses as "germanique, tudesque."

views as the rightful inhabitants of this political and geographic space. In a sense, the Empire has already been reconquered through French lyric—a corpus into which Occitan songs are inserted through Gallicization and geographic repositioning.

Conrad's Failed *Amour de loin*

Given Conrad's fascination with French art writ large, and occasionally with French royalty, we might well expect him to choose a relative of the French king as his wife. And indeed, Jouglet's initial story to Conrad, as if to hint at his recommended course of action, is one of a knight in Champagne who loves a woman in France (vv. 661–67). Confident that such exceptional people as Jouglet has described do not exist in his realm, he asks whether they exist in France (v. 728): "en mon regne n'a sa pareille" (in my kingdom she does not have an equal, v. 738). In falling for Lienor, an imperial subject, Conrad fails to make a politically savvy marriage of the sort that could actualize his desired sphere of influence, which, as we have seen, extends beyond the Empire to France. Probably because it would be so politically unsavvy, when Lienor is first described to him, Conrad rejects the idea of their marriage: "En mon roiaume n'en m'onor / n'afferroit pas q'el fust m'amie. / Mes por ce qu'el n'i porroit mie / avenir, i voel ge penser" (It would not be fitting that she be my beloved in my kingdom or lands. But because it could never happen, I would like to think about it, vv. 833–36). Even Guillaume advises Conrad that his choice of Lienor is ill advised from a strategic standpoint, warning him that his counselors would dismiss the idea immediately: "li prince et li mestre / et la hautece de l'empire, / s'il l'oënt consoner ne dire / il le tendroient a enfance. / De la fille le roi de France / fetes querre le mariage / par conseil de vostre barnage" (the princes and great lords and dignitaries of the Empire, if they heard speak or tell [of this idea] would dismiss it as childish. Seek the marriage of the king of France's daughter, according to the counsel of your barons, vv. 3036–42). Unsurprisingly, when Conrad announces to his barons his intention to marry, their expectation is that he wed a relative of the king of France. Accordingly, one asks: "Dont est ele dame de France, / ou fille le roi ou sa suer?" (So she is a lady from France, either the daughter of the king or his sister? vv. 3514–15). Shortly afterward, another reminds him that he is expected to acquire land, wealth, or allies through his choice: "Prendrez vos i terre, ou avoir, / ou amis? Icë i prent on" (Will you obtain land, wealth, or allies? This is what one takes [from marriage], vv. 3518–19).

But what begins as a mere thought experiment for Conrad quickly turns, despite abundant advice to the contrary, into a real decision. In choosing

Lienor, rather than a relative of the French king, Conrad shows himself to be only partially susceptible to the fashion for things French. In love with French clothing, French song, and the idea of governing France, but not in love with a French maiden, Conrad fails to follow the path of *amour de loin* set out in the lyrics that are feverishly circulated at his court.[40] Although he seems especially susceptible to mimetic desire, commenting that love is more pleasant when one hears someone else speak of it (vv. 3000–3001), Conrad does not follow up on the cues of cross-cultural love scattered throughout the songs that circulate at his court.

We have seen here how Conrad elsewhere fetishizes French fashions and objects. This chapter has documented the widespread fascination with French exports—including Occitan song—within Jean Renart's fictive Holy Roman Empire. Troubadour song is transformed so that it blends into this tradition of "French" song. It is thoroughly Gallicized, tagged in such a way as to give the impression that it comes from the southernmost points of *langue d'oïl* territory, and thematically similar to the genuine *oïl* pieces that surround it. Even its moments of opacity are subtly rationalized within the narrative—it is associated with insanity, unspeakable sexual desire, and birdsong, and staged as overheard (rather than heard directly) or as part of a larger sonic spectacle in which multiple voices compete. Within Jean's Empire, Occitan is never acknowledged as a foreign language—unlike Germanic languages (historically, of course, quite native to the Empire). Indeed, although one Occitan lyric is sung only lines away from Conrad's Flemish-speaking barons, it is the Germanic speech and the Germanic speech alone that is treated as a foreign entity in Jean's imagined francophone Empire. It is noteworthy that Jean's Frenchification of the Empire is much more violent than his treatment of Occitania. Transposed to the Poitou and the Auvergne, on the linguistic border between *langue d'oïl* and *langue d'oc*, Occitania is presented as a nonexistent geographical space while Occitan lyrics are linguistically colored to bring them closer to French. The geographical contours of the Empire, meanwhile, are fully registered, but its cultural landscape has been drastically altered. Although German had its own flourishing medieval lyric tradition—Minnesang—there is not a single piece from this tradition in the French soundscape of Jean's Empire, which remains resolutely francophone and francophile. Conrad's fetish for things French is enough to make him

40. Beyond the obvious instance of Jaufre Rudel's "Lanquan li jorn," with its "amor de lonc," the anonymous "Siet soi bele Aye" depicts love between Aye and her foreign (English?) lover, vv. 1183-92. The same may also be true of "Bele Aiglentine en roial chamberine," which culminates in a certain Count Henri's marriage to Aiglentine, a woman he has impregnated, and their return to "son païs" (v. 2291).

identify with the king of France, or occasionally merely to put himself in his shoes, but it is not strong enough to lead him to the politically expedient choice of marrying a relative of the French monarch. His love ultimately proves to be insufficiently *lointain* to create the Empire of his fantasies—one that is primarily francophone, and one whose borders contain both the historical Empire and the kingdom of France.

CHAPTER 3

Birdsong and the Edges of the Empire

Gerbert de Montreuil's Roman de la violette

As in Jean Renart's *Roman de la Rose*, the border foregrounded in Gerbert de Montreuil's *Roman de la Violette* (ca. 1230) lies to the east of Capetian France rather than to the south, a fact that suggests that, as was the case in the *Rose*, the Battle of Bouvines was perceived as a more pressing historical event within Gerbert de Montreuil's circles than the Albigensian Crusade. In the *Violette*, however, the Holy Roman Empire has not been annexed to francophone and French territory. Instead, as I aim to show, it is marked as a dangerous space—a valence conveyed in part through the territory's association with hunting birds, especially the eagle, probably in recognition of the most commonly deployed imperial symbol. This chapter first documents a critical blind spot in *Violette* criticism: the saturation of imperial symbolism and geography within the romance. It then turns to the text's quotation of troubadour song, which is also placed within an avian typology. If the Empire is characterized mainly by hunting birds, Occitan song is, by contrast, associated with songbirds. Unlike in Jean Renart's *Rose*, where many *grands chants* foregrounded birdsong thematically, here this association between human song and birdsong is unique to the Occitan insertions within the romance. This association works, in part, to account for the texts' moments of semantic opacity; like inarticulate birdsong, often likened in medieval thought to a foreign language, the two Occitan pieces quoted in the text occasionally veer toward the unintelligible.

Gerbert's *Violette* has long been recognized as a Capetian response to Jean's Empire-oriented *Rose*. Rita Lejeune set the tone for much future scholarship with the following position. To Jean Renart's *Rose,* written "en Terre d'Empire pour un milieu impérial [. . .] autour d'un empereur de la famille des Plantagenêts" (in imperial territory for an imperial milieu [. . .] revolving around an emperor from the Plantagenet family), she claims, the *Violette* "a tout l'air de constituer, en réplique, le roman d'une aristocratie française fidèle au roi Louis VIII et à son souvenir" (the *Roman de la Violette,* seems to be, in reply, the romance of the French aristocracy, faithful to Louis VIII and to his memory) (Lejeune 1978, 446). Indeed, instead of the emperor Conrad, the political realm of the *Violette* revolves around a certain "King Louis" (v. 78), thought by most critics to represent Louis VIII. Marie, countess of Ponthieu, is the explicit dedicatee of the romance, and Gerbert alludes in the epilogue to the Capetians' confiscation and subsequent restoration of her lands (the latter took place in 1225, providing a *terminus post quem* for the *Violette*).[1] Marie had lost her county after her husband, Simon de Dammartin, supported his brother, Renaud de Dammartin (the count of Boulogne), in a conspiracy against Philip Augustus. At the Battle of Bouvines (1214), Renaud had allied himself with Otto IV, the Welf claimant to the Holy Roman Empire, and Ferrand, count of Flanders. Following Philip Augustus's triumph at Bouvines, Simon was exiled and Marie's lands initially taken by Philip Augustus. Gerbert casts the space of the Empire in a negative light and seeks to exclude it rather than annex it. If there is a historical moment that haunts the *Violette,* it is not the Albigensian Crusade but rather the Battle of Bouvines, whose geographical proximity to Ponthieu may have left a particularly strong impression there.

As critics have long remarked, the plot of the *Violette* is reminiscent in many respects of that of Jean Renart's *Rose.* With the king's court assembled at Pont-de-l'Arche (the location of Philip Augustus's primary residence in Normandy), the protagonist Gerart boasts of his beautiful beloved, Euriaut,

1. All references are to Douglas Buffum's edition, which is based on manuscript *A* (Gerbert de Montreuil 1928). For more on the manuscript tradition of the *Violette,* see below. The allusion to Marie de Ponthieu is found in the following passage: "Gyrbers de Monsteruel define / De la Vïolete son conte, [. . .] / Pour la millour dame ki vive / A faite et rimee ceste oevre; / Toute bontés en li s'aoevre. / Tous biens, toute honours et tous pris / Est enrachinés et repris / Ou cuer la contesse Marie / De Pontiu, ki souvent marie / Fu, anchois que venist a terre. / Souventes fois l'ala requerre, / Mais sa fois et sa loiautés / Li rendi terre et yretés" (Gerbert de Montreuil finishes his story of the Violet [. . .]. For the best woman who lives he has made and rhymed this work; all goodness is at work in her. All good things, all honors, and all worthiness is rooted and planted in the heart of countess Marie of Ponthieu, who was often distressed before she came to [her] land. Often she went to ask for it, but her faith and loyalty returned to her land and inheritance, vv. 6634–35, 6638–48).

whom he claims is the most beautiful woman between Metz and Pontoise (v. 211). These two cities—one imperial and one Capetian—signal the geopolitical framework in which the *Violette* operates. Gerart's boasting provokes the jealousy of Lisiart, who wagers all of his land that he can successfully seduce Gerart's beloved. Because he has the utmost confidence in Euriaut, Gerart agrees to the wager, sending Lisiart off on his quest. Lisiart first spies Euriaut just as she is singing the first troubadour song in the romance, which is described as a "son poitevin" in all manuscripts. Euriaut politely but firmly rebuffs Lisiart's advances, only to be betrayed by her maid, the evil Gondrée, who reveals to Lisiart that her charge has a violet birthmark on her breast that only her lover has seen. Armed with this "proof" of Euriaut's supposed betrayal, Lisiart returns to court, leaving Gerart despondent at the thought of his beloved's purported infidelity. Gerart takes Euriaut to the woods, planning to kill her, but he decides merely to abandon her after she happens to save him from an errant dragon that has wandered onto the scene. The duke of Metz subsequently discovers the disheveled Euriaut and falls in love with her. Still faithful to Gerart, Euriaut tries to make herself unattractive to the duke by concocting a story of former debauchery. Meanwhile, Gerart is determined to get to the bottom of the story. He returns to Nevers and decides to dress up as a jongleur, a disguise that allows him to overhear Gondrée and Lisiart discussing their successful ploy to defame Euriaut. With renewed faith, he sets out to find Euriaut and to challenge Lisiart to a duel. The two lovers lead separate lives, Euriaut in Metz and Gerart mostly in Cologne, both within the Holy Roman Empire. After refusing to sleep with a certain Méliatir, Euriaut is framed for the murder of the duke's sister, Ismène. While Euriaut pines after her lost beloved, Gerart sets his sights elsewhere. After initially refusing the advances of a certain Aiglente, Gerart eventually succumbs under the influence of a magic potion Aiglente has cooked up for him. Like Renaud de Dammartin, he is seduced by the Empire. Out hunting one day, Gerart spies a lark, which he lets his sparrow hawk kill after he intones the second Occitan insertion in the text, described as a "son poitevin" in one manuscript and as a "son provençal" in two others. Examining the lark's corpse, he finds a ring on its neck and realizes it belongs to Euriaut, his abandoned love. After slaying several more armies and giants, Gerart is able to find the forsaken Euriaut, just in time to save her from execution. Euriaut's innocence of murder is demonstrated through a judicial ordeal. Gerart is invited to a tournament, which Euriaut encourages him to attend in order to regain the land he has lost. Successful at this exercise, Gerart returns home and accuses Lisiart of treachery. The traitor's guilt is revealed and he is executed by the king. Gerart and Euriaut are happily married, with the festivities lasting for eight days. The romance concludes with an epilogue in which Gerbert praises the countess Marie de Ponthieu and rejoices that she has had her land restored to her by the king.

Perhaps because the romance is bookended by clear evocations of the Capetian court, many critics have read the romance through a francocentric lens. Mireille Demaules (2000, 10), for example, situates the landscape of the *Violette* in the north, center, and east of France without noting the major presence of imperial territories in the text. William Paden goes one step further and claims that "the name of Germany echoes in [Gerbert's] text only as a rhetorical expression for what is faraway" (Paden 1993, 48).[2] On my count, some 2,500 lines of the *Violette* (just under 40 percent of the romance) take place in imperial territory. What is more, these imperial territories are strategically situated at moments of amorous rupture: Gerart abandons Euriaut in the (then imperial) Burgundian woods (ca. 1097ff.), which are explicitly described as *salvage* (wild, v. 5136) later in the romance, thus framing the Empire as a dumping ground for less desirable members of Capetian society. The Burgundian woods are the starting point on both lovers' paths toward symmetrical positions, both still within the Empire. Euriaut is whisked away by the duke of Metz, where—on her arrival at his home—she is threatened both by the duke himself and subsequently by the duke's courtier, Méliatir. After his separation from Euriaut, Gerart also wanders into imperial territory, where he is also hosted by a duke. After brief sojourns in Vergy, southwest of Dijon, and in Chalons (presumably Châlons-sur-Marne)—both of which were Capetian *fiefs mouvants*—he departs for (imperial) Cologne, where he is hosted by the Duke Milon (vv. 2504ff.). Like Euriaut, Gerart fends off amorous advances from two aspiring suitors: Aiglente and Aigline. Gerart allies himself politically with the duke of Metz, defending the city of Cologne from invading Saxons. He further demonstrates his prowess in tournaments in Germany and Liège (v. 3825). Gerart's political affiliations thus shift from Capetian circles to imperial ones in this section of the romance. Like Guillaume de Dole in the *Roman de la Rose*, Gerart temporarily becomes one of the most accomplished knights in the Holy Roman Empire.

The Empire in the *Violette*, unlike the *Rose*, where it was domesticated and annexed, is resolutely foreign. Gerart announces to the Duke Milon that he comes from an "estragne tierre" (foreign/strange land, v. 2964). As if to

2. John Baldwin and Kathy Krause are notable exceptions to this trend. Baldwin (2000, 13) notes that "Jean's and Gerbert's romances exhibit a predilection for lands beyond the Capetian domain and center on Lotharingia, the middle space between France and the Empire." Krause (2007) notes how the political outlook of the *Violette* can be shaped by its codicological contexts.

acknowledge the divide between his homeland and the city where he finds himself, Gerart explains his name in such a way as to suggest its lack of a cognate in Cologne: "Gerart m'apielent el païs / Dont je sui issus et naïs" (They call me Gerart in the country where I come from and was born, vv. 2968–69). The political frame of reference of the characters in this section of the romance is also decidedly imperial; Aiglente declares that she would rather have Gerart as her lover than the emperor of Germany ("n'en volroie mie avoir / d'Alemaigne l'empereour / Et avoec lui toute s'ounour / En liu de lui" [I would not like to have the emperor of Germany, and with him all of his territory (or honor), instead of him (Gerart)], vv. 4391–94). Gerart becomes, if only temporarily, the most desired and desirable figure within the Holy Roman Empire, surpassing even the emperor.

It is tempting to read the Saxon warriors Gerart confronts in this section of the romance as stock epic characters rather than as historical representatives of a politicized, historically specific Empire. Indeed, Gerbert invites this reading by drawing the name of one of his Saxons, Espaulart de Gormaise, from the *Chevalier au cygne*. But Gerbert also includes so many historical details in this section of the romance that it is impossible to dismiss the landscape as merely mythical. The city of Cologne, for example, is evoked with remarkable accuracy and specificity. Gerbert describes its "porte les Trois Rois" (Door of the Three Kings, v. 2542), alluding to the southeast gate of the Church of Saint Mary, and more broadly to Cologne's association with the Three Magi (the Three Magi's relics had been brought to Cologne from Milan in 1164) (Snowe 1839, 1:48–49). Moreover, as Cologne's champion, Gerart sports historically recognizable garb. His vibrant red armor mirrors the traditional color of both the city of Cologne and its militia (which later evolved into the famous "Roten Funken" or Red Sparks).[3] This red armor reappears later in the romance, metonymically distinguishing Gerart, who is called "li vassaus au rouge escu" (the knight with the red shield, v. 2954). Gerart's helmet is also decked out with a typically Germanic "ruee de paon" (peacock tail, v. 2593). This sartorial fashion is still visible in the early fourteenth-century Manesse Codex.[4] Likewise, the Saxons are firmly anchored in imperial geography. Both Gontart of "Covelanche" (Koblenz) (v. 2690) and Guinebaus of "Maianche" (Mainz) (v. 2881) are associated with imperial strongholds. In fact, one of Gerbert's Saxons is identifiable through his coat of arms as William Longespée, earl of Salisbury and half-brother of the king

3. "S'armeüre ert toute vermeille, / Et ses chevals refu couvers / D'un samit vermel molt divers" (His armor was completely red, and his horse was covered in a very shiny, red silk cloth, vv. 2587–89).

4. See, for example, fol. 17r (http://digi.ub.uni-heidelberg.de/diglit/cpg848/0029).

of England, who was allied with Otto IV at Bouvines.[5] This "Saxon" sports a shield with "three lion cubs very well placed," with an additional six on his tunic and an additional six on the covering: "li Saisnes [. . .] / en l'escu ot taillé d'orfrois / trois lyonchiaus molt bien assis / et en la cote en avoit sis / et sis en ot es couvretures" (vv. 2816–18).[6] This suggests that the "Saxons" may represent not only Germanic forces more broadly but also allied forces—here the Plantagenets—who fought against Philip Augustus at Bouvines.[7]

The imperial flavor of this section of the romance is also reinforced by its saturation with hunting birds, especially the eagle, a long-standing imperial symbol (as I will show later, these birds of prey are only one-half of a broader avian typology in the romance). The aquiline duo constituted by Aiglente and Aigline—Gerart's aspiring female suitors in Cologne—onomastically evokes the imperial symbol par excellence, the eagle, although they may also be intended to conjure up in deconstructed form the archetypal lyric beloved, Aiglentine.[8] Their names and their behavior in the romance frame them clearly as a pair, a fact that may render their symbolism even more precise; as documented by Matthew Paris, Otto IV's heraldic eagle was specifically bicephalous.[9] Both of these birds of prey set their sights on Gerart, trying to lure him away from his true love, Euriaut. Aiglente seems peculiarly conscious of the cynegetic implications of her own name, declaring that she will look elsewhere since she cannot obtain her amorous quarry: "Failli ai a prendre ma proie, / Si m'estuet en autre liu tendre") (I have failed to take my prey, so I must hunt elsewhere, vv. 3517–18). Like a hunting bird, she often appears perched on high at her window, attentively surveying the landscape below (vv. 3428–33; 4156–57; 4329–31). The name of Duke

5. William, because of his relationship with King John of England, was thought to be a highly valuable prisoner when he was taken by the French. He is mentioned in many of the chronicles that discuss Bouvines (Duby 1973).

6. I assume this "couverture" refers to the silk coverings with identifying coats of arms worn on top of armor. Such coverings are mentioned, for example, in William the Breton's *Philippiad* (song XI, verses 178–99) (Duby 1973).

7. Gontart of Koblenz's shield, which is "d'or et d'asur, riches et bieles / Vairies, a quartier d'argent" (vv. 2693–94), may also link him to a specific historical figure.

8. After his defeat of Otto IV and his allies at Bouvines, Philip Augustus is said to have sent Frederick II the imperial eagle that lay on the battlefield (Toch 1995, 382). Philip himself had been presented with the battered imperial insignia when Otto fled battle (Baldwin 1986, 217). Otto is repeatedly compared to an eagle in the *Philippide* (Guillaume le Breton 1825, e.g., 352).

9. In the version of Matthew Paris's *Chronica majora* in Cambridge, Corpus Christi College MS 16, Otto's shield is emblazoned with a double-headed eagle and accompanied by the inscription "Otto creatur in imperatorem Romanorum." Otto's alliance with the English is represented in a shield on the same folio, which unites the lions of England with Otto's eagle. Otto was, of course, not alone in using the double-headed eagle to symbolize imperial power. Such symbolism both predates and postdates his co-option.

Milon—Aiglente's father—also recalls the rapacious *milan*, more commonly known as the *escoufle* in Old French (and in English as a kite).[10] Milon's avian associations are intensified through the rhyme *Milon/talon* (vv. 2554–55), *talon* referring to the human heel but also to an avian claw.[11]

The density of hunting birds in the Empire may reflect not just the historic symbol of the territory but also, perhaps, Frederick II's fascination with falconry. Although the treatise itself likely postdates the *Violette*, Frederick II's *De arte venandi cum avibus* is one of the longest texts on the topic in the Middle Ages, and Frederick II's interest—if not the text itself—might well have been known to Gerbert de Montreuil.[12] In any case, these birds of prey all play antagonistic roles in the plot. True to the lover-as-hunter trope, these imperial hunting birds pursue their amorous quarry (Gerart and Euriaut, respectively), threatening to separate the two lovers indefinitely by luring them permanently into imperial space. Ultimately the two lovers—and the Capetians—prevail, with Gerart and Euriaut happily married by the king (v. 6574) at the end of the text.

If the Empire is associated with hunting birds, Occitan song is linked instead to songbirds, although, as we will see, it may still be associated with imperial or pro-imperial territories. Of the forty lyric insertions in the *Roman de la violette*, only the two Occitan insertions occur in proximity to evocations of birdsong. Mirroring the narrative that introduces them, the actual quoted songs almost always allude to birdsong, and in one instance the lyric has demonstrably been rewritten to include this allusion. That this association of Occitan lyric with birdsong is not coincidental is further suggested by the fact that, outside of these two pieces and their narrative introductions, birdsong is mentioned only twice in the romance.[13] The precise relationship between birdsong and these two *sons* is never explicated, but in both instances a character in the romance overhears the sounds of birds before going on to sing

10. Louison (2009) and Abeele (1988, 5–15) have written about the significance of this bird.

11. See "talun, talon, taloun" glossed as "hinder claw of bird of prey" (Gregory et al. 2005).

12. On the other hand, it is not clear that Gerbert de Montreuil would have had Frederick II rather than Otto IV in mind as a representative of the Empire. Although Frederick II was certainly emperor by the time of the composition of the *Violette*, Frederick II was allied with Philip Augustus at Bouvines.

13. When Gerart arrives in Nevers dressed as a jongleur, he is informed that music and birdsong will no longer be appreciated there, because everyone is so upset by Euriaut's situation: "Son de note ne cri d'oisiel / N'ierent mais chaiens chier tenu" (no melody or bird cry will be valued here anymore, vv. 1373–74). Later on, the lark sings just before the tournament at which Gerart conquers Lisiart: "L'aloëte lieve ses chans, / Qui por le douch tans se depieche, / S'a grant voie dusch'a la pieche" (The lark, who rushes because of the mild weather, lifts its song, and the path is long to the field, vv. 5875–77).

his or her own *son*, often featuring, as already mentioned, a sonic encounter with birdsong, thus creating an echo effect. This is the narrative introduction to the first inset troubadour song, which is labeled as a "son poitevin":

Vint a Nevers li desloiaus [Lisiart];
Et ma damoisele Orïaus
Fu en haut a la tour montee,
A la feniestre est akeutee;
Si a entendu des oysiaus
Les cans dous et plaisans et biaus.
Lors li souvint de son ami,
Lors souspire et plaint et gemi.
Apriés, quant elle [Euriaut] a souspiré
L'a un poi amours aspiré
A chanter, si com jou devin,
D'un vier d'un boin son poitevin
Dont il li estoit pris talens.

He came to Nevers, the disloyal one [Lisiart]; And my lady Euriaut was at the top of the tower, leaning at the window; She heard from the birds the sweet and pleasant and beautiful songs. And then she remembered her beloved and then she sighed and lamented and moaned. Afterward, when she sighed a little, Love inspired her a little to sing, as I imagine it, from a stanza of a good poitevin song, which she felt a wish to sing. (vv. 311–23)

The relationship between the birds' *cans* and Euriaut's *son* is not explicitly one of imitation. In fact, the *cans* of the birds might seem to suggest a rational cultural artifact more than the term *son*—which literally means "sound"—used to describe Euriaut's song.[14] Nevertheless, the immediate contiguity of the sonic objects suffices to invite us to draw an analogy between them. Moreover, the three adjectives applied to the birds' songs ("dous et plaisans et biaus"), all linked via the repeated conjunction *et*, are echoed in the formula used to describe Euriaut's actions preceding her own song ("souspire et plaint et gemi")—although here, of course, the linked terms in the polysyndeton are verbs rather than adjectives. Curiously, the modifiers of the birds' *cans* ("sweet and pleasant and beautiful") frame them as more aesthetically desirable than the "son poitevin" that follows shortly. And, what is more,

14. Gilles Eckard (1999, 680) argues for a similar reversal of "natural" and "cultural" terms in the Châtelain de Couci's "La douce voiz du louseignol sauvage."

this swerve toward formulae involving repetition extends to the subsequent description of Euriaut's actions—with its anaphoric repetition of *lors* and the subsequent verbs beginning with S (*souvint* and *souspire*)—as if to signal the recursive sonic qualities of birdsong.

Are we to understand that Euriaut is, in this passage, akin to a bird? Euriat's name supports this hypothesis, in its proximity to Old French *euriel*, or oriole.[15] So does Euriaut's physical position, at the edge of a window ledge, perched on high when Lisiart encounters her. Orioles are, in fact, known for residing so high in the tree canopy that they are more easily recognizable through their song than through visual cues (Mason and Allsop 2010, 13; Beaman and Madge 1998, 724). This is, in fact, precisely how Lisiart both encounters and identifies Euriaut: "Lisïars a la vois oüe, / Dreche son chief, si l'a veüe / A la feniestre ou elle sist" (Lisiart heard the voice, he lifts his head, and saw her / at the window where she was sitting, vv. 334–36). Given that Lisiart has never met Euriaut, and that nothing about her song would obviously indicate her identity, the only way to make sense of this acousmatic sonic identification is, in fact, to imagine that Euriaut *is* a bird whose distinctive call indexes her species identity. Medieval theorists (following some classical ones) generally posited that bird names derived from the sounds produced by various species, mapping ontological difference onto not physiological distinction but sonic traits.[16] In short, in light of Euriaut's avian name, her position at a windowsill, and the threefold quasi-pleonastic characterization of her behavior, which mirrors the (equally pleonastic) threefold characterization of birdsong in the same passage, it seems clear that Gerbert invites us to understand Euriaut's sonic production as a species of birdsong. Perhaps it is a kind of echolalia, an unconscious imitation on Euriaut's part of the birdsong she has just heard.

But why frame Euriaut's song in this way, as something akin to avian vocalization? Part of the answer, I think, lies in the status of birdsong in medieval grammatical treatises. As we saw in this book's introduction, birdsong occupied a specific category in these treatises, where it was conceived as a type of *vox* (voice) that was scriptable (*literata*) but meaningless (*inarticulata*). To frame an utterance as birdsong was thus to prime listeners or readers for incomprehensibility. And, indeed, as we will see, Euriaut's song at

15. The spelling of Euriaut's name cycles between Euriaut, Euriaus, and Oriaus. The spellings Godefroy gives for "oriole" are *oriel*, *orial*, and *euriel*.

16. Pliny, for example, describes birds solely in terms of their voices. Isidore follows Pliny in seeing avian species names as non-arbitrary signifiers, either because of imitation (like the *bubo*, the owl whose name onomatopoeically reproduces its cry) or because the name "derives" from its behavior (the *luscinia*—nightingale—indicates daybreak with her song) (Cannon 2004, 257).

this moment in the narrative is nonsensical to varying degrees in many of the manuscript variants. But the comparison to birdsong also, I would suggest, invites the audience to listen to Euriaut's vocal production as a sonic entity whose status as decipherable within traditional semantic linguistic codes is secondary. In other words, the narrative lead-up to Euriaut's song prepares the audience to attend to sound over sense, to the acoustic fabric of language as opposed to its referential content. We saw a similar gesture in Renart's *Rose* through the framing of the Occitan songs as ones overheard from a distance, part of a larger sonic spectacle, or, as here, likened to birdsong. The same sort of priming—for the acoustic as opposed to the referential—is achieved in the verbs used to describe Euriaut's actions just before she begins to sing. Euriaut's sighing, complaining, and moaning (we are told that she "souspire et plaint et gemi"), which come in between her aural encounter with birdsong and her singing, also occupy a particular category in medieval grammatical treatises. Sighing and moaning were generally theorized in treatises as instances of *vox inarticulata et illiterata*, voice that is both meaningless and unwritable. Gerbert's choice to cue the first "son poitevin" in the text with these two types of utterances drawn from widely circulated grammatical treatises, both nonreferential and, in the case of one, not even transcribable within traditional language, cues an auditory encounter with the lyric to follow that frames it not primarily as sung referential speech but as *sound*. In the terms of medieval theory, we are invited to understand this sonic event not as *vox literata et articulata* (writable and meaningful voice) but as *vox inarticulata*. To use the vocabulary of contemporary sound studies, the type of listening solicited is not semantic listening—listening whose primary function is to interpret a referential code such as language—but rather reduced listening (listening to the sound itself, independent of its cause and meaning). This mode of listening proves to be a productive one, since, as we will see below, many versions of Euriaut's song border on unintelligibility.

The actual "son poitevin" given in the narrative at this point varies across manuscripts.[17] Three of the four manuscripts of the *Violette* (*BCD*) transmit a related but elsewhere unknown stanza while *A* (BnF MS fr. 1553) gives a

17. There are four extant manuscripts of the verse *Violette* (as well as a fifteenth-century prose redaction, discussed later in this chapter). These are Bibliothèque nationale de France, MS. fr. 1553 (*A*), BnF MS. fr. 1374 (*B*), St. Petersburg, National Library of Russia, Fr. Q. v. XIV. 3 (*C*), and New York, Pierpont Morgan Library MS. 36 (*D*). Manuscript *A*, written in a Franco-Picard *scripta*, is from the late thirteenth century, probably in the vicinity of Cambrai. *B*, from the middle of the thirteenth century, is the oldest manuscript, and its *scripta* indicates compilation near the southeast border of *langue d'oïl*. See Krause (2007, 82). *C* was copied between 1400 and 1420 and was compiled in Paris for the duke of Burgundy (83). *D* dates from the middle of the fifteenth century.

Gallicized version of the fourth stanza of Bernart de Ventadorn's "Ab joi mou lo vers e·l commens" (PC 70.1). In this manuscript, Euriaut appears preemptively to condemn Lisiart for his future behavior and to predict her imminent trouble as a result of jealous courtiers before her speech drifts to an only semi-intelligible conclusion. Here is how the insertion appears on folio 289v:[18]

> Il nest anuis ne faillemens
> Ne villonie che mest vis
> Fors dome ki se fait devins
> Dautrui amour ne con*n*issans.
> Enuieus q*ue* vous en avanche
> De moi faire anui ne pesanche
> Chascuns se velt de son mestier
> garir. Moi confondes
> *et* vous n'en voi joir

> There is no trouble or fault or evil deed, it seems to me, [greater] than the man who tries to divine and obtain knowledge of someone else's love. Jealous ones, how does it advance you to cause me harm or injury? Everyone wants to [?] his needs [?]. You destroy me and I do not see you rejoice as a result.

The implied parallel between birdsong and this troubadour stanza thus rationalizes both its moments of opacity and its hint of linguistic strangeness. Although it looks mostly like the Picard French found in the rest of this version of the narrative, there is an occasional Occitanism: "Faillemens" (v. 1), for example, approximates Occitan *falhimens* without being an exact translation (cf. French *faillement*). Other than this term, the text blends in linguistically with the surrounding manuscript, but it veers toward the nonsensical in its final lines. In the original Occitan, the penultimate line of the *cobla* reads: "Chascus se vol de so mestier formir" (may everyone occupy themselves with their [own] affairs). In the Gallicized version presented in *A*, it is not clear what this line is supposed to mean. Godefroy and the *DEAF* gloss *garir*, the verb that replaces Occitan *formir*, as some version of "garantir, protéger, défendre," or else as "fournir." But none of these acceptations makes any sense with *mestier*, in any sense of that word. The effect of Gallicization here

18. I quote directly from the manuscript rather than from Buffum's edition. I have not added punctuation. Realizations of abbreviations are indicated in italics. Line divisions reflect those in the manuscript.

Table 3.1 Euriaut's song in the three manuscripts of the *Violette*

B (BnF MS fr. 1374)	*C* (Saint Petersburg, National Library of Russia, Fr. Q. v. XIV. 3)	*D*, New York, Pierpont Morgan Library MS. 36, fol. 7r
[. . .]	[. . .]	[. . .]
Un vier d'un boin son poitevin Dont amors la fait esbaudir:	Un vier d'un bon son poitevin Dont amors la fait esbaudir	D'un vier d'un boin son poitevin Dont amors la fait esbaudir:
	Par ung amoureux souvenir:	
En inqual tans que never dausir Bois et pras vergiers et flors espanausir Et voi bien que jois enance sans / faillir Plus que cors n'en puet pensar ne / bouce dir Et sui jausie d'un riceau Qui plus me place a ma partie	En cel temps que la verdure Est ou bois et ou vergier Et je oy ces oyseaulx chanter Et de mon ami me souvient Que je prens a regretter.	En ce doux temps que je voy revverdir Bois prez vergiers et fleurs espenir Et voy que joie en aise sans faillir Par fine amours en doulx espoir duire Plus que ne peult nul cuer ne bouche dire Et suis du cuer durement ravie D'un doulx raissiau qui plaist a ma partie
In that time when [*never* = *Nevers? never dausir?*] woods and fields, orchards and flowers blossom, And I see that joy advances without fault, more than anyone can conceive or a mouth say, and I am delighted by a river that pleases me at my departure . . .	In that time when greenery is in the woods and the orchard and I hear these birds sing and I remember my beloved, whom I begin to regret...	In this sweet time when I see become green woods, fields, orchards and flowers blossom, and I see joy at ease without fault, through true love leading to sweet hope, more than any heart or mouth can say, and I am very uplifted in my heart because of a sweet river that pleases me at my departure . . .

is thus (as elsewhere) to produce a text that sounds and looks like French but does not wholly make sense *as* French. The song's framing as birdsong works, arguably, to account for this breakdown in language's referential function.

In the three other manuscripts of the *Violette*, Euriaut's song is more comprehensible but strange in other ways. These manuscripts, instead of stanza IV of Bernart's "Ab joi mou lo vers," transmit a related but thus far unidentified piece. Table 3.1 shows how it appears in all three manuscripts, with introductory lines of narrative. This insertion has been classified as PC 461.103a, although there is still no scholarly consensus on whether the original behind these three variants was composed in Occitan or Old French.[19]

19. There is nothing resembling the piece in the *Concordance de l'occitan médiéval* (Ricketts 2001) (henceforth abbreviated as *COM*). Douglas Buffum (1911, 141) notes a similarity to the first stanza of one of Bernart de Ventadorn's songs, "Can par la flors josta·l vert folh." The stanza reads as follows: "Can par la flors josta·l vert folh / e vei lo tems clar e sere / e·l doutz chans dels auzels per brolh / m'adousa lo cor e·m reve, / pos l'auzel chanton a lor for, / eu, c'ai mais de joi en mo cor, / dei be

It is unattested elsewhere, although in its hypervernality it is highly reminiscent of the opening stanzas of many troubadour lyrics, including Raimon Jordan's "Lou clar tans vei brunazir" (PC 404.4), a lyric whose first stanza is transmitted in BnF MS fr. 844. All three variants read like stalled springtime exordia of the sort that mark the beginnings of myriad troubadour (and trouvère) songs. All set the stage of abundant greenery and emotional effusion so typical of the *Natureingang*. In this, they perform a type of hyperlyricization similar to the francophone versions of Occitan song discussed in chapter 1.

Unsurprisingly, this hypervernality includes, in two of the three variants, an allusion to the auditory. For the *joie* (joy) of the *BD* readings, manuscript *C* substitutes an acoustic encounter: "je oy ces oyseaulx chanter" (I hear these birds sing). The *B* variant also alludes to the auditory in its opening line, "En inqual tans que never dausir." It is not immediately apparent what this line means (like the *A* variant, this one shifts in and out of making sense). Is "never" a reference to the city of Nevers, the location of Euriaut's performance? "Ausir" means "to hear" in Occitan, but how could the speaker *hear* the "bois et pras vergiers et flors" of the following line, except perhaps by inferring their presence from the birdsong that is absent in this variant?[20] How could one hear the apparition of greenery? In any case, the *BC* variants foreground an auditory encounter, one that is in fact only a constitutive link in a chain of such encounters: Euriaut hears the birdsong at her window and subsequently sighs and moans, both acts that prime the listener for reduced listening. Within her song, she sings about her own auditory experience in an auditory event designed for the aural consumption of the audience. *What* one hears in this instance—that is, the actual, referential content of the song—seems secondary to the very act of hearing, which is thematized again and again both within the song and in the narrative lead-up to it, as if to encourage reduced listening.

This type of listening helps account for the various linguistic peculiarities of the *B* variant, which conjures up the sounds of Occitan more than it faithfully reproduces Occitan forms. This conjuring is mostly achieved via

chantar, pois tuilh li mei jornai / son joi e chan / qu'eu no pes de ren al" (When the flower appears among the green leaves and I see the clear and calm weather and [when] the sweet song of birds in the woods softens my heart and revives me, since the birds sing in their manner I—since I have more joy in my heart—must sing well, since all my days are joy and song for I do not think of anything else) (Bernart de Ventadorn 1966, 152). I would note that the first two lines at least resemble Raimbaut de Vaqueiras's famous multilingual descort: "Eras quan vey verdeyar / Pratz e vergiers e boscatges" (Now when I see growing green fields and orchards and woods) (Raimbaut de Vaqueiras 1964).

20. I am very grateful to Marion Uhlig for pointing out this appearance, in absentia, of birdsong.

diphthongs (*dausir, espanausir, jausie*) and through Occitanizing forms such as *inqual*, a form that falls between Occitan *aquel* and French *(i)cel*. Likewise, the verb in *B*'s last line—*place*—may be an attempt to reproduce the Occitan *platz*. Although phonologically the piece serves as a veneer of Occitaneity, its forms—as just described—do not actually correspond to real Occitan; the piece *connotes* Occitan more than it actually reproduces it. The soundscape of Occitania seems to be of equal or greater interest to the poet (or scribe) than the content of the song, which, in this variant as in others, reads like an unfinished thought; though the piece sets the stage for later development, beginning with well-worn allusions to birdsong and greenery, it stalls rather than proceeding.

Mirroring this stasis of content, the rhyme scheme of all variants fails to go anywhere, either through the absence of a real rhyme scheme or through monorhyme, depending on the manuscript. Just as the speaker of the *BCD* variants never seems to finish her thought, so does the rhyme scheme either anchor the stanza in one place, in the case of monorhyme, or else dissolve entirely. In the former category are the *B* and *D* variants, which, except for the last two lines, are monorhymed; they return repeatedly to *-ir*, perhaps an attempt to evoke the oriole's fast chirping on the same sound. In any case, the song's heightened sonic focus on closural moments highlights the stanza's inability to conclude. At the opposite end of the spectrum, the *C* variant does not contain a single rhyme sound (the closest is a near rhyme between a noun in *-ier* and an *-er* infinitive). Depending on the manuscript, the stanza either returns obsessively to the same rhyme sound or completely rejects rhyme. That this should formally represent stasis is suggested, elsewhere in the *Violette*, by Gerbert's association of the process of rhyming with movement. In the epilogue, he deploys the metaphor of rhyming and rowing—a metaphor itself constructed on sonic self-sameness: "Gyrbers de Mosteruel define son conte; / N'en velt plus faire lonc aconte. / Tant a rimé k'il est a rive" (Gerbert de Montreuil ends his story; he does not wish to lengthen it further. He has rowed/rhymed so much that he has reached the shore, vv. 6634–35).[21] The semantic failure of the stanza—its inability to complete the thought introduced—is thus mirrored in the formal structures of the variants, which either row in place or fail to row at all. Both poetic moves—the saturation of the same rhyme sound or the absence of any rhyme sound at all—draw the audience's attention to the insertion at the sonic level, since they represent a rupture in the poetic soundscape of the surrounding narrative. That all the insertions are implicitly compared to birdsong (in the narrative lead-up in all

21. Quintilian also uses rowing as a metaphor for rhetoric (Curtius 1953, 436).

cases and in the opening lines of the song in some) justifies their sonic and/or semantic strangeness.

The second Occitan insertion in the narrative is also associated with birdsong—and was in fact demonstrably rewritten to intensify this association. The song—a Gallicized version of the first stanza of Bernart de Ventadorn's famous "Can vei la lauzeta mover" (PC 70.43)—is performed by Gerart for Aiglente in the imperial section of the romance. Gerart embarks on an afternoon of hunting larks and quails (v. 4149) along the banks of the Rhine (v. 4176). The lark he overhears—which also happens to bear Euriaut's ring around its neck—inspires him to sing the first stanza of Bernart's lyric. Just as Euriaut overhears the *cans* of the birds before beginning to sing, and just as Lisiart overhears Euriaut before he actually sees her, so does Gerart hear the lark before he sees it: "une vois a entendu / D'une aloe ki ot tendu / Ses heles et vait haletant, / Et si aloit molt cler chantant" (he heard the voice of a lark that had stretched its wings and goes fluttering and singing very clearly, vv. 4178–81). These references to the lark's song and to its halting movements, like the mention of the lark's song, will be echoed in the lyric insertion. Both of the manuscripts that transmit a lyric insertion at this point in the narrative (*AB*) supplement what is an exclusively *visual* encounter in Bernart de Ventadorn's original (the speaker spies the lark against the backdrop of the sun, visually observes its movements, and is moved to envy) with a sonic dimension. In the *Violette*'s rendition of this famous troubadour lyric, as shown in table 3.2, Gerart does not just see the lark in the sky; he overhears the lark's *song*.

As if to acknowledge the long-standing link between birdsong and opaque language, both scribes insert the allusion to the lark's song precisely at the moment when they seem to have had the most difficulty making sense of the original Occitan. What is more, as will be clear from the question marks in my translation, this allusion to birdsong is itself only semi-intelligible (what is, exactly, "miravilment du cant *de se*"?), thus performing a kind of avian garbling. This is Bernart's hypothetical original, according to Appel:

Can vei la lauzeta mover
de joi sas alas contral rai,
Que s'oblid' e·s laissa chazer
Per la doussor c'al cor li vai
ai! tan grans enveya m'en ve
de cui qu'eu veya jauzion,
meravilhas ai, car desse
lo cor de dezirer no·m fon.

When I see the lark move
out of joy its wings against the ray [of the sun],
[and] that it forgets itself and lets itself fall
because of the sweetness that goes through its body;
oh! such great envy comes to me of those whom I see rejoicing. It is a miracle that
my heart does not immediately melt from desire.

The Occitan adverb *desse* (immediately) has no cognate in French and, as we saw in chapter 2, was obscure to French readers and scribes. Here manuscripts *A* and *B* take the opportunity to inscribe an allusion to the miracles of the lark's song, which does indeed work as a kind of antidote to Aiglente's magic potion. Like these allusions, which appear only in these two variants of the song, the reference to the "felon" at the end of the *A* variant seems like a bespoke addition; it is likely an allusion to Aiglente and her machinations. At precisely the moment in which the lyrics turn to the apotropaic power

Table 3.2 The *Violette*'s rendition of Bernart de Ventadorn's famous "Can vei la lauzeta mover"

A (BnF MS fr. 1553)	*B* (BnF MS fr. 1374)	*C* (Saint Petersburg, National Library of Russia, Fr. Q. v. XIV. 3)	*D* (New York, Pierpont Morgan Library, MS. 36)
Pour Aiglente talens lin vint De cest son poitevin chanter	Pour Aiglente talens li vint De cest son provençal chanter	De Aiglente talens li vint Et de son provençal chanter Adonc a prins a commencer	[Manuscript lacks passage containing this insertion (vv. 3666–4223).]
Quant voi la loete moder De ioi ses ele contre rai Qui soblide et laisse cader Pour la douchour cal cor li / vai Dex tant grant anvide mi fai de li quant vi la jausion mirabillas son cant fait Anui le felon	Quant voi la loete moder De jau ses ales contre el rai Que soblide et laisser cader per la douçor c'al cor mi [sic] vai, Dex cal grant envide mi fai De li quant vi la jaucion Miravilment du cant de se Lou cor de desier me fon	[Insertion omitted.]	
When I see the lark move / out of joy its wings against rays / And forget itself and let itself fall / Because of the sweetness that moves through its body, / God, what great envy it inspires in me / Of it, when I see the rejoicing [when I see it rejoicing?] / Its song makes miracles / To the detriment of the evil one.	When I see the lark move / out of joy its wings against the rays / And forget itself and let itself fall / because of the sweetness that goes through my heart, / God, what great envy it inspires in me / Of it when I see the rejoicing [?] / Miraculously, because of its song [?], My heart melts from desire.]		

of song, their own referential operations begin to falter, leaving it up to the reader or listener to piece together meaning. As in many incantations (abracadabra!), the referential function of language is downplayed.

What identifies these stanzas as Occitan is not so much the actual remnants of the Occitan language but the forms that imitate Occitan sonorities as well as intermediate forms that fall somewhere between French and Occitan (as was the case in the *B* variant of the first "son poitevin" in the romance). Occitan *joi* has been rendered as *jau* in the *B* variant and is probably modeled on the later term *jauzion* (an adjective in Occitan but perhaps a noun here). As is the case elsewhere, the diphthong /aʊ/ serves to cue a sense of Occitaneity. Some forms fall somewhere between Occitan and French: *cader*, for example, is neither French *cheoir* nor Occitan *chazer*. The form obviously approximates the Latin *cadere*, and in this instance proximity to Latin may also be an attempt to signal the Occitan language, or perhaps the clichéd "Latinity" of birdsong.[22] On the whole, however, both variants read as French, albeit it a French that is strange and sometimes ungrammatical. Once again, this strangeness is accounted for within the narrative via the piece's association with birdsong and the concomitant mode of listening—"reduced listening"—that this analogy invites. In light of this association, we are not troubled by the fact that our hearing of the song does not result in perfect understanding, since we are invited to treat the lyrics as a variety of noise poetry.

This particular Occitan song is clearly more than a vehicle for referential human language. Although it can be (mostly) parsed semantically, the primary function of the denotative linguistic function of this song seems to be to tell us of its *other* functions. The song explicitly announces its miraculous properties—"mirabillas son cant fait" in one variant and "miravilment du cant de se" in another—and the narrative confirms the song's exceptional, apotropaic status: though he begins to sing this song for Aiglente, Gerart's performance of this reincarnated troubadour song initiates the chain of events that leads Aiglente's potion to lose its potency (after intoning the song, Gerart allows his sparrow hawk to kill the lark, and thereby discovers the ring that Euriaut has placed around its neck). *Chant* here is conflated with *enchantement*, as is etymologically appropriate. Bernart's lark song has been transformed into an all-encompassing sonic event. The same could be said of the initial Occitan (or, in some variants, perhaps Occitanizing) song. Only these two insertions are associated with birdsong, and, arguably, only these

22. I am indebted to Marion Uhlig for this suggestion regarding Latinity.

two insertions are framed in such a way as to encourage us to listen to them in ways that exceed semantic listening.

Along with the implied comparisons to birdsong within and around both Occitan(izing) pieces, and their moments of semantic opacity, the pieces are also set apart by the geographical tags assigned to them. Unlike in Renart's *Rose*, where the two Occitan insertions were not the only ones marked in such a way, here only these two pieces are associated with a particular provenance. As we have already seen, the first insertion is tagged as a "son poitevin" in all manuscripts, while the second is sometimes a "son poitevin" and sometimes a "son provençal." These labels do not correlate strongly either with the linguistic features of the insertions in a given manuscript or with the overall provenance of the manuscript. Initially, based on the first insertion, the *B* variant of the first insertion, which is transmitted in a manuscript from the southeastern border of *langue d'oïl*, would seem to confirm the hypothesis that the more proximate the provenance of a given manuscript was to Occitan territory, the more its insertions resembled Occitan; the *B* variant of the first insertion does on the whole look the most Occitan, although this is a result of creative phonological coloring and not a reflection of genuine Occitan forms. However, the *B* variant of the second insertion, despite its "provençal" label, does not really look much more Occitan than the *A* variant. This suggests that the choice between "poitevin" and "provençal" does not correspond to the degree of Occitan phonological coloring present in the associated insertion.

Alongside language, the political valence of the two spaces would constitute another plausible rationale for the labels, but the political valence of "poitevin" and "provençal" within the broader context of the romance is unclear. Poitou was a hotly contested territory in the years leading up to the composition of the *Violette*. Since 1154, the Plantagenets had held Poitou; it was only in 1204 that Philip Augustus reclaimed part of the region (Sivéry 1995, 65). In 1206, however, some major Poitevins, including the counts of Eu and La Marche, sided with King John of England instead of Philip Augustus (Baldwin 1986, 219). The barons of Poitou continued to earn their reputation for a lack of loyalty. In 1214, at the Battle of Bouvines, some Poitevin barons sided with the English king, and King John of England was absent from the battle because he was occupied attempting to secure Poitou. In fact, Philip's son, Louis VIII, was sent to Poitou to protect the territory at the same time as Philip Augustus warded off imperial forces at Bouvines (Sivéry 1995, 240).[23] Around 1225–30, during the period of the

23. Poitou is repeatedly mentioned in chronicles that discuss Bouvines. See, for example, Roger of Wendover, William the Breton, and the Minstrel of Reims (Duby 1973).

Violette's composition, Poitou was officially Capetian territory, but it could hardly have felt like "home turf." As recently as 1198, Otto IV, foster son of Richard I of England and the emperor who led the charge at the Battle of Bouvines, had been made count of Poitou. Thus, the label "poitevin" might have conjured up either pride at a recent Capetian conquest or a suspicious, disloyal Plantagenet space.

If Poitou was formerly Plantagenet territory, Provence was at the time partly imperial. The part of Provence beyond the Rhône lay within the Kingdom of Burgundy and was thus part of the Holy Roman Empire (Strayer 1992, 12). Does "provençal" signal this part of Occitania? The valence of the labels remains unclear. Both could be intended to cue for the audience the Plantagenet and imperial coalition, or they could instead point to two prized recent Capetian conquests (Poitou and the part of Provence recently conquered through the Albigensian Crusade). If the former is true, it would explain why the two Occitan insertions act as bookends to the imperial section of the romance. After the first, both Euriaut and Gerart depart for imperial territories, and after the second they take leave of them and return to Capetian France. I have already described the broader geographical contours of the romance; suffice it to say here that Lisiart's encounter with Euriaut (which is triggered by the first *son poitevin*) and Gerart's with the lark that wears Euriaut's ring around its neck (triggered by the second) mark crucial moments of rupture and reunion in the lovers' relationship. The lark's death also leads to Aiglente's rejection, and to Gerart's departure from imperial territory. Having emerged from his narcotic-induced stupor, Gerart remembers Euriaut and abruptly takes leave of both the duke of Metz and his daughter (vv. 4320ff.) before beginning his journey back to Capetian France. After Gerart has rescued Euriaut, the two lovers return to Capetian France via the court of King Louis (v. 6573). Even Aiglente understands the pivotal role the lark has played; true to her predatory nature, she attempts to kill the sparrow hawk that has killed the lark (v. 4369) as punishment for killing the bird through which Gerart was reminded of his true love ("l'oisiel prist / Par coi Gerars nouviele aprist / De cheli pour cui m'a laissie" [she took the bird through which Gerart received news of the one for whom he has left me], vv. 4376–78). In this, her behavior further conforms to the underlying cynegetic structure of the romance, since sparrow hawks are natural prey of many varieties of eagle. In any case, that the apparition of the lark should mark the separation of two lovers—Gerart and Aiglente—and a "new dawn" in the romance (in which Gerart departs and eventually reunites with his first love) is apposite, given the medieval traits of the lark, which often warned lovers of the approach of day and the need to take leave of each other.

Given the uncertainty surrounding the political space of these two *sons*, William Paden's (1993) reading of the romance as anti-Occitan seems questionable (in his assessment, "the romance is played out against an implicit background, a political, social, and cultural framework which privileges the north of France and condemns the south" (48–49). Paden's reading depends, in part, on the notion of the lark as "an allegorization of Bernart's lark as the voice of the troubadours" and of the "murderous response" provoked as a "rejection of the troubadour model in favor of the snatches of French lyric" (49). That the scene surrounding the second Occitan insertion is a violent one is indisputable.[24] The killing of the lark by Gerart's sparrow hawk is gruesome and described in gory detail. Gerart himself seems to fall into a kind of stupor, extracting pleasure from the spectacle of the sparrow hawk's slaying of the lark: "De la cervele le repeut, / Puis li oste au plus tost k'il puet" (He fed it [the sparrow hawk] on its [the lark's] brain / Then removed it from him as fast as he could, vv. 4217–18). It is not clear to me, however, that the lark represents "an allegorization of Bernart's lark as the voice of the troubadours," as Paden (50) sees it. In many variants, these two *sons* do not look especially Occitan, and their tags of "poitevin" and "provençal" do not firmly associate them with Occitania (as indicated above, "poitevin" might mean Plantagenet or Capetian, while "provençal" could indicate Capetian, Occitan, or imperial territory). Moreover, as we have already seen, the two troubadour songs are caught up in the romance's anti-imperial thrust in that they bookend the imperial sojourns of Euriaut and Gerart. They are not clearly associated with Occitania politically or linguistically, and they are in some instances barely recognizable as troubadour songs. Transmitted anonymously, and in the heavily Gallicized form of some variants, these pieces would likely have been unidentifiable as originally Occitan to most medieval audiences.

In Paden's reading of the *Violette*, the historical moment that haunts the text is the Albigensian Crusade. As I have shown, however, the memory of Bouvines, much more than that of the Albigensian Crusade, inflects the geopolitical space of the text. It is the Empire that is depicted as the negative space—one dominated by birds of prey—rather than Occitania. It is the Empire that threatens to destroy the Capetian-sanctioned romance at the center of the plot, with its hunting birds luring Gerart and Euriaut into

24. The scene is also a reworking of Jean Renart's *Escoufle*. Marion Vuagnoux-Uhlig (2009, 360) has looked in detail at the parallel scene in the *Escoufle*.

imperial space, threatening to capture them indefinitely. That the memory of Bouvines shapes the text much more than that of the Albigensian Crusade is clear in the composition of the tournament at Montargis, which Paden reads as reenacting the sides of the Albigensian Crusade. Five members of Gerart's party had fought for the Capetians at Bouvines: the count of Ponthieu (v. 5922), the lords of Barres and Garlande (v. 5926), and the counts of Dreux and Saint-Pol (vv. 5914, 5928). In John Baldwin's (2000, 63) reading, Gerart's side of the tournament is composed of individuals faithful to the Capetians and may even be considered "a royal party." In Baldwin's reckoning, four are related to the king by blood, with the count of Bologne (v. 5921) representing Philippe Hurepel, son of Philip Augustus (64). The counts of Brittany and Dreux (v. 5914) were royal cousins, and the count of Saint-Pol (v. 5928) was a royal cousin (Baldwin 2000, 64). Lisiart's side, meanwhile, does not allude to Occitania but is rather composed, according to Baldwin, of "turbulent barons [. . .] from the mountainous regions of the Massif Central" (65). Baldwin singles out the houses of Beaujeu and Auvergne, which had long been disruptive to the Capetians.

Moreover, Occitania is always evoked neutrally in the romance. It is first mentioned via the town of Saint-Gilles (Gard *département*), described as the site of the fake pilgrimage Lisiart stages in order to have an excuse to visit Euriaut in Nevers: "Or oiés dou mal trahitour: / Com pelerins quist son atour, / Aussi com alast a Saint-Gilles" (Now hear about the evil traitor: as a pilgrim would leave his home, as if he were going to Saint-Gilles) (vv. 305–7). In Paden's reading, this is an allusion to the site of the assassination of Pierre de Castelnau, the papal legate, in 1208. Pierre's death was critical in sparking the Albigensian Crusade because of the alleged involvement of Raymond, count of Toulouse, in the event (Paden 1993, 48). I remain unconvinced that there is anything symbolically significant to this mention of Saint-Gilles given that the town was, in in fact, the third most popular pilgrimage site after Jerusalem and Santiago de Compostela, as well as a frequent stopping point on the way to the latter (Vuagnoux-Uhlig 2011). Indeed, the same pilgrimage route is mentioned elsewhere in the text in relation to the duke of Metz (v. 1119, v. 5134). If anything, Saint-Gilles seems to stand as an immediately legible synecdoche for the Camino de Santiago.

A second southern area is evoked via Lisiart's county, Forez, now part of the Haute Loire department. Franco-Provençal was the historic language of this region. Paden (1993, 49) interprets Lisiart as a symbol of southern treachery because he is from Forez. At the time of the *Violette*'s composition, however, the county of Forez was linked politically to Nevers (through the marriage of Mathilde of Nevers and Guy IV, count of Forez) (Baldwin 2000, 61).

This suggests that Nevers and Forez are part of the same political sphere in the romance, and indeed, Lisiart and Gerart squabble over Gerart's ownership of Nevers (v. 994).

The city of Toulouse makes a brief appearance via a mention of the count of Toulouse, who is upheld as an example of extreme wealth. The fabric of Euriaut's dress is said to be so opulent that not even the count of Toulouse could buy it: "En quel onques liu que je soie, / Oseroie dire pour voir / Que n'esligast de son avoir / Le tissu li quens de Toulouse" (In whatever place I might be, I would truly say that the wealth of the count of Toulouse could not acquire the fabric, vv. 831–34). The specific count Gerbert has in mind is probably Raymond VII, who was one of the wealthiest vassals of the French king until he ceded his territory to Louis VIII in 1226 (Sivéry 1995, 369).[25] Even when speaking of a historic figure who played a significant role in the Albigensian Crusade, Gerbert's tone could be read as either neutral or complimentary, but certainly not as antagonistic. In short, allusions to Occitan space are few and far between, and their tone entirely neutral. By contrast, the Empire is clearly marked as a dangerous space in the romance—one dominated by hunting birds who prey on the songbirds Euriaut and Gerart, threatening to keep the couple apart.

Strangely, the framing of troubadour lyric as a kind of birdsong in the *Roman de la Violette* is less exoticizing than we might expect, given that so many characters in the romance have an avian quality. Nevertheless, the text does stage a boundary between francophone human art song and the inarticulate Occitanizing or formerly Occitan songs of birds. Through this comparison to birdsong, the two Occitan pieces are framed to solicit a type of listening that attends to sound over sense, accounting for their garbled status in some manuscripts. In the case of the first insertion, this attention to sound over sense is further cultivated through the use of monorhyme or through the total absence of rhyme. Occitan song is transformed into a kind of noise poetry, one whose value in the text lies less in its ability to serve as a vehicle for referential language (indeed, a *sine qua non* of song, according to many medieval treatises, which declared rationality to be its constitutive feature) but in one instance at least, in its ability to serve an incantatory function. Although they are marked as somewhat foreign, through the geographical tags associated with them, the insertions are nevertheless not always clearly distinguishable as Occitan ("poitevin," as we have seen, lay on the border

25. Gerbert's comment about Raymond's wealth may suggest that the *Violette* was composed before 1226.

between France and Occitania, and the label "provençal" appears in only two of the four manuscripts). Their provenance in the cultural tradition of the troubadours is concealed, and their status as human interrogated. The sounds of the Occitan are not part of the fabric of a distinct and historical language, recognizable within the text as such, but rather part of the soundscape of a type of noise poetry associated with avian vocalization.

CHAPTER 4

From Beak to Quill

Troubadour Lyric in Richard de Fournival's Bestiaire d'amour

We saw in the previous two chapters that an association with songbirds was one feature that served to "explain" the occasional unintelligibility of Gallicized Occitan in Jean Renart's *Rose* and Gerbert de Montreuil's *Violette* (where it was one of a handful of such features in the *Rose* but the primary feature in the *Violette*). Richard de Fournival's *Bestiaire d'amour*, the third French narrative to incorporate Occitan (or formerly Occitan) material, might well have taken this latent "explanation" of Gallicized Occitan as birdsong to its acme. Birds are, after all, more at home in a bestiary than in a lyric-interpolated romance, and they abound in Richard's *Bestiaire d'amour*, a bestiary-cum-love narrative.[1] Richard's songbirds are not, however, associated with Occitan song.[2] Instead, the troubadours are quoted in the *Bestiaire*'s account of the hoopoe, a bird not treated as a songbird by medieval bestiaries or treatises.[3] That Richard would maintain the association

1. All references are to Segre's critical edition of the *Bestiaire* (Richard de Fournival 1957). All translations from the French are mine. Gabriel Bianciotto's 2009 translation into modern French, which also includes an edition based on manuscript *A* on the facing page, is the most accessible (Richard de Fournival 2009).

2. Margarida Madureira (2009) has discussed the staging of songbirds in Richard's *Bestiaire*.

3. The hoopoe is, in fact, a songbird, but only its cry is discussed in medieval bestiaries, and even this comes up only occasionally. In his survey of the hoopoe, Lops (1982, 179) quotes a passage from Philippe de Thaon concerning the hoopoe's cry.

of Occitan song with birds but divorce it from its association with birdsong specifically reads like something of a joke against the backdrop of the persistent association we have seen thus far in the French songbooks and narratives. I argue in this chapter that Richard's perpetuation of the linkage between troubadour lyric and birds, on the one hand, combined with his decoupling of the linkage between troubadour lyric and avian song, on the other, is indicative of a broader delyricization of Occitan lyric in the *Bestiaire*. This chapter documents the ways in which troubadour song is transformed from poetry into prose and the troubadours inserted into a writerly genealogy. Moreover, even if Richard acknowledges the individuality—if not the identity—of the troubadours whose songs he quotes, the manuscript transmission of the relevant passage of the *Bestiaire* was uniquely unstable, with most manuscripts subjecting the Occitan quotations to several more stages of oblivion.

Born on October 10, 1201, Richard de Fournival was deacon, canon, and chancellor of the Amiens chapter of Notre Dame and canon of Rouen.[4] His *Nativitas*, an astrological autobiography, describes the alignment of the stars at the moment of his birth.[5] A remarkable polymath, Richard was also a licensed surgeon, an accomplished astronomer, a composer of some eighteen lyrics, and a forerunner in the domain of motet composition.[6] Richard's *Biblionomia*, an elaborate library catalog, may represent at least partially the contents of his own library, which was bequeathed to Amiens after his death.[7] Despite the fact that Richard was likely no stranger to vernacular literary production, the *Biblionomia* bears no trace of it, although it includes some Latin works by Richard's contemporaries.[8] Richard may also have penned

---

4. Richard's connections to the city of Amiens have not been sufficiently explored. In addition to promoting Amiens-based writers (see note 8), he states in the preface to the *Biblionomia* that the astrological alignment of the day of his birth mirrored that of the city of Amiens (Richard de Fournival 1874, 520). A romance titled *Abladane*, describing the history of the city of Amiens, is ascribed to him (erroneously, according to Paulin Paris [1856, 714]). His affiliation with the city is analogous to Adam de la Halle's connection to Arras and Guillaume de Machaut's to Reims.

5. The *Nativitas* has been edited by Alexandre Birkenmajer (1949). The *Nativitas* was glossed by Pierre de Limoges in the second half of the thirteenth century.

6. These lyrics have been edited most recently, without music, by Yvan Lepage (Richard de Fournival 1981). To my knowledge, the most extensive discussion of Richard's lyric production from a musical point of view remains that of Glenn Pierr Johnson (1991, 283–383). Four of Richard's lyrics appear (with music notation) in Samuel Rosenberg, Hans Tischler, and Marie-Geneviève Grossel's 1995 anthology of trouvère song as numbers 149–52. See also Tischler's own 1997 anthology.

7. The only edition of Richard's *Biblionomia* is from the late nineteenth century (Richard de Fournival 1874).

8. Thomas Haye (2010, 226) also notes the absence of texts in the vernacular. The writers with a connection to Amiens are Nicolas of Amiens (ca. 1147–1200) and Richard de Gerberoy, bishop of Amiens from 1205 to 1210. Haye considers Richard's inclusion of these two writers to be indicative of a certain "esprit de clocher" (221).

several treatises on love, although the authorship of many is disputed: the *Consaus d'amours*, the *Poissance d'amours*, and the *Commens d'amour*.[9]

The list in the front matter of this book ("Manuscripts and Sigla of Richard de Fournival's *Bestiaire d'amour*") documents the twenty-three manuscripts, including fragments, that either transmit or are known to have transmitted the prose version of Richard's *Bestiaire d'amour*, which also sparked various continuations (including a distinct redaction in Italy), responses (including the famous female-voiced response), translations (into Middle Low Franconian, Flemish, and Welsh), and a verse *remaniement* known as the *Bestiaire d'amour rimé*. Richard may also have authored a verse version of the *Bestiaire* himself, known today as the *Bestiaire d'amour en vers*, but only a fragment of this version has survived.[10] Among the twenty-three manuscripts that transmit the prose *Bestiaire d'amour*, three are of Italian provenance: New York, Pierpont Morgan MS. 459 and Florence, Biblioteca Laurenziana, Ashburnham 123, which both contain an anonymous French-language continuation and several additional exempla, and Biblioteca Laurenziana, Plut. 76,79.[11] Of the twenty other manuscripts, the two oldest are Paris, Bibl. Ste. Geneviève 2200, compiled in 1277, and the most recent manuscript to be discovered, compiled in the 1260s.[12] The latest manuscript, according to Christopher Lucken (2010, 114), is from the fifteenth century.

Richard's incorporation of troubadour song into his narrative is unusual within the early French reception of Occitan lyric, and the text is rarely discussed in relationship to the *Rose* or the *Violette*, despite the fact that its lyrical mode of writing, its date of composition, and its inclusion of fragments of troubadour song clearly invite such a comparison. Maureen Boulton (1993, 295), for example, cites the *Bestiaire* in her index of French narratives containing lyric insertion, but she does not actually discuss it in the course of her study. Although Boulton offers no explanation for her exclusion, it may result from Richard's presentation of the troubadour lyrics he quotes not as karaoke-style song intoned by characters within the diegesis but instead as

9. The *Consaus* was edited by Gian Battista Speroni (Richard de Fournival 1974), who has also edited the *Poissance* (pseudo-Richard de Fournival 1975). And for the *Commens d'amours*, in which Richard de Fournival—forerunner to Jean Froissart—invents mythological exempla, see Antoinette Saly's edition (Richard de Fournival 1972).

10. The *Bestiaire d'amour en vers* survives in fragmentary form in only one manuscript (Paris, Bibliothèque nationale de France, MS fr. 25545).

11. For an edition of these manuscripts, see Coltelli (2014). On the transmission of the text in Italy, see the introduction to Segre's edition, Casapullo's *Lo Diretano bando* (1997), articles by Jeanette Beer (1991, 2007), and my recent discussion of Pierpont Morgan MS 459 (Zingesser 2015).

12. Roy (2006, 205) proposes the siglum *T* for this manuscript. For an excellent overview of the manuscript tradition, see Lucken's (2010) survey.

speech or writing.[13] In this respect, the case of the *Bestiaire* is unique within the French transmission of the troubadours. Richard's mode of incorporation bears no resemblance at all to the procedure of "lyric insertion" deployed in the *Rose*, *Violette*, and other narratives that form the object of Boulton's study, all of which quote songs in a way that suggests performance. Richard was demonstrably familiar with this mode of lyric insertion, which he uses in his *Commens d'amour*, and his move away from lyric insertion as diegetic performance must be read as a deliberate and calculated move. Meanwhile, for reasons that are less clear, the text is also omitted entirely from the Raupachs' study of Gallicized Occitan lyric.

The passage of the *Bestiaire* in which Richard quotes from troubadour song occurs, as I have already noted, within the section on the hoopoe. I will return to the significance of this location later. I quote the passage here as edited by Segre, using italics to emphasize the quotations:

> . . . il n'est riens c'amours ne face ivel. Quar en amours n'a ne val ne tertre, ains est aussi ounnie coume mers sans ondes.[14] Dont uns poitevins dist que *riens ne vaut l'amour qui ensi endoie*; et pour c[h]ou dist Ovides que amours et segnourie ne puent demourer ensanlle en une caiere. Et li poitevins qui ensievi Ovide si dist: "*Non pot l'orgueill od l'amour remanoir*"; et li autres qui redist: "*Non pos poiar s'el non descen.*" Il le dist pour c[h]ou que puis qu'ele estoit plus haute et il plus bas, que a c[h]ou que il fuissent ouni il couvenoit que ele descendit et il montast. Et la raisons de ceste iveleté si est prise de c[h]ou que c[h]ou est uns meïsmes chemins qui va de Saint Denis a Paris et qui vient de Paris a Saint Denise [*sic*]. Ausi di jou ke se vous voliés ke nous nos entramissiesmes, ke chu seroit une misme amors de vous a moi et de moi a vous, et tout d'autretel lignage seroit l'une comme l'autre. Et por ce dist li poitevins: "*Se tout vos est, bele, de rien lignage, l'amour ki emport est ingaus de parage.*" (Richard de Fournival 1957, 88–90)

> There is nothing that love does not make equal, for in love there is neither valley nor mountain, and it is as unified as the sea without

13. Speech and writing are two textual modes that are not fundamentally opposed in the *Bestiaire*, whose prologue claims that all writing is intended to be revoiced through *parole* ("toute escripture si est faite pour parole monstrer et pour che ke on le lise; et quant on le list, si revient elle a nature de parole" (Richard de Fournival 1957, 6–7)).

14. For these lines, Segre compares the following passage from Mathieu de Gand's *De faire chanson envoisie*: "Amors doit estre tote ounie / Sans orgueil et sans vilenie" (Richard de Fournival 1957, x). Richard's oceanic imagery is absent from this lyric, and is also textually rather distant.

> waves. For this reason a Poitevin says that *"love that undulates in this way is worth nothing."* And it is for this reason that Ovid says that "love and lordship cannot remain together on the same seat for long"; and the Poitevin, who followed Ovid, says: *"Pride cannot remain with love."* The other says: *"I cannot rise if she does not fall."* He says this because she had risen higher and he lower, and for them to be on the same level it was necessary that she descend and that he ascend. And the reason for this equality is that it is the same road that goes from Saint-Denis to Paris, and from Paris to Saint-Denis. And, for this reason, I say that if you wanted us to love each other, it would be the same love from me to you and from you to me, and everything from the same lineage; and, for this reason, the Poitevin says: *"if [your friend?] is of poor lineage compared to you, beautiful one, the love he bears within himself is of equal rank."*[15]

All of the attributed quotations in this passage have now been identified. The words attributed to Ovid are thought to be a translation of lines 844–46 of Book II of the *Metamorphoses*, "non bene conveniunt nec in sede morantur / maiestas et amor" (majesty and love don't fit together well and don't linger in the [same] place). The quotation is specifically from the Rape of Europa episode, in which Jove transforms himself into a bull in order not to scare off Europa with his godly attributes (these lines are part of Jove's justification of his animal metamorphosis).[16] Beyond the phrase attributed to Ovid, three are attributed to a "poitevin" and one to an "autre." The first, "riens ne vaut l'amour qui ensi endoie" (love that wavers in this way is worth nothing), is taken from Bernart of Ventadorn's "Can vei la flor" (PC 70.42), where, in the original Occitan, it reads as "re no vol amors qu'esser no deya" (love does not want anything that is not fitting).[17] The verb *voler* has been misconstrued—either by Richard or by the songbook from which he quotes—as *valoir*, while the combined sonority of *no deya* has been interpreted as a form of the verb

15. This last sentence is an approximation of the French; Richard's formulation is unclear. Bianciotto translates the sentence as "Belle, si à comparaison de vous votre ami n'est en rien votre égal par la race, l'amour qu'il porte en lui est l'égal du vôtre par le rang" (Richard de Fournival 2009, 259). This whole passage was subject to frequent alteration in the manuscript tradition of the *Bestiaire*, as I describe later. Throughout this section, Richard's hypothetical original is that of Segre's edition.

16. A variation on the same idea appears, unattributed, as a "parole" in Jean de Meun's portion of the *Roman de la rose*: "Bien savoient ceste parole / Qui n'est mensongiere ne fole, / C'onques amours et seignorie / Ne s'entrefirent conpaingnie / Ne ne demorerent ensamble" (Guillaume de Lorris and Jean de Meun 1992, vv. 8453–57).

17. Cf. Jeanette Beer's theory that the lines in question are from Bernart de Ventadorn's "Tant ai mo cor ple de joya" (PC 70.44). She compares them to "c'atressi·m ten en balansa / com la naus en l'onda" (for she keeps me rising and falling like a boat on the waves) (Beer 2003, 100).

ondoier (Kay 2011, 480). BnF MS fr. 20050, the sole French songbook to transmit this piece, does not make this mistake, which may indicate that it is Richard's invention.[18] In any case, the reading is naturalized in the *Bestiaire*, where the quotation about undulating love is made to echo and confirm Richard's own comment that love is like a sea without waves. The next line attributed to the Poitevin, "non pot l'orgueill ad l'amour remanoir" (pride cannot remain with love), is drawn from the same song by Bernart of Ventadorn, where, in its original Occitan, it reads: "pauc pot amors ab ergolh remaner, / qu'ergolhs dechaiu e fin'amors capdolha" (love cannot remain with pride for long / for pride descends and *fin'amors* conquers). Both of these quotations are drawn from stanza III. In fr. 20050 this line reads: "greu poc amors a orgoil remaner." Jumping to the end of the passage, the last quotation attributed to the Poitevin, "se tos vous est bele, de riens lingnage, l'amours k'il em port est ingaus de parage," is from "Destregz d'amor veing denan vos" (PC 16.9), thought by most scholars today to be by Albertet de Sestaro but attributed to Bernart of Ventadorn (albeit in a modern hand) in the sole French songbook to transmit it—BnF MS fr. 844 (*W*).[19] In the Occitan, it reads: "si tot vos etz belha e d'aut linhatge, / lo ben qu'ie·us vuelh es egal del paratge" (if you are noble and from a high lineage, the good that I wish you is of equal rank). *W* does not transmit the relevant stanza (IV), pointing to a broader French transmission of this piece than the extant evidence would indicate. Taken collectively, I would argue that this evidence indicates that behind Richard de Fournival's "poitevin" stands Bernart de Ventadorn, whose identity Richard has chosen not to transmit.[20]

That Richard was well aware that the songs from which he was quoting had two distinct authors is confirmed by his choice of the term "autre." If

18. In BnF MS fr. 20050, the line reads "ren non vol amor q'esser non deie" (fol. 88r).

19. See fol. 192r. Segre proposed as a source for this quotation another line from "Can vei la flor" (PC 70.42): "Paubres e rics fai ambdos d'un paratge" ([Love] makes the poor and the rich of one rank) (Richard de Fournival 1957, xi).

20. Richard's source songbook may have resembled BnF fr. 844, which supplies a similar sequence of songs: *coblas* from the lyrics from which Richard's last two quotations are taken (Albertet de Sestaro's "Destregz d'amor" and Guilhem Magret's "Enaissi·m pren cum fai al pescador") are transmitted one after the other on fol. 192 of *W*. Moreover, although *W* does not transmit Bernart de Ventadorn's "Can vei la flor," source of Richard's first two quotations, what might be considered the "Bernart section" of *W*—a series of eight lyrics that have been attributed to him—precedes the Albertet and Guilhem *coblas* almost directly (fols. 190–91). It seems possible, then, that Richard was working with a source whose ordering of lyrics closely resembled *W*'s: first a section of Bernart de Ventadorn's lyrics (this time including "Can vei la flor"), then PC 16.9, then PC 223.3. Whichever modern reader added attributions to Bernart de Ventadorn to three lyrics of this section of *W*, including the source of Richard's last quotation by the "Poitevin," may even have come into contact with Richard's source manuscript.

Richard had been working with a songbook in which these particular pieces were anonymous, there would be no reason for him to distinguish between a "Poitevin" and an "autre." Although Richard does acknowledge two distinct "Poitevins," he nevertheless does not transmit their names, unlike the name of Ovid. To this nebulous "other" Poitevin, Richard attributes the dictum "non pos poiar s'el non descen." I follow Jeanette Beer's suggestion (2003: 101) that this line is adapted from Guilhem Magret's "Enaissi·m pren cum fai al pescador" (PC 223.3). In the Occitan, the passage from which these lines are drawn reads: "Quar ses lieys non ay guerimen / ni puesc poiar s'il non dissen" (For without her I have no remedy, nor can I rise if she does not come down).[21] Both this piece and another by Guillem Magret are transmitted in fr. 844—and this inclusion represents the only trace of Guillem's poetry in French transmission.

Were it not for the single vowel A in the verb *puiar*, we might well read these quotations as French (Kay 2011, 479). What is more, this verb appears only in six of the twenty-three manuscripts of the *Bestiaire*; the others are either too fragmentary to transmit this passage, or else they abridge it, or else they substitute the verb *monter* for *puiar*.[22] In his Gallicization, Richard follows the pattern of Jean Renart and Gerbert de Montreuil before him. However, Richard's transposition into French has not produced any moments of semantic opacity, as was the case in the *Rose* and the *Violette*, although on one occasion (*ondoie* for *no deya*), the transposition prioritizes sound over sense. Richard's label of "poitevin" is the only indication of the texts' Occitan provenance, although it is unclear whether "poitevin" should be read as a cipher for "Occitan," as indicative of the border region of Poitou, or as something else entirely. In any case, we will see below that much of the manuscript transmission of the *Bestiaire* bears witness to the erasure of the Occitan language; many versions of this passage omit the "Poitevin" label entirely.

The Poet as Parrot in *Quant jou voi*

Before turning to the various other erasures to which troubadour lyric is subjected in the *Bestiaire*, I want to explore briefly one of Richard's love lyrics, because it clearly demonstrates both Richard's attentiveness to rhyme

21. Beer (2003, 186–87) readily admits that such metaphors of ascent and descent are legion in the troubadour corpus. Segre thought the source was Folquet de Marselha's "S'al cor plagues" (PC 155.18) (Richard de Fournival 1957, xi).

22. Florence Biblioteca Medicea-Laurenziana, Plut. 76.79, Vienna Österreichische Nationalbibliothek MS 2609, Pierpont Morgan MS 459, and Florence Biblioteca Medicea-Laurenziana, Cod. Ashburnhamiani 123 substitute the verb *monter*.

elsewhere in his corpus (an attentiveness he does not extend to troubadour song) and his deployment of rhyme and other sound effects as part of an exploration of avian language.[23] This lyric, which reflects thinking on birdsong akin to what we have already seen in this book, represents, in short, what Richard *might* have done with his poitevin quotations. Following in the tradition of many troubadour and trouvère lyrics, the song, "Quant jou voi" (song XI in Lepage's edition), evokes, in its exordium, the incipient birdsong of warmer seasons (see table 4.1).

Because it is composed of stanzas with lines as short as three and four syllables (lines 1, 3, and 5 and lines 9 and 11, respectively), the song already, by virtue of its form, foregrounds the sonic dimension of language, in the sense that its naturally occurring repetition of rhyme sounds occurs much more frequently due to the lower number of syllables in the text as a whole. This lays the groundwork for what is, I would argue, a broader exploration of the sonic dimension of language in the piece. This begins with an allusion to birdsong that is more than an allusion. Richard's language in this particular passage actually *performs* the birdsong (and perhaps also the insanity) it describes. As was the case in BnF MS fr. 844, insanity is associated with acoustic disregulation on the level of the signifier (see chapter 1). The third line of the poem splits the word *oiscillon* in two, as if to find the music within the bird, thereby transforming its first syllable, *oi*, into a rhyme sound. This procedure of breaking a word in two over a line break in order to use an internal syllable as the rhyme sound, called *rim trencat* in Occitan poetic theory, is extremely unusual in medieval French. Via *rim trencat*, Richard invites us, like Jean Renart and Gerbert de Montreuil before him, to listen to lyric as sound disassociated from semantic meaning. Here, he calls attention to the recursive sonic structure that *is* poetic song. The initial *oi* of line 3's *oiseillon* finds an echo in line 5's *oi* ("I hear"), a lexical choice that further encourages a kind of close listening going beyond language's denotative function. That Richard's lyric flags this feature of song *within* the word *oiseillon* also acknowledges the deep kinship between human recursive sonic structures and avian ones. Through his acoustic reduplication, he *becomes*—or at least comes to resemble—the birds he describes. Other figures of acoustic reduplication proliferate in the song, which deploys identical rhyme ("fait" in lines 25 and 29), a *rime léonine* (involving homonyms) with similar alveolar onset consonants ("d'esté" and "ont esté" in lines 2 and 4), *rime paronyme* ("vis"

23. I discuss elsewhere this piece's position within a broader tradition of avian zoopoetics in medieval French and Occitan in "Pidgin Poetics: Bird Talk in Medieval France and Occitania" (Zingesser 2017).

Table 4.1 "Quant jou voi" (song XI in Lepage's edition)

Quant jou voi	When I see
La douce saison d'esté,	The sweet season of summer,
Que cist oi-	And that those birds
seillon qi trop ont esté	who have been too long
mu et coi	Silent and calm,
Se sont reconforté.	Have revived themselves,
Et quant je les oi,	And when I hear them,
Si m'ont tel atourné	They have affected me so much
Qu'en la folie	That into the folly
Qu'avoie laissie	Which I had left behind
M'ont retourné.	They send me back.
Pas ne di	I am not saying
Que folie soit d'amer,	That it would be folly to love,
Mais ainsi	But as
Con j'en pens fais fol penser	I see it, I have crazy thoughts
Quant celi	When she to whom
M'estuet mon cuer douner	I must give my heart
Qi moi a gerpi	—[She] who has abandoned me
Pour pïeur acoster,	To become close to a lesser man—,
Se n'i pert mie	Loses nothing
Tant con sa boidie	As much as her treachery
Li peut grever.	Can hurt her.
Car qi laist	For whoever leaves
Son bon ami pour felon	His good friend for a traitor
Vers lui fait	Toward him commits
En tel guise traïson	Treachery in such a way
Qu'il mesfait	That he does wrong
Meïsme a vengison,	Even against vengeance,
Et se honte en fait,	And if he brings shame on himself,
Ja ne grouchera on;	One will never grumble as a result;
Mais en ma vie	But in my life
De sa felounie	Of this misdeed
N'avrai renon.	I will not have the reputation.
Si m'est vis	It seems to me
Que bien m'en deliverrai,	That I would happily be rid of her,
Car toudis	For constantly now
Desdaigneus cuer or avrai:	I will have a disdainful heart:
Por c'envis	For with difficulty
Son dangier souferrai,	I will suffer her power,
Puis qu'ele m'a mis	Since she makes me
Muser au papegai;	Think of the parrot;
Mout le fornie,	She contests it,
Mais, que qu'ele en die,	But, whatever she says,
Maugré l'en sai.	I hold it against her.
Neporqant,	Nevertheless,
S'ele m'amer me revoloit	If she wanted to love me again,
Et samblant	And if she showed me a semblance
De loiauté me moustroit,	Of loyalty,
Je dout tant,	I strongly fear that,
S'ele m'i renbatoit,	If she rejected me,
Que che que j'en chant	She would make me atone for
Conperer me feroit,	What I am singing about her,
Si que vengie	Such that she would have vengeance
Par sa tricherie	Through her treachery
De moi seroit.	On me.

and "envis" in lines 34 and 38), *rimes dérivées* ("atourné" and "retourné" in lines 8 and 11; "fait" and "mesfait" in lines 25, 27, and 29) and a *figura etymologica* ("felon" and "felounie" in lines 24 and 32).[24] All of these poetic figures amplify the acoustic reduplication that is constitutive of most trouvère song beyond the requisite final vowel, thereby forging a psittacine language in which the same sounds constantly surface.

As if to hammer in the affinity between avian and human *poesis*, the speaker of this lyric regrets that his beloved turns his thoughts toward the parrot: "ele m'a mis / muser au papegai" (she made me think of the parrot, vv. 40–41).[25] Lepage suggests, following Jeanroy and Långfors (1921, 137), that these lines be translated as "since she condemned me to waiting in vain" (Richard de Fournival 1981, 80). While these lines are certainly startling, I see no need to resort to a figurative interpretation. We should, I think, take the lyric voice literally, that is, both nonfiguratively and with attention to its *litterae* or letters. His beloved, Richard tells us here, makes him think of a parrot (and the verb used to describe this thinking—*muser*—suggests not just a fleeting thought, but a more profound type of mental reflection). Once again, Richard's language takes a performative turn via alliteration, with its insistent M's ("*m*'a *m*is / *m*user"), each followed by a different vowel, in a birdlike vocalization. And, indeed, the speaker's parrotese continues in the following lines, each of which begins with M: "Mout le fornie, / Mais, que qu'ele en die, / Maugré l'en sai" (She contests it, but whatever she says, I hold it against her, vv. 42–44). These four consecutive lines are, except for the repeated Q at the start of lines 9 and 10 (a repetition arguably triggered by the poem's evocation of insanity at precisely that moment), the only instance of a recurring initial consonant in the song, and they constitute a kind of onomatopoeia.

Moreover, Richard's parrot allusion does not just spark a series of sonic reduplications. It also retrospectively explains a sonic reduplication that has taken place throughout the entire song as avian in origin: the piece is *almost* composed of *coblas singulars* (that is, stanzas that preserve a rhyme scheme but do not reuse rhyme sounds). I say "almost" because the *c* rhyme of the song (*-ie*) stays the same throughout. In the case of the fourth stanza, where the parrot allusion appears, this *c* rhyme, which has echoed throughout the song, makes an appearance directly after Richard mentions a *papegai* (v. 41). The placement of this structural echo in the song immediately after

24. These rhymes are noted by Lepage, who does not link them to the avian turn in the poem (Richard de Fournival 1981, 80).

25. This interest in the voice in relation to love lyric reappears—via a comparison to Echo—in song IX. Christopher Lucken (1999, 2002) has explored this aspect of Richard de Fournival's work.

Richard's mention of the bird suggestively links the two ideas—parrot and repeated sound. That the speaker's rather cryptic allusion should be followed so shortly by the reappearance of the single rhyme sound that has echoed throughout the song invites us to hear this repeated rhyme sound as yet another indication of Richard's psittacine qualities. And this allusion to the *papegai* is itself located at the rhyme, a location that transforms its name into a local sonic echo, the rhyme sound *ai* having already appeared three times in this stanza. The mention of the parrot thus explains various acoustic repetitions as psittacine in origin, both on the level of the stanza (in which the rhyme in *papegai* rings for the fourth time) and on the level of the whole composition (by having the sole repeated rhyme sound in the song follow directly the evocation of the bird). I want to emphasize here that Richard's parrotese does *not* involve code-switching into an avian language that can be circumscribed, but rather the increased and strategic use of formal and poetic devices that draw attention to language as sound. This suggests, I think, that Richard's lyric metamorphosis into a parrot should not be read exclusively as local and transitory. His sound effects here are nothing but an exaggeration of the repetitive sounds any lyricist must produce in the making of song. All poets, he suggests, are already parrots. And a poet who is obliged to repeat his songs endlessly, as he tells us that he himself must, in an ongoing attempt to secure his lady's affections, is the parrot of a parrot.[26]

The avian linguistic turn I have just outlined is, curiously enough, *not* associated with troubadour quotation in the *Bestiaire*. We have already seen similar linguistic experimentation—the foregrounding of the sonic, nondenotative function of language of the sort demonstrated in the song above—in Jean's *Rose* and Gerbert's *Violette*—yet the *Bestiaire* does not place its poitevin quotations in the beaks of any of its manifold birds. Although it associates the quotations with the hoopoe (which I discuss in the next section), it does not stage them in relation to avian speech. Richard, unlike Jean Renart and Gerbert de Montreuil, seems entirely uninterested in the *sound* of Occitan song, which he imagines as neither song nor poetry.

From Songbird to Hoopoe: Delyricizing the Troubadours

Richard's forgetting of the names of the troubadours behind his "Poitevin" and "other," and his forgetting of the original Occitan in which these Poitevins

26. Regarding the poet as parrot, Sarah Kay (2010, 25) suggests that all troubadours are parrots in another sense—that they must learn literary Occitan and compose in a language that is not strictly native to them.

composed, are complemented by several other dimensions of erasure, the first of which is his obliteration of any traces of lyricism in the troubadours' texts. The *Bestiaire* author has subtly shifted the troubadours' words toward impersonal, third-person statements. This is mostly achieved through judicious excerpting: the third stanza of Bernart's "Can vei la flor"—the stanza from which Richard has drawn two of his quotations—is the *only* stanza in the piece that contains third-person sentences (Bernart de Ventadorn 1966, 86–89). In this case, Richard seems merely to be selecting for the most sententious and impersonal passage in his source lyric. Sometimes Richard goes further, however: in the last quotation, he has changed Albertet's original declaration, "si tot vos etz belha e d'aut linhatge, / lo ben qu'ie·us vuelh es egal del paratge" (even if you are beautiful and from a high lineage, the good *I wish for you* is of equal rank) into a third-person statement: "Se tos vous est, bele, de riens lignage, l'amours k'i emport est ingaus de parage" (Beautiful woman, if [your friend?] is of poor lineage compared to you, the love he bears within himself is of equal rank). In the passage in which Richard quotes the troubadours, the only hint of the first-person voice of most Occitan lyric is the verb ending in S of the quotation attributed to the "other" ("Non pos poiar s'el non descen"). Barring this single verb form, the troubadours are well on the way to looking like coiners of *sententiae* rather than composers of lyric poetry. We will see later that part of the manuscript transmission of the *Bestiaire* exploits this latent tendency away from lyric and toward the sententious.

This shift toward the third person is not the only way in which the troubadours are delyricized: Richard's selection of quotations is also so abbreviated that the only hint of their original poetic form is in the last quotation—the quotation which, as we will see below, was the most often forgotten in the manuscript transmission of the passage. Only in the *-age* ending does the rhyme scheme of the original Occitan songs still ring: "Se tout vos est, bele, de rien lign*age*, / l'amour ki emport est ingaus de par*age*." As a lyric poet himself, as we saw in the case of "Quant je voi," Richard was highly attuned to rhyme schemes, and the oblivion into which rhyme sounds have fallen in the *Bestiaire* as a result of the tendency toward extreme abbreviation effectively writes the troubadours out of the tradition of lyric poetry—a tradition in whose numbers Richard counted himself, as he acknowledges at the beginning of the *Bestiaire*. There, the narrator explains that he will divert his efforts away from song: "Et por chu me convient il, quant je ne puis en vous trover merci, metre grengnor paine c'onques mais, ne mie a forment canter, mais a forment et atangnamment dire. Car le canter doi jou bien avoir perdu, si vous dirai par quel raison" (And for this reason, since I cannot find mercy in you, I must exert greater effort than ever before, no longer in singing loudly, but in strongly and appropriately saying. For I must have lost song, and I will tell you for what reason) (Richard de Fournival 1957, 10–11). The narrator later expresses his desire to retract his earlier (lyric) pleas, just as a dog eats its vomit: "Car se jou puisse faire ausi come li chiens, ki est de tel nature ke quant il a vomi, k'i repaire a son vomite et le remangüe, jou eüse volentiers me proiere rengloutie cent fois, puis k'ele me fu volee des dens" (if I could do as the dog, which is of such a nature that when it has vomited, he returns to his vomit and eats it, I would gladly eat my prayer a hundred times, since it flew from my teeth) (14–15). In delyricizing his poitevin quotations, then, Richard transports the troubadours to his postlyric, prosaic landscape. The near obliteration of rhyme sounds allows the troubadours' words to blend formally into the background of Richard's surrounding prose.

A further strategy of delyricization is Richard's decoupling of the term *poitevin* from *son* (melody)—the most common label for Occitan song in France, as we saw in several songbooks, the *Rose* and the *Violette*. This decoupling is indicative of the *Bestiaire*'s treatment of the quotations, which are mined as a text rather than used to suggest performance, as was the case in Jean Renart's *Rose* and Gerbert de Montreuil's *Violette*. While we might say that Richard's memory of the troubadours is greater than Jean Renart's or Gerbert de Montreuil's, in the sense that he acknowledges the distinct identities of a "poitevin" and "other"—even if he does not name them—he nevertheless forgets the specificity of their medium: *song*. This is mirrored in the verb used to introduce the quotation: *dire*. This saying or writing of troubadour lyric invites us to view it not as a sonic object, as was the case in the *Rose* and the *Violette*, but instead as a text that is to be mined for its content. Our attention is directed, unlike in the *Rose* and the *Violette*, not to song as sonic spectacle but to the semantic dimension of the utterances.

Finally, and perhaps most obviously, it is difficult to imagine a scenario in which the music that initially served as the medium for these poitevin utterances was conjured up, either in silent reading or in performance.[27] If, in the case of the *Rose* and the *Violette*, the fiction of diegetic performance invites readers to call to mind the melodies behind the trouvère and troubadour songs they quote—or at least to acknowledge them as sonic and potentially musical objects—in the *Bestiaire* everything works *against* such a melodic remediation. First of all, as we have seen, the quotations are introduced not

27. Cf. Elizabeth E. Leach and Jonathan Morton (2017, 349), who argue that the melodic snippets quoted here would have been particularly memorable.

with a verb suggesting musical performance but with the term *dire*. Even if we acknowledge that singing and saying are not incompatible vocal modes, it is difficult to imagine traces of melody slipping back into this literally prosaic passage, where the quotations are so heavily abbreviated that the corresponding melodies—assuming they were known—would, of necessity, have been correspondingly truncated. The assimilation of the poitevin utterances to the quotation from Ovid's nonmusical *Metamorphoses* makes a sudden turn to song even more unthinkable. And it seems unlikely that Ovid's "saying" and the Poitevins' "saying" are intended to call to mind two different types of vocalization—nonmusical on the one hand and musical on the other. Instead, I would argue, both the Poitevins and Ovid are recast in a thoroughly writerly tradition.[28]

Richard's evocation of the "Poitevin" (and the "other" Poitevin!) within the section of the *Bestiaire* on the hoopoe confirms and develops Richard's delyricization of the troubadours. It is hard not to think that Richard consciously composed this passage against the grain of certain songbooks, the *Rose*, and the *Violette*—all of which associate Occitan lyric with birdsong (and the *Rose* and BnF MS fr. 844 with a broader range of nonsemantic sonic phenomena). In inserting his quotations in the hoopoe section, Richard maintains the link between troubadour song and birds, all the while shifting this association away specifically from songbirds. Although hoopoes do sing, their song is not mentioned in any extant medieval bestiary. In fact, Richard's narrative description of the hoopoe serves as the perfect figure for Richard's reframing of troubadour song as a *written* text. Here is the passage, as edited by Segre:

> [. . .] li faon de la huple [. . .] quant ele est mal empenee, jamais ne mueroit ele a par li, aussi com autre oisel font, ains vienent li hupelot, si li esrachent a lour bes les vies pennes et puis si le keuvent et norrissent tant qu'ele est toute rempenee. Et bien metent autrestant de tans a li couver et a li nourrir, com ele mist a aus, quant ele les couva. (Richard de Fournival 1957, 87)

> [. . .] the offspring of the hoopoe, when it is poorly feathered, never leave her, as other birds do; rather, the little hoopoes come and tear off with their beaks the old feathers and then they brood and nourish her

28. I stress, again, that writing and speech are presented as complementary in the *Bestiaire*. See pp. 6–7 of Segre's edition.

until she is refeathered. And they put as much time into brooding and nourishing her as she devoted to them, when she brooded.

Richard's account of the hoopoe's behavior follows the bestiary tradition relatively closely. Here is the description in the long version of Pierre de Beauvais's *Bestiaire*:

> [. . .] Physiologes dist un example de sa nature. La hupe, quant ele a ses oes, ele les aime molt et keuve molt volentiers; et quant ses oes escloent, ele aime molt ses pocins et tient chierement et soef tant que il sont grant et que il se sacent bien porchasier. Physiologes nos dist ke li huplot sont de tel nature que quant il voient lor perre et lor mere enviellir, il en sont tot triste. Et nature de le hupe est tele qu'ele pert le voler et le veïr par viellece. Et quant li joene hupelot voient lor perre et lor merre si a meschief, si esrachent les vielles penes de lor pere et de lor mere; si les norissent sous lors eles tant que lor penes sont creues, et lor oeil renluminé, et renovelé tout lor cors, qu'il poent bien veoir et voler si come devant. (Pierre de Beauvais 2010, 171)
>
> Physiologus gives an example of its nature [the hoopoe's]. The hoopoe, when it has its eggs, loves them greatly and broods very willingly. And when its eggs have hatched, it loves its chicks greatly and cares for them until they are big and they know how to hunt well. Physiologus tells us that the little hoopoes are of such a nature that when they see their father and mother get old, they are sad. And the nature of the hoopoe is such that it loses its ability to fly and to see in old age. And when the young hoopoes see their father and mother in such misfortune, they pluck out the old feathers of their father and mother; they nourish them under their wings until their feathers have [re]grown and their eye regained its luster, and their body [is] renewed, so that they can see and fly again as before.

The general contours of the hoopoe bestiary exemplum will be clear. In Pierre de Beauvais's account—and in most other contemporaneous bestiaries—the hoopoe removes the feathers of its parents and nurses them until their feathers regrow.[29] Parallel to this replacement of antiquated, defunct *pennes* (feathers) with new ones is Richard's rescripting—with his

29. In Isidore of Seville's *Etymologies*, the hoopoe is associated with filth and excrement and has no association with filial piety, an association that seems to originate in the *Physiologus*. In Guillaume le Clerc, Philippe de Thaon, and Pierre de Beauvais, the hoopoe is lauded for its filial piety.

own quill, of course—of troubadour song. Richard's shift from song to script is perfectly encapsulated in the hoopoe, whose feathers are the focus of most bestiary accounts.

Ovid's *Metamorphoses*—which Richard clearly knew, as evinced by his quotation of the text and his naming of Ovid—also imagines the hoopoe in opposition to lyric and, specifically, to that paradigmatic incarnation of lyricism, the nightingale.[30] There, the Thracian king Tereus, who lusts after his wife's sister, Philomela, and subsequently assaults her, is transformed by the gods into a hoopoe, while his victim more famously becomes a nightingale. This Ovidian intertext strengthens the *Bestiaire*'s positioning of the hoopoe as anti-songbird. Indeed, Tereus's metamorphosis into a hoopoe only confirms his violent inclinations toward Philomela. While the hoopoe's crest signals his royal status, the rest of the hoopoe's physical traits signal his readiness for violence—his spearlike beak points analeptically both to Philomela's rape and to the severing of her tongue: "prominet inmodicum pro longa cuspide rostrum; / Nomen epops volucri, facies armata videtur" (an immoderate beak with a long tip juts out; the name of the bird is 'hoopoe'; it seems to have the appearance of being armed, VI.673–74) (Ovid 1972).[31] This predatory slant of the hoopoe is echoed earlier in the Philomela tale, where Tereus is compared to Jupiter's eagle and to a raptor gazing at its quarry ("Iovis ales," "spectat sua praemia raptor," vv. 517, 518). For Ovid, at least, the hoopoe does not just lack song; it is violent toward that songbird par excellence, the nightingale, a bird whose call—as registered in French and other medieval languages (*oci*)—subsumes both the valence of death (as a form of the verb *ocire*) and the identifying sound of the Occitan language or the *langue d'oc*—*oc*, or "yes." Like King Tereus, "King" Richard—who has summoned his prose rearguard in the *Bestiaire*—has stifled the lyric *langue*, or tongue, of those former songbirds, the troubadours, whose call would in fact reveal their Occitan origin.[32] Instead, Richard scripts them into a prosaic lineage. Via this

30. The *Metamorphoses* also figure in Richard's *Biblionomia*, where it is number 119 in the catalog ("Ejusdem liber Metamorphoses, in quo laudans Augustum ex successione ab antecessoribus per Eneam, sperabat saltem sic ipsius sibi graciam comparare [. . .]" [In the same book, *Metamorphoses* in which he praises Augustus in succession from his ancestors all the way back to Aeneas, he hopes at the same time to secure favor for himself], p. 531). Richard presumably alludes here to the concluding lines of the *Metamorphoses*, in which Ovid glorifies Augustus. Ovid does not state explicitly that he glorifies Augustus in order to secure his own position, although he does glorify himself and his work directly after Augustus. Lepage (1982) and Michèle Gally (2002) have explored other references to the *Metamorphoses*, especially Narcissus, this time in Richard's lyric corpus. Gally notes an exploration of Daedalus's labyrinth similar to Richard's in Aimeric de Peguilhan's "Atressi m·pren" (PC 10.12). She suggests that Richard may even have known this piece (8n7).

31. My translation. The severing of Philomela's tongue with a sword is described in VI.549–70.

32. On Richard as a king, see Segre, p. 7.

Ovidian intertext, and the memory of the association between Occitan lyric and birdsong, the *Bestiaire* recapitulates obliquely the cynegetic framework of the *Roman de la violette* (albeit in somewhat lopsided fashion: since both "King" Richard and the troubadours are aligned with the hoopoe, the distinction between predator and quarry is not upheld).

Troubadours of Yore

In addition to rewriting their language and medium of performance, Richard also rescripts the troubadours' position in literary history. His series of quotations, embedded within the hoopoe exemplum, also double the temporal framework of the hoopoe and its progeny. The passage suggests a textual genealogy in which Ovid is followed by the two Poitevins, who are in turn presumably followed by Richard. This genealogical structure is manifest in the verbs used to introduce two of the quotations: "Et li poitevins qui *ensievi* Ovide si dist," "et li autres qui *re*dist." The Poitevin does not just follow Ovid in his thought; he follows him chronologically. Temporal distance may also be implied by the verb *redire*, associated with the quotation of the "other" Poitevin (the prefix "re" suggests repetition, which, by definition, assumes temporal distance). And indeed, we will see below that the "other" Poitevin did indeed follow the first Poitevin chronologically. Richard is clearly the youngest hoopoe of the flock, since it is he whose philological doting "saves" his textual forbears from oblivion.

At the same time as it implies affection, however, this literary genealogy, as read through the filter of the hoopoe exemplum, clearly implies that Ovid and the Poitevins are outmoded, and, indeed, quasi-defunct. While Richard's quotation of Ovid and the Poitevins would seem to imply a kind of reverence toward them, the hoopoe framing suggests simultaneously that this "filial" doting is necessary because both Ovid and the Poitevins have been superseded. Their quills—or more properly, the metonymic products of their quills—survive only thanks to Richard's quotational eldercare. With a few marks of his own quill, Richard relegates the troubadours to the dusty shelves of literary history. They are treated as remnants of a distant literary past—one worthy of partial recollection, but one that is nevertheless a product of an irrevocably bygone era.

This avian genealogy, both reverent and insulting, is also factually absurd. While Richard's hoopoe analogy would seem to imply that the troubadours—like Ovid, with whom they are quoted—lived and worked in days of yore, Richard's "Poitevins" were in fact more or less his contemporaries. Even if we concede that Bernart de Ventadorn, whose compositional activity centered around the 1150s and 1160s, may have seemed like a remnant of the past to Richard (ca. 1200–1270)—although hardly a classical one—the career of Guilhem Magret (fl. ca. 1195–1210) overlapped with Richard's own.[33] Richard's introductory verb (*redire*) for Guilhem Magret, whom Richard says "restates" what has already been said by the "Poitevin" (Bernart de Ventadorn), suggests his awareness of the temporal divide between his "Poitevin" and "other," but despite this he relegates both to a classical past alongside Ovid.[34] This represents a bold move, since many troubadours were still flourishing around the time of the *Bestiaire*'s composition.

Richard's relegation of the Poitevins to the past is also performed by his gloss of erotic dynamics, in which he likens the equalizing forces of love to the selfsame road between Paris and Saint-Denis. With long-standing historic links to the French monarchy, Saint-Denis had long been the royal necropolis, and the road from Paris had on occasion served as the site of funeral processions when a monarch died in that city.[35] Although there were, of course, other processions on the road between Paris and Saint-Denis, and although not all French monarchs chose to be buried at Saint-Denis, Richard's surrounding discussion of lineage and the Ovidian intertext—which features both the regal hoopoe (King Tereus) and the regal Jupiter—invites a reading of the "road from Paris to Saint-Denis" as the path to the royal necropolis—a path whose very contours were said to have been traced by Saint Denis, who carried his severed head to the place he desired to be buried.[36] The troubadours are not just near-dead hoopoes, in this paradigm, but deceased monarchs who have been replaced by a worthy heir: Richard de Fournival.

In fact, Richard compares himself at the beginning of the *Bestiaire* to a king who has to deploy his prose *arriereban*:

> Et cis escris est ausi come l'arierebans de tous chaus ke je vous ai envoié dusques a ore. Car ausi comme uns rois, quant il va guerroier fors de son roialme, il en maine de ses melleurs hommes une partie, et s'en

33. The same is true of Albertet de Sestaro (ca. 1194–1221), but, as discussed above, Richard may have thought "Destregz d'amor veing devant vos" to have been composed by Bernart de Ventadorn.

34. Godefroy glosses *redire* as "dire de nouveau; dire à plusieurs reprises; dire encore." However, it could also mean "for his part" or "in his turn."

35. Gabrielle Spiegel (1975) and Elizabeth A. R. Brown (1980) have explored the links between Saint-Denis and the Capetians.

36. According to his astrological autobiography, known as the *Nativitas*, Richard was reputedly born on October 10, the day after the feast of Saint Denis (Birkenmajer 1949, 19).

> lasse encore gringnor partie a sa terre garder; mais quant il voit qu'il ne se puet soufire a tant de gent com il a mené, si parmande tous chiax qu'il a laissiés et fait son ariereban: ausi me covient il faire. (Richard de Fournival 1957, 7–8)
>
> And this writing is like the rearguard of all those I have sent you up to this point. For just as a king, when he must go to war outside of his kingdom, brings some of his best men and leaves behind more of them to guard his kingdom, but when he sees that the number he has brought is not enough, he sends for those he has left behind and composes his rearguard—thus must I act.

Several of the manuscripts of the *Bestiaire* amplify this textual analogy, in which Richard depicts himself as a king, on a visual plane as well. Folio 228v of BnF MS fr. 412, for example, shows a king preparing to attack a tower. With Richard's establishment of himself as a kind of king in the earliest lines of the *Bestiaire*, this passage on lineage, with its backdrop of the road between Paris and Saint-Denis, becomes one in which both royal and literary succession is established.

A fascination with lineage thus manifests itself in several dimensions of this passage: first, and most obviously, in the hoopoe exemplum, in which the young hoopoes dote on their aging parents. That this avian species was *not* registered as a songbird in medieval thought, but rather as a bird whose textual legacy focused on its *feathers*, draws the "Poitevins" into an avian typology that is scriptural rather than song-based. Second, the troubadour quotations both mention lineage explicitly (in the case of the passage from Albertet de Sestaro's *Destregz d'amor*) and are made to conform to a textual lineage, through Richard's suggestion that the Poitevins "followed" Ovid and that one Poitevin "said again" what another Poitevin had already said. The imbrication of this lineage with royalty is also made clear here, both in the regal hoopoe (via the intertext of Ovid's *Metamorphoses*, quoted explicitly here) and also in Richard's "road from Paris to Saint-Denis." Richard frames himself as a king in the earliest lines of the *Bestiaire*, and in this passage he makes clear that he is the worthy heir to his textual "forebears," some of whom—the troubadours—were not as decrepit or dead as the text makes them out to be. Thus, while on the one hand Richard's treatment of the troubadours as on par with classical *auctores* is reverent, this reverence comes at the cost of both premature mourning (for poets who are not yet dead) and forgetting (of the troubadours' names, region of origin, language, and mode of composition). In fact, Richard's memorialization of the troubadours is, in the ways just described, more an act of oblivion and obliteration than an act of commemoration, although it is framed as such.

Manuscript Metamorphoses

The manuscript transmission of Richard's hoopoe passage testifies to further levels of oblivion. While Richard likely had no control over the manuscript dissemination of the *Bestiaire*, it is remarkable that this passage in particular seems to have been especially subject to scribal reworkings. Richard's forgetting of the troubadours was thus just the first in a series of acts of creative forgetfulness to which they were subjected in the transmission of the *Bestiaire d'amour*. Table 4.2 outlines the placement and reworkings of the "Poitevin" quotations across manuscripts. Eighteen of the twenty-three extant manuscripts of the *Bestiaire* transmit some version of the hoopoe passage.[37] Of those eighteen manuscripts, only two—BnF MS fr. 1444 and Milan Ambrosiana 78 sup.—could be said to get everything "right," assuming that Segre's edition reflects Richard's text (a proposition that seems somewhat dubious in light of this statistic). The following analysis, which assumes Segre's version as authorial, moves from most to least faithful, showing the various forms and levels of textual transformation.

At the next level of remove from Segre's proposed authorial version are a handful of manuscripts. Florence, Plut. 76.79 approximates it most faithfully after the two manuscripts just mentioned, but it omits the end of the last quotation (thereby wiping out the sole trace of rhyme) and rebaptizes one of Richard's Poitevins (on which more below). Arras BM 139, Oxford Douce 308, and Vienna 2609 also come close in the sense that they register the right number of quotations, but they miss the mark in interesting ways: the Arras manuscript is generally very approximative, occasionally devolving into quasi-nonsensicality. Its first quotation, for instance, reads as follows: "dont uns poitevins dist. Car riens fait il ne vaut lamors qui est es ondes" (because of which a Poitevin says: "for he does nothing, he is not worth love that is in the waves," or, differently punctuated: because of which a Poitevin says—for he does nothing—: "he is not worth love that is in the waves").[38] Neither proposition coheres entirely. The manuscript's fourth quotation is similarly befuddling: "Et li autres le redist non fait sil i est il li couvient a descendre."

37. I am unsure about Milan, Biblioteca nazionale Braidense AC.X.10, which I have been unable to consult, but I am told by the librarians there that it is badly damaged.

38. I have realized abbreviations throughout.

Table 4.2 "Poitevin" quotations across all manuscripts of Richard de Fournival's *Bestiaire d'amour*[1]

SIGLA PROPOSED BY LUCKEN	MANUSCRIPT	"A REBOURS NON EST L'AMORS"	"RIENS NE VAUT L'AMOUR QUI ENSI ENDOIE" ("UNS / LI POITEVINS")	"AMOURS ET SIGNERIE NE PUENT LONGES DEMOURER ENSANLE EN UNE CAIIERE" (OVID)	"NON POT L'ORGUEILL OD L'AMOUR REMANOIR" ("LI POITEVINS QUI ENSIEVI OVIDE")	"NON POS POIAR S'EL NON DESCEN" ("LI AUTRES")	"SE TOUT VOS EST, BELE, DE RIEN LIGNAGE, L'AMOUR KI EMPORT EST INGAUS DE PARAGE" ("LI POITEVINS")
A	Paris, BnF, MS fr. 25566		1	2	3	4	---
B	Paris, BnF, MS fr. 412		---	---	faint reminiscence ("mais il me samble qe vous avez plus qe mestiers ne me fust de cel orgueil qui aveuc amors ne puet durer")	---	---
C	Paris, BnF, MS fr. 12786		1	2	3 ("ne pot leur ieus ou l'amor remanoir")	4	---
D	Paris, BnF, MS fr. 12469	1	4 ("en l'autre proverbe'")	2	3	---	---
E	Paris, BnF, MS fr. 1444		1	2	3	4	5
F	Paris, BnF, MS fr. 24406	1	4 ("en l'autre proverbe")	2	3	---	---
G	Paris, BnF, MS fr. 15213	1	4 ("en l'autre proverbe")	2	3	---	---
H	Dijon, Bibliothèque municipale MS 526		1	2	3	4	---
I	Paris, Bibliothèque Sainte-Geneviève MS fr. 2200		---	---	faint reminiscence, see fr. 412	---	---
J	Arras, Bibliothèque municipale, MS 139 (anc. 657)		1 ("dont uns poitevins dist. Car riens fait il ne vaut lamors qui est es ondes")	2	3 ("non pas [*sic*] lorgieus en amour remanoir")	4, ("Et li autres le redist non fait sil i est il li couvient a descendre")	5, ("se tout li cuers de cascun estoit de commun lingnage lamours que on porte seroit veignans de parage")
K	Brussels, Bibliothèque royale de Belgique, MS 10349-414 *[does not transmit relevant passage]*						

L	London, British Library Harley 273	1	2	3	---	4
M	New York, Pierpont Morgan Library MS 459	1 ("un poetes")	2	—	3 ("li poetes qui ensivi Ovides")	4 ("por ce dist uns poetes: se vos estes bele et de roial parage, il n'est pas ygaus au mien parage")
O	Oxford, Bodleian Library Douce 308	1	2 (attributed to Love, Ovid mentioned *in* the quotation): "pour ceu dit amor ovides *et* orgueil ne puent bien estre an samble en une chaiere"	3 (attributed to "li poetevins," present tense)	4	5 "si tost vos estes belle de grant lignai ge lamor ki am porte est igal de parage"
P	Florence, Biblioteca Mediceo-Laurenziana, Plut. LXXVI, 79	1 ("un poites")	2	3 (present tense)	4 ("monter")	5 omits end of quotation ("et por ce dist uns poiteus se vos estes belle e de roial paraie ne qi nest pas igaus")
Q	Florence, Biblioteca Mediceo-Laurenziana, Cod. Ashburnhamiani, Fondo Libri 123	---	1 ("un poetes")	---	2 (" et li poetes dit ce est ovide") / monter	3 "un poete": "se vos estez belle et de roial parage et il nest pas ingal a mon parage"
S	Geneva, Bibliothèque publique et universitaire, Fonds *Comites Latenses,* no. 179 [*fragment; does not transmit relevant passage*]					
T	Turin, Biblioteca nazionale universitaria, L.III.22 [*manuscript mostly destroyed in fire; did not transmit relevant passage according to Vitale Brovarone's transcription at IRHT*]					

(Continued)

Table 4.2 (Continued)

SIGLA PROPOSED BY LUCKEN	MANUSCRIPT	"A REBOURS NON EST L'AMORS"	"RIENS NE VAUT L'AMOUR QUI ENSI ENDOIE" ("UNS / LI POITEVINS")	"AMOURS ET SIGNERIE NE PUENT LONGES DEMOURER ENSANLE EN UNE CAIIERE" (OVID)	"NON POT L'ORGUEILL OD L'AMOUR REMANOIR" ("LI POITEVINS QUI ENSIEVI OVIDE")	"NON POS POIAR S'EL NON DESCEN" ("LI AUTRES")	"SE TOUT VOS EST, BELE, DE RIEN LIGNAGE, L'AMOUR KI EMPORT EST INGAUS DE PARAGE" ("LI POITEVINS")
R	Private collection (Heribert Tenschert). Facsimile available (Muratova and Roy 2006)		1	2	3 "ne pot lor geus o lamour remanoir"	4	---
V	Vienna, Österreichische Nationalbibliothek MS 2609		1 "amors ne vaut riens qui sor- ondoie"	2 "amors ne vaut riens qui si est on-diere" + "amors et seurtes et segnourie ne pueent en un cuer remanoir ensanle ne lonc estage faire ne seoir en une kaiiere sans tencon"	3 (present tense)	4 also attributed to "li poitevins" / monter	5 "Et pour cou dist .i. prouvenciaus se viers vous n'est bielle ingal de linage, l'amours qu'il porte est ingal de parage"
W	Milan, Biblioteca Ambrosiana l. 78 sup.		1	2	3 (present tense)	4	5
Y	Milan, Biblioteca nazionale Braidense AC.X.10 [manuscript badly damaged]						
Z	fragment preserved in Saint Petersburg [does not transmit relevant passage]						

1. Numbers indicate the sequence in which the quotations appear. I have not been able to consult the manuscripts with call numbers in italics.

This could be translated either as: "And the other says it again but does not do it: 'if he is there, it behooves him to descend'" or instead, with different punctuation assumed: "And the other says it again: 'he does not do [it]; if he is there it is fitting that he should descend.'" The quasi-repetition of the idea that someone (the Poitevin and the other?) fails to do something ("riens fait," "non fait") is a curious addition. If the subject of these verbs is indeed the Poitevin and the other, respectively—and this is the most logical way of parsing them—this represents a rather bizarre commentary on the scribe's part on the inability of the "Poitevins" to practice what they preach: if we are to take the scribe at his word, both Poitevins would seem to talk the talk (that is, to proffer amorous advice) but not walk the walk.

Although it does not accuse the Poitevin of erotic ineptitude, the second quotation attributed to him in the Arras manuscript is also creative: rather than "Et li poitevins qui ensievi Ovide si dist: '*Non pot l'orgueill od l'amour remanoir*'" (and the Poitevin, who followed Ovid, says: "*Pride cannot remain with love*"), it reads: "Et li poitevins dist qui ensivi Ovide non pas [sic] lorgieus en amour remanoir" (And the Poitevin who followed Ovid says: "the prideful one [?] not in love to remain"). The lack of a main verb in the quotation makes it difficult to make heads or tails of the passage, as does the unusual form *orgieus*. The negation "non pas"—probably a misreading of the authorial "non pot"—has the curious effect of crafting symmetry between almost all of the Poitevin quotations ("riens fait," "non fait," "non pas"). And in all instances, the grammatical function of the negation is somewhat nebulous. The Arras manuscript's rendering of the fifth quotation is similarly interventionist, though devoid of a mystery negation. It reads as follows: "se tout li cuers de cascun estoit de commun lingnage l'amours que on porte seroit veignans de parage" (if the whole heart of each were of a common lineage, the love one bears would come from rank). This is a far cry from "Se tout vos est, bele, de rien lignage, l'amour ki emport est ingaus de parage" (if [your friend?] is of poor lineage compared to you, beautiful one, the love he bears within himself is of equal rank), although it has the merit of making considerably more sense. But the Arras scribe seems to arrive at the opposite meaning of Segre's proposed authorial text; in the scribe's rendering, *both* lovers would appear to be of common lineage, with love having an ennobling effect on both of them. This is a perfectly plausible idea, admittedly, but it deviates dramatically from Richard's illustration of the equalizing force of love on two partners of unequal social status. All in all, then, the Arras manuscript approximates Segre's version of Richard's authorial text only in the sense that it registers the same number of quotations and assigns them to the same speakers. The actual quotations are significantly altered.

Oxford Douce 308 also comes close to Segre's authorial version of the hoopoe passage but with two fascinating alterations. The scribe has switched the positions of "Ovid" and "Love," thereby managing to attribute Ovid's quotation not to Ovid but instead to a presumably personified Love, with Ovid appearing instead *within* the quotation: "pour ceu dit amor ovides et orgueil ne puent bien estre an samble en une chaiere" (Because of this Love says: "Ovid and pride cannot remain well in one seat").[39] The manuscript's other significant alteration concerns chronology rather than identity. The Oxford manuscript, along with three others—Florence, Plut. 76.79, Vienna MS 2609, and Milan, Ambrosiana I. 78—substitutes a present-tense form of the verb *ensuivre* to describe the Poitevin's relationship to Ovid. In Douce 308 the passage reads: "li poetevins ki ansuet ovide dist ne puet orguille o amor remanoir" (the Poitevin who follows Ovid says: "pride cannot remain with love"). The other three manuscripts register alternate spellings of the present singular.[40] All four scribes seem to offer a corrective to Richard's strange suggestion that the Poitevin is a fragment of a quondam literary moment, rather than part of a still-active literary school. With their verb forms, these four scribes bring the Poitevin back into the realm of the contemporary. Douce 308 even registers this temporal reworking in its term for the Poitevin—"li poetevins"—halfway between a classical *poete* and Richard's *Poitevin*.

Segre's authorial version is also visible but receding in Vienna 2609, which does a significant bit of rewriting and embellishing. The manuscript attributes two quotations to Ovid, the first a clear echo of what was originally the first Poitevin quotation, "amors ne vaut riens qui si est ondiere." And, in fact, a similar quotation—in botched form—has just been attributed to the first Poitevin. Here it reads: "amors ne vaut riens qui sorondoie" (love that superundulates [!] is not worth anything). It would appear that, rather than correcting this delightful misreading—which anticipates the rhetoric of accumulation underlying the rest of the passage—the scribe has let it stand and instead attributed to Ovid only a few words later the correct version of the first Poitevin quotation. This gesture compounds Richard's collapsing of the troubadour tradition into an Ovidian one, in the sense that Ovid's thoughts and those of the "Poitevin" become near-verbatim echoes of each other. The second quotation credited to Ovid also elaborates rhetorically on the original phraseology. Instead of the pithy Ovidian dictum, "amours et signerie ne puent longes demourer ensanle en une caiiere," the scribe

39. The form *amor* is used—without an S—for the *cas sujet* throughout this whole passage.

40. The spelling is *ensui* in Florence Biblioteca Mediceo-Laurenziana, Plut. 76.70 and in the Vienna manuscript, and *ensuit* in the Milan manuscript.

proposes the following prolix formulation: "amors et seurtes et segnourie ne pueent en un cuer remanoir ensanle ne lonc estage faire ne seoir en une kaiiere sans tencon" (love and safety and lordship cannot remain together in a heart or have a lengthy sojourn or sit on [the same] seat without disagreement). This is quite a feat of rhetorical embroidery; we move from a simple sentence with two subject nouns ("amours et signerie") to one with three ("amours et seurtes et segnourie"), mirrored by a triplication of predicates ("ne puent en un cuer remanoir ensanle *ne* lonc estage faire *ne* seoir en une kaiiere sans tencon") in a veritable (and arguably pleonastic) *surenchère* of metaphors. Ovid's image of love and lordship being unable to remain in a single *caiiere* is reduplicated but has also blossomed in two additional directions—a lengthy sojourn and coexistence in a single heart. The scribe has also clarified the meaning of the last quotation in the hoopoe section, which he—and he alone—attributes to ".i. prouvenciaus."[41] This manuscript alone, and only for this quotation, unambiguously recognizes the Occitan origin of one of Richard's troubadour quotations. The other quotations, excepts for Ovid's, are attributed to a sole "Poitevin" (that is, without any "other") and the only trace of Occitan in Richard's original—the *a* in the verb *puiar*—has been replaced by the verb *monter*.[42] One wonders how the scribe recognized this quotation as originally Occitan without this linguistic trace, and also why he recognized this quotation as Occitan but not the others.

At the other end of the spectrum—that is to say, at the furthest remove from Segre's proposed authorial text—two manuscripts omit all quotations, producing a highly abridged account of the hoopoe and quickly moving on to the next exemplum (BnF MS. 412 and Paris, Sainte-Geneviève 2200). These same two manuscripts nevertheless contain a faint reminiscence of the second quotation from "Can vei la flor," although they do not register it as a quotation. After glossing the hoopoe, both have the narrator accuse the woman of excessive pride of the sort that cannot exist with love: "Mes il me samble qe vous avez plus qe mestiers ne me fust *de cel orgueil qui aveuc amors ne puet durer*" (But it seems to me that you have more than is necessary to me of that pride which cannot last alongside love) (BnF MS fr. 412, fol. 235r). This would seem to be a reminiscence of Bernart de Ventadorn's "Non pot l'orgueill od l'amour remanoir," although its source is not identified, and indeed, despite the fact that the demonstrative adjective would lead one to

41. In this manuscript, the quotation reads: "Et pour cou dist .i. prouvenciaus se viers vous n'est bielle ingal de linage l'amours qu'il porte est ingal de parage" (And for this reason a Provençal says: "If, beautiful one, the love he carries is not of equal lineage to you, it is equal in rank").

42. This is also the case in a cluster of other manuscripts, as I discuss in note 20.

think otherwise, the manuscripts have not made any previous mention of a type of pride that cannot coexist with love. Just a faint trace, then, of the "Poitevin" quotations remains, and this trace is not registered as a quotation at all.

Taking a step back and surveying the manuscript tradition of the passage more globally, we see that only ten of the twenty-three extant manuscripts register at least three distinct authorial identities behind the set of quotations, but these identities are not always Richard's Poitevin, the "other" Poitevin, and Ovid. In Oxford Douce 308, as discussed above, one of the "authors" quoted is Love. In the Vienna manuscript, quotations are attributed both to a "Poitevin" and to a "Prouvenciaus," a distinction that gives the impression that one troubadour was from Poitou and another from Provence—true of neither of the troubadours in question. The three Italian manuscripts of the *Bestiaire* are particularly blind to Richard's various "Poitevin" identities. Pierpont Morgan MS 459 attributes all the non-Ovidian quotations to "un poetes," as does Florence Biblioteca Medicea-Laurenziana, Cod. Ash. 123. The latter manuscript further blurs the question of authorship by conflating this "poete" *with* Ovid; all of its quotations are attributed to the "poete," glossed in one instance by the scribe as a reference to Ovid ("et li poetes dit—ce est Ovide"). Florence Biblioteca Medicea-Laurenziana, Plut. 76.79 attributes its first quotation to "un poites," its second to Ovid, its third to "li poitevin," and its last to "uns poiteus." It is tempting to see these last two labels as references to two distinct people rather than merely as spelling variants—why the need for these two forms, given that both are grammatically in the nominative case? One senses the scribe's hesitation as to how many individuals are quoted in the passage. In sum, Richard's three distinct authorial voices—already anonymous though they were, in the case of the two troubadours—have been further obscured in most of the manuscript transmission of the *Bestiaire*.

The "other" Poitevin seems to have been especially susceptible to omission. While his words are acknowledged in twelve manuscripts, that these words originate in the authorial voice of a distinct troubadour, rather than the one already quoted, is registered only in nine manuscripts. In three manuscripts, the "other" has not entirely disappeared but instead metamorphosed from a unique individual to an adjective modifying not another *Poitevin* but a "proverb."[43] This is a mysterious transformation, since there is no mention of proverbs in Richard's authorial version of the passage. The same cluster of manuscripts also, in fact, supplies an otherwise unattested proverb-like

43. These are BnF MSS fr. 12469, 15213, and 24406.

sentence, which they attribute to the Poitevin: "a rebours non est l'amors" (love is not upside down). And to the same Poitevin the manuscripts attribute what was originally the first Poitevin quotation, which they introduce as follows: "Et en l'autre proverbe dist il: 'riens ne vaut l'amour qui ainsi ondelle'" (And in the other proverb he says: "love that undulates in this way is worth nothing"). Furthering this shift toward the paroemiological, these manuscripts also omit the least sententious of the cluster of Richard's original quotations, "Non pos poiar s'el non descen" (I cannot rise if she does not fall) and "Se tout vos est, bele, de rien lignage, l'amour ki emport est ingaus de parage" (if [your friend?] is of poor lineage compared to you, beautiful one, the love he bears within himself is of equal rank). In sum, then, these three manuscripts thrust the passage toward the proverbial—by inserting a proverbial phrase, by labeling one of the troubadour quotations as a proverb, and by omitting the quotations that least resemble proverbs. Although these additions and subtractions represent a significant modification of the authorial version of the passage, this paroemiological frame is an obvious leap from Richard's third-person rewriting and his predilection for extreme abbreviation (proverbs are, of course, short, sententious statements that are almost always composed in the third person).

It is obviously impossible to say how much the scribes and compilers of these three manuscripts knew of the rest of Richard's corpus (none of the codices in question includes other works by Richard), but this reframing of the quotations as proverbial actually has the effect of aligning the passage with several of Richard's other texts. As a handful of modern critics have already observed, a predilection for proverbs is a distinguishing trait of Richard de Fournival's writings (Dragonetti 1960, 51–53; Crespo 1991).[44] Perhaps coincidentally, some of Richard's preferred proverbs concern metaphors of ascent and descent, much like the third "Poitevin" quotation. For instance, as already noted by Crespo and Dragonetti, an echo of the proverb "Qui plus haut monte qu'il ne doit / De plus haut chiet qu'il ne voldroit" (Morawski 2091) can be seen in the second stanza of one of Richard's lyrics, R 1278 (Crespo 1991, 544). The *Consaus d'amours*, sometimes attributed to Richard, is also riddled with proverbs, some of which are unique to the *Consaus* and may be the author's own invention (Richard de Fournival 1974, e.g., 242 I.5). The *Consaus* contains textual overlap with the *Bestiaire*, showing that even if it was not by Richard, it was nevertheless a pastiche of Richard's style. Like Dragonetti and Crespo, the author of this pastiche of the Poitevin passage

44. Dragonetti identifies echoes of Morawski 800, 769, 1881, and 2091, to which Crespo adds, among others, Morawski 847. All references are to Morawski's (1925) catalog of proverbs.

clearly viewed both general stylistic sententiousness and the actual quotation of proverbs as a defining feature of Richard's corpus. This branch of the manuscript transmission of the *Bestiaire* thus erases Richard's acknowledgment of two distinct "Poitevins" and transforms their lyrics into proverbial nuggets, thereby aligning the passage with Richard's style in the rest of his corpus. Even if unconsciously, then, this cluster of manuscripts builds on several dimensions of forgetfulness—of composers (in this set of manuscripts we are down from three to two) and of form (proverbs vs. song)—already present in the authorial version of the *Bestiaire*.

If the proverb-oriented manuscripts bring the number of Poitevins from two to one, most of the Italian transmission of the *Bestiaire* obliterates the Poitevins entirely, transforming them into a single "poete" whom, as we have seen, they in some instances conflate with Ovid. Pierpont Morgan 459 rewrites both Richard's attribution and the last quotation. In this manuscript, both for this quotation and for all others, Richard's "poitevin" has been transformed into a "poete," thereby aligning him more obviously with Ovid, and the last quotation in the passage now suggests the opposite of its original meaning. Segre's proposed original, "Se tout vos est, bele, de rien lignage, l'amour ki emport est ingaus de parage," suggests the equalizing force of love—and this is indeed how Richard glosses it—while Pierpont Morgan 459 supplies the following: "por ce dist uns poetes: 'se vos estes bele et de roial parage, il n'est pas ygaus au mien parage" (if you are beautiful and of royal rank, it is not equal to my rank). Rather than asserting the ability of love to upend hierarchy, Pierpont Morgan 459 instead insists on love's class-based nature. One other manuscript of Italian provenance also transforms Richard's Poitevins into a sole "poetes." Florence Ash. 123 attributes all quotations to a single "poete," which it explicitly identifies as Ovid. Florence Laur. 76.79, for its part, attributes its quotations variously to a "poites," "Ovides," "li Poitevin," "li autres," and "uns Poiteus." While the Poitevins are not collapsed into a single "poete" as in the other Florence manuscript, in the case of the first quotation they are partially conflated with the term. This lexical confusion (is "poites" a compromise between "Poitevin" and "poete"?) furthers Richard's relegation of the troubadours to a classical past, the term *poete* being reserved before the fourteenth century for classical *auctores* (Brownlee 1984, 7).[45]

---

45. New York, Pierpont Morgan MS 459's rescripting of the *Bestiaire* in relationship to the Occitan tradition is more complex than can be accounted for here; it supplies a prologue in the form of a *vida* for Richard de Fournival before the *Bestiaire* proper. I describe this manuscript in greater depth elsewhere (Zingesser 2015).

As the above analysis suggests, this passage of the *Bestiaire* seems to have provoked serious and disproportionate confusion. A glance through Segre's variants would seem to indicate that this passage as a whole is one of the most unstable passages in the text, with modifications going far beyond orthography. If Richard forgets the language, form, period of activity, and names of his two Poitevins, the manuscript transmission sometimes goes even further in metamorphosing them into either a single Poitevin or into a classical *poete*, and in registering the fragments of their songs as proverbs. The quotations seem to have become progressively more difficult to recall: the manuscripts record the first and second quotations in roughly equal numbers (fifteen and sixteen, respectively), fourteen the third quotation, twelve the fourth quotation, and nine the last quotation. Among Richard's entire set of quotations (which, as we have seen, includes a selection from Ovid), the Poitevin quotations are especially subject to oblivion, with all manuscripts—except for those that heavily abridge the passage—remembering both the content of Ovid's quotation and the attribution to Ovid, but only a few remembering both the Poitevins' distinct identities and words.

French Troubadours

Richard's linguistic erasure of Occitan, and his association of two Poitevins with utterances that look almost exclusively French, paved the way for one manuscript of the *Bestiaire* to apply the label "son poitevin" to a trouvère lyric with no relationship at all to the troubadours. BnF fr. 12786 appends, to the end of the *Bestiaire*, the first stanza of "Puis qu'en moi a recovrée seignorie" (RS 1208), elsewhere attributed to Gautier d'Épinal (see figure 0.2 in the introduction). The piece is not a contrafactum of any known troubadour song, and it does not display any Occitanizing linguistic traits in this manuscript. Although it is francophone—or perhaps, *because* it is francophone—it looks very much like Richard's other quoted "Poitevins," both in its language and in its treatment of erotic themes. While Lori Walters (1994, 12–13) has argued that the label "son poitevin" is applied in situations where Occitan themes have been transposed into French, there is nothing discernably Occitan—in language or in theme—about this song. I would argue instead that Richard's Gallicization of troubadour song and his remapping of its origins onto Poitou have paved the way for the view of a typical trouvère lyric with no relationship at all to Occitania as "poitevin." Walters's assertion that the "son poitevin" label "indicat[es] the origins of the lyric" (13) is difficult to accept: neither Gautier d'Épinal, from the Empire, nor any of the troubadours quoted was from Poitou. Instead of assuming that this

Poitevin label stood transparently for Occitan culture, as Walters seems to do, I would argue that this extension of the term to what is indisputably a French-language lyric shows just how thoroughly the term "poitevin" has been bleached of its Occitan connotations in the *Bestiaire*. For the scribe of fr. 12786, the Gallicization of "poitevin" songs in French manuscripts such as the *Bestiaire* had rendered the fictional *francophonie* of the troubadours so convincing that it seemed plausible to label an actual *langue d'oïl* poem with the label normally reserved for the troubadours. A "Poitevin," or so the manuscript tradition of the text would lead us to believe, is someone who writes about erotic themes in French.

We have seen in this chapter how Richard de Fournival both upholds and disrupts the association of troubadour lyric with avian song—a frame first visible in Jean Renart's *Roman de la rose* but then taken to new heights in Gerbert de Montreuil's *Roman de la violette*. Richard preserves the troubadours' avian ties by inserting his quotations in the hoopoe section of his *Bestiaire*. However, in medieval thought, the hoopoe's defining feature was not its song but its quills, supplying the perfect symbol of Richard's broader delyricization of troubadour song. As we have seen, the troubadour quotations are presented as speech, with only the faintest trace of rhyme remaining. Likewise, the original language of the Occitan songs has been obscured and their cultural identity transformed. These newly baptized "Poitevins" are inserted into a literary lineage that suggests that their heyday is long gone (quite a fiction, given that Richard's life overlapped with that of some of the troubadours). The manuscript tradition of the *Bestiaire* compounds Richard's various modes of forgetfulness. In much of the manuscript tradition, the distinction between two "Poitevins" is not upheld, or they are conflated with a single "poete" who in one instance is glossed as Ovid. These codices thus bring to full fruition—and multiply exponentially—Richard's partial oblivion (of the form of Occitan song, of the names of its composers, and of its language).

Chapter 5

The Rustic Troubadours

Occitanizing Lyrics in France

This book has thus far explored the ways in which troubadour songs were adapted or framed in such a way as to make them appear as part of a francophone cultural space or tradition. But at the same time as this process of assimilation was occurring, another corpus—in some sense diametrically opposed to that of Gallicized Occitan song—was emerging. This is a corpus I propose to call Occitanizing French song. If the Gallicization of genuine Occitan compositions, the quotation of them by French speakers, and their compilation in French songbooks assimilates troubadour lyric into a French-language trajectory, the composition of Occitanizing lyrics moves in the opposite direction, suggesting a desire not just to make the troubadours French but also to make French poetry Occitan. These two impulses might initially seem contradictory, but they operate on different levels. I show in this chapter that the pieces that were cast as related to Occitan occur primarily in the lower register. This division of register, in turn, frames Occitan as less prestigious than French. In parallel to this generic hierarchy, which positions Occitan within a body of "lesser" forms and dissociates it from the *canso*, the use of scatological, rustic, and sexual themes confers a primitive quality on the texts. Some are explicitly associated with border linguistic territories, which gives the impression—like the geographical labels discussed earlier in this book—that Occitan poetry is not a separate corpus but rather a linguistic coloring used within French poetry to artistic effect. Indeed, both the Gallicizing and Occitanizing corpora undermine rather than shore up the boundary between two languages we would today consider distinct, following some medieval thinkers.

For nineteenth-century philologists, and possibly for medieval audiences as well, the pseudo-folkloric form and content of many of these pieces served as evidence of early composition. For these critics, the rustic quality of the corpus gave the impression that it was anterior to—but not quite distinct from—*oïl* lyric. Indeed, a handful of nineteenth-century philologists adduced precisely these poems as the earliest extant in French (and Occitan) literary history, with some taking the linguistic borderlands mentioned in a few poems of the Occitanizing corpus as the true birthplace of both troubadour and trouvère song. For those nineteenth-century philologists who had a particular stake in the preeminence of the French (as opposed to the Occitan) *patrimoine*, this theory had the great advantage of either situating the origins of *oïl* lyric in a moment anterior to the troubadour tradition or imagining that the *oïl* and *oc* repertoires emerged from a single moment and space. These theories go against the considerable evidence that troubadour poetry antedates its northern counterpart.

The Occitanizing Corpus

I have limited my corpus to lyric poems with Occitan traits that are transmitted *exclusively* in francophone territories and do not exist in a version without French linguistic traits. Both of these facts suggest that they were composed by native francophones, as does the absence of generic analogs in Occitan lyric for many of the pieces. Nevertheless, I have chosen not to restrict myself to the corpus in which this francophone origin can be demonstrated beyond any doubt to be true. Nor have I limited my corpus to texts where both Occitan and French occur at the rhyme, though this would be the surest indicator that their fusion of languages was intentional, because this would artificially restrict a corpus whose contours are probably wider.[1] Table 0.1 in the introduction marks all Occitanizing songs with an "O."[2] These are,

1. This restriction to linguistic hybridity at the rhyme sound was proposed by Marshall (Marshall 1987).

2. There is a considerable amount of overlap with the corpus discussed by Robert Taylor (1993). However, I have eliminated one of the pieces included in Taylor's corpus because it is not extant in French transmission: "Ara lausetz, lauset, lauset" (PC 461.27b), a satire of monastic life. It is transmitted on two paper sheets in the archives of the abbey of San Juan de las Abadesas and may be Italian in origin (Bond 1985). I have also broadened Taylor's count to include several motet texts with Occitan traits, the *rêverdie* "Volez vos que je vous chant" (RS 318), and a refrain with Occitan coloring transmitted only in two of the three manuscripts of the late thirteenth-century *Court de*

to recap: "A l'entrade del tens clar—eya" (PC 461.12), "A l'entrada del tans florit" (PC 461.13), "En aquel temps que vezem verdezir," the second "Occitan" insertion in some manuscripts of the *Violette* (PC 461.103a), the "Lai Nonpar" (PC 461.122), the "Lai Markiol" (PC 461.124), "L'autrier cuidai aber druda" (PC 461.146), "L'altrier m'iere levatz" (PC 461.148), "Li jalous per tout sunt fustat" (PC 461.148a), "Molt m'abellist l'amoros pensamen" (PC 460.170a), "Per vous m'esjau" (PC 461.192), "Tuit cil qui sunt enamourat" (PC 461.240a / van den Boogaard 1822), "Volez vos que je vous chant" (RS 318), and "El mois d'avril qu'ivers va departant / Al cor ai une alegrance / Et gaudebit" (Gennrich 319). This corpus of roughly twelve songs is not large (although I would wager that some of the anonymous *unica* transmitted only in francophone songbooks catalogued under PC 461 are in fact also Occitanizing songs of francophone origin).[3] I would argue, however, that it held a disproportionate influence in shaping nineteenth-century audiences' views—and perhaps those of medieval audiences as well—on the history of the French lyric.

Like most Gallicized Occitan songs, these pieces are anonymous. None is associated with an authorial name in any songbook or lyric-interpolated romance in which it is transmitted. And, like Gallicized Occitan songs, they exist on a linguistic spectrum. Some contain such a high degree of Occitan coloring that they were included in Pillet and Carstens's standard catalog of troubadour lyric and have only recently seen their status as troubadour song questioned.[4] These pieces have often been discussed in relation to the question of their "convincingness," a prism that assumes an underlying intent to

paradis. Anna Zayaruznaya kindly brought two Franco-Occitan pieces to my attention, although I have excluded them on the grounds that they are not extant in French transmission. These are "A l'entrade d'avrillo," a *pastourelle* hocket transmitted in the *Speculum musicae* (Bent 2015, 160–62), and the fragmentary motet . . . *Bon milgrana de valor / Mon gauch, mon ris, ma salut e ma laus / [tenor]* (Harrison 1956, 5:185–87). The sole manuscript to transmit the part of the *Speculum* containing "A l'entrade d'avrillo" is Paris, BnF fr. lat. 7207, thought to be from the Veneto. The motet is extant only in the Treasury of the Cathedral of Gerona (Gerona, Archivo Capitular, frag. 33/1).

3. The corpus is difficult to quantify exactly because of the pieces that appear in both refrain and motet form. It is also a challenge to delimit its contours definitively. As István Frank (1953, xxii) has remarked, it is difficult to distinguish between three categories: first, songs by troubadours, second, "des pastiches composés 'à la manière' provençale," and third, "de[s] pièces provenant de ces régions intermédiaires entre le Nord et le Midi dont les caractères linguistiques sont, pour ce qui concerne la critique textuelle, si fuyants."

4. The provenance of "L'altrier cuidai aber druda" and "A l'entrade del tens clar," which both show a very high concentration of Occitan linguistic traits, has been especially contested. The status of the former remained unquestioned until a 1986 article by Robert Taylor. On "A l'entrade," see Taylor (1993, 464). The motet "Li jalous par tout sunt fustat / Tuit cil qui sunt enamourat / Veritatem" also falls on this end of the linguistic spectrum. Frank (1954) demonstrated its French provenance in the middle of the twentieth century.

deceive audiences.[5] In some cases this may well have been the intent. In others, however, it undoubtedly was not: the scattered Occitanesque sounds in a piece I discuss at length below, "Volez vos que je vous chant," are too few and far between to have deceived anyone. I want to suggest here that, rather than always viewing the Occitan traits of these texts as an attempt to reproduce (usually unsuccessfully) correct Occitan phonology and morphology, it might be more accurate to think of them as a coloring within French, a kind of dialect, which gives the pieces a more "southern" feeling without constituting a real imitation of Occitan as a language. Those pieces that include geographic indications are located in border territories between French- and Occitan-speaking regions, and their linguistic admixture may be intended to evoke the language of these liminal spaces.[6] They are also often transmitted in the same manuscripts as Gallicized troubadour song, a fact that suggests that both sets of pieces were perceived on a single continuum.[7] But however we choose to interpret their linguistic status, the pieces contain, on average, a higher concentration of Occitanisms than do the Gallicized troubadour songs. Thus, to a French reader with no outside knowledge of the troubadour tradition, this corpus would have looked much more like Occitan than did most of the actual troubadour lyric transmitted in francophone territories. Such a reader's idea of what Occitan poetry *was*—its themes, its form, and so on—might consequently have come more from this corpus than from the corpus of Gallicized troubadour lyric, a corpus that, as we have seen, was not readily identifiable as foreign in origin in its francophone transmission. Occitan, in the body of Occitanizing poetry, is generally not associated with the sorts of first-person declarations of unrequited love we are accustomed to coming across in the *canso*, but with baser themes and lower registers.

Much ink has been spilled in an attempt to establish a hierarchy among medieval lyric genres.[8] I will limit my discussion to medieval evidence for

5. See, for instance, Taylor (1993), who argues that, in an early period, these "pastiches" must have been good enough to evoke the proper "Occitan" signal, but not complete enough to fool an enlightened audience. Taylor hypothesizes that the audiences became less and less savvy over time and were eventually duped into thinking they were real (468).

6. As we will see below, some have argued that the pieces are, in fact, from border territories.

7. BnF MS fr. 20050, fr. 844, and Bern MS 389 transmit Gallicized troubadour poetry and Occitanizing song together.

8. Pierre Bec's model, which has probably been the most influential, sets out three registers: *aristocratisant*, *hybride*, and *popularisant*—terms that emphasize the effect of certain stylistic choices rather than suggesting origin in a particular class (Bec 1977, 35). Paul Zumthor (1972, 299) proposes two registers: that of the "requête d'amour" and that of the "bonne vie." Zumthor's distinction—at least as he discusses it in his *Essai de poétique médiévale*—is primarily stylistic (hypotaxis vs. parataxis, regular nouns vs. diminutives, etc.). Christopher Page's (1987, 16) typology involves "high" and "low" styles; his criteria include the use of refrains and isometric lines as well as the explicitness with which the beloved is named.

such a hierarchy. Johannes de Grocheio's treatise, *De musica* (ca. 1300), outlines a system of correspondence between song types and class. The genre he calls the *cantus coronatus*—a genre that corresponds to what scholars today call the *canso* or *grand chant courtois*—is especially associated with the upper echelons of society. About the *cantus coronatus*, Grocheio remarks: "This kind of song is customarily composed by kings and nobles and sung in the presence of kings and princes of the land so that it may move their minds to boldness and fortitude, magnanimity and liberality, all of which things lead to good government. This kind of *cantus* deals with delightful and lofty subject-matter, such as friendship and love" (qui etiam a regibus et nobilibus solet componi et etiam coram regibus et principibus terre decantari, ut eorum animos ad audaciam et fortitudinem, magnanimitatem et liberalitatem commoveat, quae omnia faciunt ad bonum regimen. Est enim cantus iste de delectabili materia et ardua, sicut de amicitia et caritate) (Johannes de Grocheio 1993, 23). Dante's discussion of the same genre also emphasizes its nobility. The *canso*, he says in *De vulgari eloquentia*, is "far and away the most excellent [form]" (horum autem modorum cantionum modum excellentissimum putamus) (Dante Alighieri 1996, II.3). The tragic style (of the *canso*) is to be used "whenever both the magnificence of the verses and the lofty excellence of construction and vocabulary accord with the gravity of the subject matter" (stilo equidem tragico tunc uti videmur quando cum gravitate sententie tam superbia carminum quam constructionis elatio et excellentia vocabulorum concordat) (II.4). In Dante's formulation, then, the *canso* is associated with especially refined construction, and a lexicon with *gravitas*. Dante also adduces on behalf of the prestige of the genre of the *canso* the care with which it—above all other genres—is preserved within songbooks (II.3).

What emerges from these comments on the part of medieval poets and theorists is the preeminence of the *canso*. That this is the genre least represented in the corpus of Occitanizing songs suggests a desire to dissociate the troubadour tradition from the form in which it was, demonstrably, most frequently actually encountered in francophone spaces (as discussed in chapter 1, the *canso* is by far the form most represented in the francophone transmission of actual troubadour songs). That this form was also the most prestigious, both "domestically" and "internationally" (according to both Grocheio and Dante, among other theorists), also suggests a desire to demote Occitan to less prestigious registers. In the Occitanizing corpus, only PC 461.103a, Euriaut's song in some manuscripts of the *Roman de la violette*, and PC 461.13 could be described as *cansos*. The other genres represented include the lai (twice), the *pastorela*, the motet (twice), and a dance. In terms of genre, then, the Occitanizing corpus is diametrically opposed to that of Gallicized song, which, as we saw in chapter 1, favors the *canso* by a wide margin. If the Gallicized corpus associates the *canso* with the French language (via linguistic transformation), the Occitanizing corpus instead associates other, less prestigious genres with Occitan.[9]

This demotion of Occitan is also evident in the themes of some of the songs, a few of which are associated with the rustic.[10] This is clear especially in the triplum of the motet "Li jalous par tout sunt fustat / Tuit cil qui sunt enamourat / Veritatem," in which the jealous are supposed to be kicked out of the circle "comme garçon" (like lackeys) (Tischler 1978, 63). "L'autrier m'iere levaz," a *pastorela*, obviously represents an encounter with the lower classes (via the figure of the shepherdess), and "L'altrier cuidai aber druda" further heaps on rusticity. In this bawdy piece in which the male narrator expects his mistress in bed one night but is instead confronted with an old hag, the narrator says he has proffered "vels vin . . . peis et por salat" (old and cloudy wine . . . fish, and salt pork) to try to win over his mistress (R. A. Taylor 1986, vv. 10–11). Accordingly, he asks that she be punished with "pan mesalat, et carne de vella truda ou porc sorsemat, pis de mar qui de loig puda, vin cras et boutat" (moldy bread and meat from an old sow, or tainted pork, seafish which stinks from afar, and coarse, spoiled wine) (vv. 54–58). The shepherdess's body is also condescendingly rusticized: her sagging breasts are compared to a "borsa pastor" (shepherd's bag) (v. 22). Even the speaker of "Nonpar" declares that he speaks "com hom vilains" (like a peasant) (Billy 1995a, v. 99). This focus on the lower classes constitutes another way in which the Occitan language is rescripted away from its association with the *canso* and toward lower registers.

The Occitanizing songs' focus on sex is another. If the typical *canso* evokes erotic satisfaction only obliquely, these pieces foreground it unabashedly. In "L'altrier cuidai aber druda," as described above, the narrator recounts an evening in which an old hag came into his bed, sparing us no details on the woman's aging body parts. "L'autrier m'iere levaz," which I discuss at greater length below, recounts a knight's rape of an (Occitan?) shepherdess. The explicit language and the violent nature of the sexual act in both of these pieces contrast starkly with the elliptical language and unsatisfied desire of the *canso*.

---

9. It is possible that the later additions to BnF MS fr. 844, all of which are in un-Gallicized Occitan and many of which are dance songs, are in fact of francophone manufacture. If this is the case, the association of Occitan with less prestigious forms would be stronger. Stefano Asperti (1995, 131–32) has postulated a possible Angevin connection to these additions. See also Anna Radaelli's (2004, 217–43) edition of the dances.

10. I am not the first person to have noticed the fact that many of these poems are composed in what might be called a "low register." Marshall (1987, 38), for example, makes this observation from the perspective primarily of form. He notes that "les traits métriques de type popularisant sont nombreux dans ces œuvres," In particular, he notes that the majority of the pieces are "heteromorphic,"

Occitanizing Low Style and Gallicized High Style in the Montpellier Codex

As a case study, I want to turn briefly to the Montpellier Codex (Montpellier, Faculté de Médecine, MS H 196), because its use of Occitan coloring is reflective of the broader trends this book outlines: the Gallicization and domestication of the *canso* and the Occitanization of less prestigious genres and/or themes. Compiled sometime in the second half of the thirteenth century (Wolinski 1992, 265), the codex includes three motets in its fifth fascicle that bear some relation to either the Occitan language or to the troubadour repertoire.[11] The first of these, a motet with strong Occitan coloring in the motetus and triplum, is "Li jalous par tout sunt fustat / Tuit cil qui sunt enamourat / Veritatem" (fols. 218v–219).[12] Another motet has only faint Occitan coloring but is demonstrably inspired by a famous troubadour *canso*: "Onques n'ama loiaument / Mout m'abelist / Flos filius eius" (fols. 151v–152r). And finally one, also inspired by a troubadour *canso*, contains no Occitan coloring at all: "Quant voi l'aloete / Dieus, je ne m'en partirai ja / Benedictus dominus deus meus" (fols. 117v–118r). I will argue here that this gradation of linguistic coloring is indicative of the register of each set of texts: the most rustic of the three appears in the strongest Occitan garb, while the two *canso*-inspired motets contain very little and no Occitan coloring, respectively. This gradation is emblematic, in microcosm, of the procedures of Occitanizing and Gallicization. The Occitanizing motet is the one in a low register, while the two others, while not strictly speaking Gallicizations of troubadour songs, are nevertheless "Frenchified" riffs on two distinct troubadour *cansos* in a high register.

I begin with the motet with the highest degree of Occitan coloring, "Li jalous par tout sunt fustat / Tuit cil qui sunt enamourat / Veritatem," which, as mentioned, contains this coloring in both the triplum and the motetus.[13] Here is the motetus:

Tuit cil qui sunt enamourat
veignent dançar, li autre non.
La regine le commendat

---

which is to say neither heterostrophic nor isostrophic (40). Billy (1995a, 2), meanwhile, notes that these lyric "hybrids" were almost always composed in "des genres secondaires sinon mineurs." To my knowledge, however, Billy and Marshall do not seem to impute any significance to this pattern.

11. The fifth fascicle spans fols. 111 to 228 (Tischler 1978, xxix).

12. Elizabeth Aubrey (1997, 8–16) has discussed this piece at some length.

13. The piece echoes a refrain in the *Court de paradis*. See no. 98 in introduction, table 0.1. In both the motet and the *Court de paradis*, there is a queenlike figure who commands the dance and decides whom to include (in the *Court*, this queen is the Virgin).

tuit cil que sunt enamourat
que li jalous soient fustat
fors de la dance d'un baston.
Tuit cil qui sunt enamourat
viegnent avant, li autre non.[14]

May all those who are in love
Come to dance, not the others.
The queen orders this:
May all those who are in love . . .
[and] that jealous ones be beaten
out of the dance with a stick.
May all those who are in love
come forward, not the others.

As it stands, there are three traits of the piece that evoke Occitan: the adjectival ending in *-at* (Occitan *-ar* verbs have past participles in *-at*), the form *regine* (Occitan *regina/reïna*; French *reine/raine/roine*) and the verb *dançar* (Occitan *dansar*; French *dancier*) (Frank 1954, 102). The first of these features, the rhyme sound in *-at*, is musically highlighted since it almost always sounds simultaneously in the top two voices (measures 3, 6, 8, 10, 12, and 16) (Tischler 1978, 188; see figure 5.1). This sonic emphasis is the result of two highly unusual procedures: on the one hand, the rhyming of the top two voices with each other completely, and on the other, a setting that places this rhyme in the spotlight by having the two voices sing it simultaneously. Both of these procedures are rare within the Montpellier Codex.[15] This suggests a desire not just to Occitanize but to make the particular sonorities evoking Occitan especially audible.

The piece's Occitan veneer is convincing enough that it was taken for years as a genuine Occitan composition. Pillet and Carstens, for example, included it in their catalog of troubadour lyric (PC 461,148a), but so did Linker in his catalog of French lyric (Linker 1979, 265–1070).[16] In 1954 István Frank argued that the piece was a French composition designed to give the illusion of Occitan origin, and his views have generally been accepted: Chambers is the only scholar since Frank to view the piece as Occitan (Chambers 1985, 228). Querying the piece's French origin, Frank points, first of all, to the

14. For the French text, I have relied on Tischler's 1978 edition of the motet, which is number 169 in his count (p. 63). I have modified his translation slightly.

15. In fascicle 5, they occur elsewhere only in pieces nos. 116 and 127.

16. It does not, however, appear in Raynaud and Spanke's catalog.

FIGURE 5.1 Occitanizing motet "Li jalous par tout sunt fustat / Tuit cil qui sunt enamourat / Veritatem" as edited by Tischler.

preterite form *commendat*, which looks more French than Occitan (in Occitan, one would expect *comandét*). As Frank points out, the clearest indication that the piece was composed by a native speaker of *langue d'oïl* is the series of rhymes pairing *-on* and *-ont* (*non* and *baston* in the motetus and *front*, *larron*, and *garçon* in the triplum, on which see below) (Frank 1954, 102). In Occitan, the expected terms would be *non*, *baston*, *fron*, and *lairon* (there is nothing in Occitan approximating *garçon*, which is a term of Germanic origin).[17]

Alongside its linguistic traits, the poetic form of "Tuit cil" suggests a French origin. Most critics consider the piece to be a rondeau, a form whose essential feature is the use of a final refrain that also appears at the beginning of the poem, usually in the second line.[18] Whatever formal label one considers most apt, it remains that the contemporaneous pieces closest to "Tuit cil" formally are all French. As Elizabeth Aubrey points out, "The only extant examples of this musico-poetic form are found exclusively in northern sources" (Aubrey 1997, 16). Frank Chambers has dissented from this view, describing the piece as a *balada*, a relatively uncommon Occitan dance form involving the repetition of a refrain after each stanza and the repetition of the first line of the refrain after the first and second line of each stanza. Frank's metrical catalog documents only nine such pieces, most of which are anonymous (Frank 1953, 2:70). In fact, Chambers (1985) acknowledged how rare the piece is in its full repetition of the refrain at the end of the stanza. As he puts it, "It is the only piece in Old Provençal literature to do so [give the refrain in full], as far I have been able to discover; elsewhere, the repeated verses are indicated in abbreviated and possibly ambiguous form" (228). Some refrain-based dance forms, such as the *retroencha*, were cultivated in Occitan poetry, but mostly not until the fourteenth century.[19] They are discussed, for example, in the *Leys d'amors* (ca. 1341), but they do not seem to have been cultivated in Occitan language production much earlier than the beginning of the fourteenth century.[20] That formal analogs to the piece

---

17. As is the case with most hybrid language pieces, it is possible that the mixed linguistic traits are the result of composition in a border region between *langue d'oc* and *langue d'oïl*. This is the hypothesis Meyer (1872, 405) proposes, suggesting that the pieces may have been composed in either the Auvergne or the Limousin. He also, however, raises the possibility that the pieces were composed by a northern composer in imitation of Occitan, a hypothesis accepted and developed by István Frank (1954, 101–2), whose conclusion about both pieces is that their linguistic traits are designed to create a "fausse couleur locale." The fact that the rhyme sounds of the poem only function in French, of course, points very strongly to a French origin, and I am inclined to agree with Frank.

18. Mark Everist (1994, 106) gives a survey of the various theories on the form of the piece.

19. The earliest mention I have found of the refrain-based *retroencha* is in the *Doctrina de compondre dictatz*, probably from the late thirteenth century (Marshall 1972, 96, lxxvii).

20. For the discussion of refrain-based dance forms in the *Leys*, see Molinier (1977, 202). On the rarity of the refrain in Occitan poetry, see Bec (1977, 43).

can be found almost exclusively in French rather than in Occitan also points toward a French provenance.

The linguistic characteristics of the triplum of the piece point even more clearly toward a French origin than the motetus.[21] The triplum reads as follows:

Li jalous par tout sunt fustat
et portent corne en mi le front;
par tout doivent estre huat.
La regine le commendat
que d'un baston soient frapat
et chacie hors comme larron.
S'en dancade veillent entrar,
fier le[s] du pie comme garcon.

The jealous ones are chastised everywhere
And wear a horn on their foreheads;
everywhere they must be booed.
The queen orders
that they be struck with a stick
and chased away like thieves.
If they want to enter the dance,
kick them like lackeys.

Paul Meyer was the first to point to linguistic elements that suggest that the piece's Occitan coloring is mere veneer. The form *huat* is neither French (*huchié*) nor Occitan (*ucat*). The verb *frapar* is attested in Occitan but was not common, while *fustar* existed but only with an unrelated meaning.[22] The subjunctive form *soient* is clearly French (cf. Occitan *sion*). Similarly, the form *chacie* (cf. Occitan *cassat*) is closer to French than to Occitan. The suffix *-ade* ("dançade") is in fact a hypercorrection (the correct Occitan form is *dansa*) resulting from the frequency of the suffix *-ada* in Occitan.[23] As I describe below, it is used in one French poem as the sole method of conveying Occitan linguistic color. In short, all signs point to composition by a francophone composer familiar primarily with French forms.

---

21. If the linguistic features of "Li jalous" point more strongly toward a French origin than those of "Tuit cil," its formal properties are more ambiguous, and thus harder to localize. The rhymes are those of a rondeau (*abaaabab*) but the piece contains no refrain.

22. Frank (1954, 101) claimed that the verb *frapar* does not exist in Occitan, but it is attested in Raynouard. Raynouard glosses *fustar* as "raccomoder, radouber."

23. It originally was derived from the Latin verbal suffix *-ta* but also came to be used as a suffix in nouns, perhaps with a connotation of containment (Adams 1913, 24–30).

It is no coincidence, I would argue, that this motet, with the strongest Occitan coloring of those with an Occitan connection in the Montpellier Codex, is also the one that reads as the most primitive. In its evocation of dancing, its suggestion that those who are jealous be kept away from the dance with a stick, and its allusion to the horns of the cuckold, the piece trades in material associated with low-register pieces. The motet is, moreover, not the only piece in the Occitanizing corpus with a connection to dancing. "A l'entrade del tens clar, eya" similarly conjures up a queen who presides over a dance, warning the jealous to keep their distance. Similar pieces to these are mentioned in Grocheio's *De musica*, where he claims that the broader genre of which such pieces are a subset (the *cantus versualis*) "lacks the inherent virtue" of the *grand chant* ("Cantus versualis est qui ab aliquibus cantilena dicitur respectu coronati et ab eius bonitate in dictamine et concordantia deficit" [The *cantus versualis* is a species of *cantus* which is called a *cantilena* by some with respect to their (*cantus*) *coronatus* and which lacks (its) inherent virtue in poetry and melody]) (Johannes de Grocheio 1993, 24).[24]

The second motet with an Occitan connection in the Montpellier Codex is part of another thematic world entirely, one drawn from the restrained world of the *canso* or high-style love song. The motetus of "Onques n'ama loiaument / Mout m'abelist / Flos filius eius" contains a clear allusion to a well-known piece by Folquet de Marselha.[25] In the Montpellier Codex, the motetus reads as follows:

Mout m'abelis
l'amouros pensement,
qui soutilment
a mon cuer assailli
et la biauté de ma dame ensement,
qui tout contient sens et vaillance en li.
Car quant remir son sens et sa valor,
ne puis avoir tristece ne dolor,
mes nuit et jor
joie et baudour
et grant aliegement.

24. In positing similarity to the *cantus versualis*, I am, obviously, considering each voice in isolation. Grocheio discusses motets elsewhere in the treatise.

25. The triplum, however, is not reminiscent of any particular song by Folquet. It evokes the notion of placing oneself at love's mercy no matter what the pain and suffering caused. The torments of devotion to love are a recurring theme in Folquet de Marselha's poetry, but the triplum's text is not reminiscent of any one piece in particular.

The amorous thought which has subtly assailed my heart pleases me, as well as the beauty of my lady, who contains all sense and worth in her. For, when I see her sense and valor, I cannot experience sadness or pain, but [rather], night and day, joy and gladness and great levity.

The Occitan piece that the motetus seems to be attempting to evoke through its incipit is Folquet de Marselha's "Tant m'abellis l'amoros pessamens" (PC 155.22).[26] In Stroński's edition, the first stanza of this piece reads as follows:

Tant m'abellis l'amoros pessamens
que s'es vengutz e mon fin cor assire
per que no·i pot nuills autre pes caber
ni mais negus no m'es dous ni plazens,
qu'adonc viu sas quan m'aucizo·l cossire
e fin'amors aleuja·m mo martire
que·m promet joi, mas trop lo·m dona len,
qu'ap bel semblan m'a trainat longamen.

The amorous thought that has come to sit in my heart pleases me so much that no other can find a place there, nor is any other [thought] sweet or pleasing. For I live then in good health however much worries kill me and fine love lightens my martyrdom. For it promises me joy but gives it to me too slowly, for it has attracted me with beautiful appearances for a long time.

Folquet's song was transmitted in France—in BnF MS fr. 844—and, indeed, the reminiscences seem to be confined to the part of stanza I extant in that manuscript (i.e., the first half of the first stanza). Except for the first two lines, it is not exactly accurate to call the motetus a translation of Folquet's poem. Outside of the initial lines of Folquet's poem, the only potential reminiscence is the last word of the motetus—*aliegement*—which may be intended to evoke the verb *aleujar* in the sixth line of Folquet's stanza. And in one instance, what is preserved in the French text is less semantic content than sonority: the verb *assire* ("to sit, to take root") in Folquet's poem has been confused with the verb *assaillir* ("to attack"), even though the verb *assire* existed in Old French. Other than these brief reminiscences, only one other element of Folquet's poem has been preserved.

26. Elizabeth Aubrey (1997, 24–33) has explored this motet at some length, as have G. A. Anderson (1973) and Paul Meyer (1872).

FIGURE 5.2 Occitanizing motet "Onques n'ama loiaument / Mout m'abelist / Flos filius eius" as edited by Tischler.

The nonnasalized *a* rhyme *-ens* in Folquet's poem has been maintained via the word *pensement* (Occitan *pessamens*) but transformed into the nasalized French *b* rhyme *-ent*. If the Occitanizing motet discussed above emphasized its Occitan sonority through rhyme and simultaneous voicings of rhyme, this one uses similar procedures to emphasize the newly Gallicized sound. Although the motetus and triplum do not rhyme with each other (as was the case in "Li jalous par tout sunt fustat / Tuit cil qui sunt enamourat / Veritatem"), they share rhyme sounds in *-ent* and *-i*. Each line ending with the rhyme *-ent* is foregrounded in the motet by the use of a rest after each iteration of the syllable (triplum measures 3, 11, 19, 21; motetus measures 4, 12; see figure 5.2). The (wholly French) triplum's use of the sound outnumbers the motetus's, as if to appropriate the newly nasalized sound as French through repeated iteration. And if sound it is used to appropriate, it is also used to efface: there are no melodic resemblances between the motet and Folquet's *canso*.

The visual program associated with the motet arguably also subtly associates the motetus with French. Next to that voice, on folio 152r, a rooster surveys the scene above him (figure 5.3). The Latin term for rooster, *gallus*, homonym of the term for a resident of Gaul, may be intended to mark the motetus as part of a French patrimony. This might seem like a stretch, but next to the tenor—*flos filius eius* (her son, the flower)—sits a pelican, a bird regularly associated with Christ in bestiaries (figure 5.4). There, the pelican pierces her breast in order to feed her young—a symbol of Christ's sacrifice. The choice of birds plays off the texts with which they are associated, reframing a troubadour-inspired motetus as French in one instance and nodding to Christological bestiary iconography in another.

In sum, this motet, which unlike that discussed above, downplays its connections to the Occitan language and to the troubadour tradition, is—not coincidentally—in the high style of the *canso*. Its first-person declaration of love to a female beloved who remains absent is the paradigm adopted in most of the Gallicized troubadour songs transmitted in France, and as we saw in chapter 1, there, too, traces of the Occitan original were suppressed.

A similarly submerged reminiscence of a well-known Occitan lyric is visible in another motet of the codex. This time it is the triplum of "Quant voi l'aloete / Dieus, je ne m'en partirai ja / Benedictus dominus deus meus" that echoes a troubadour song: the opening of Bernart de Ventadorn's "Can vei la lauzeta mover." As was the case with Folquet's lyric, reminiscences are

FIGURE 5.3 Montpellier, Faculté de Médecine, MS H 196, fol. 152r.

FIGURE 5.4 Montpellier, Faculté de Médecine, MS H 196, fol. 151v.

more or less confined to the first two lines of the original Occitan. This is the triplum in the Montpellier Codex:

Quant voi l'aloete,
qui saut et volete
en l'air contremont,
adonc me halete
le cuer et semont,
Dieus, d'amer la plus bele del mont!
Les ieus a vairs, le chief a blont,
bele bouche et poli front;
la char a blanchete
plus que la noif, que vient d'amont:
S'est bele joenete.
Mes mesdisant grevé m'i ont:
Dieus leur pait leur dete,
si leur criet les ieus du front!
Adonques en pais seront
amoretes.

When I see the lark that jumps and flies in the air, then my heart trembles and invites me—oh God!—to love the most beautiful woman in the world! She has sparkling eyes and blonde hair, a beautiful mouth and a shining forehead, skin whiter than the snow that comes from on high. She is a beautiful young creature. But evil tongues have injured me; may God pay them their debt, and may he poke their eyes out! Then those in love will find peace.

And here is the first stanza of Bernart de Ventadorn's "Can vei":

Can vei la lauzeta mover
de joi sas alas contral rai,
que s'oblid' e·s laissa chazer
per la doussor c'al cor li vai,
ai! tan grans enveya m'en ve
de cui qu'eu veya jauzion,
meravilhas ai, car desse
lo cor de dezirer no·m fon.

(When I see the lark move its wings against the rays [of the sun] in joy, that it forgets itself and lets itself fall because of the sweetness that goes through its heart—ah!—such great envy comes to me of those whom I see rejoicing. It is a miracle that my heart does not melt from desire.)

As we have already seen, this poem was widely transmitted in the north. In addition to being transmitted in Gallicized form, it was also contrafacted on several occasions by *langue d'oïl* composers (Stevens, Butterfield, and Karp 2009). The poem also clearly stands behind this French triplum in the Montpellier Codex. Both pieces begin with the speaker's encounter with a lark in the sky. "Can vei" is translated exactly before the French lyric veers slightly off course. In Bernart's poem, the lark is backlit by the sun ("contral rai"), whereas in the French piece it is merely in the air ("contremont"). The preposition *contre*, however, is enough to recall the original Occitan. In both pieces, the encounter with the lark provokes a response anchored in the heart (line 8 in Bernart de Ventadorn, line 5 in the French triplum). Although encounters with larks were far from unprecedented in French lyric (e.g., Moniot d'Arras's "Quant je oi chanter l'alöete," RS 969), there are just enough phraseological reminiscences of Bernart de Ventadorn's "Can vei la lauzeta mover" to confirm that the French composer had it in mind. Musically, however, there are no reminiscences of Bernart's original, and unlike the motet just discussed, this one contains no linguistic echoes of Occitan. An audience member with no knowledge of Bernart's original would fail to see anything unusual about this motet.

The gradations of Occitan linguistic coloring evident in these three motets (with the highest degree found in the Occitanizing motet with no relationship to actual troubadour song, a faint amount present in a Gallicized rendering of a Folquet de Marselha lyric, and finally none at all in a motet inspired by Bernart de Ventadorn's famous lark song) reflect, in microcosm, the two trends described in this book: the Occitanization of pieces in a low register and the Gallicization and domestication of the high-style *canso*. For a reader with no independent knowledge of the troubadour repertoire, Occitan appears in the Montpellier Codex only as a variant of French—one used in a popularizing dance piece that sonically highlights its Occitan coloring. Those motets with a demonstrable connection to genuine troubadour lyric betray no evidence of such a connection. Only to readers familiar with Folquet's and Bernart's songs would their relationship to the manuscript be evident through such faint signals as rhyme sounds reminiscent of Folquet's, or the rooster whose presence on the folio subtly remaps the provenance of the motetus with which it is associated.

Ambivalent Desire: "L'autrier m'iere levaz" and "Volez vos que je vous chant"

This divergent treatment of Occitan—the repurposing of genuine Occitan cultural material in such a way as to render that debt invisible, alongside the deployment of faux Occitan coloring in pieces with less prestigious generic associations—suggests an ambivalent attitude toward Occitan culture overall. On the one hand, it was admired enough to be circulated, quoted, and requoted, but, on the other hand, genuine Occitan songs were rarely if ever acknowledged as such, and the Occitan language was demoted from its status as a distinct language to that of poetic coloring. While such coloring could be read as an acknowledgment of Occitan, it associates the language with poetic genres and themes that were not actually cultivated in it (outside of this corpus), all the while disavowing real borrowings from the Occitan tradition. I want to turn to two pieces in which this ambivalence is especially visible: a *pastourelle*, "L'autrier m'iere levaz," and a piece often described as a "rêverdie," "Volez vos que je vous chant." These two pieces both uphold and dissolve a linguistic boundary between French and Occitan, and both allude to a separate cultural space in which the latter language is spoken only to negate the existence of such a space. Both include a set of characters in which one is easily legible as "Occitan" and the other as "French" (assuming the availability of these conceptual categories—an availability compromised by the work of appropriation and domestication documented in chapters 1–4). But such labels are *not* applied, and the linguistic traits used to conjure up Occitan identity are not systematically applied to any one character in either song, although they are concentrated enough in the speech of a particular character to raise the specter of cultural alterity. The contradictions with which these pieces are shot through, I argue, are indicative of broader attitudes toward Occitan culture in francophone territories: on the one hand, they suggest a perception of Occitania as a distinct cultural space—one with a distinct language and especially prestigious cultural tradition—but they also vigorously deny both distinctions. Their attitude toward Occitan itself is decidedly ambivalent: in the *pastourelle*, Occitan linguistic traits are depicted as something through which one can (and should) be cured through corrective rape. In the other song, by contrast, Occitan linguistic traits are a constitutive feature of French identity.

I turn first to the *pastourelle* "L'autrier m'iere levaz" (PC 461.148). Were it not for its unusual linguistic features, which, in fact, appear only in one of the two manuscripts that transmit the piece (BnF MS fr. 20050), "L'autrier" would seem to be a fairly standard-issue *pastourelle* within the *oïl* tradition.[27] The scene begins with a mounted knight who approaches a pretty shepherdess named Ermoison. The shepherdess initially resists the knight's advances and warns him that her shepherd friend Perrin remains nearby. Unimpressed by the shepherdess's reticence, the knight resorts to rape. Ermoison's reaction

27. On the differences between the *pastourelle* as cultivated in France and Occitania, see Callahan (2002).

to the sexual encounter is to declare that the knight has rescued her from sadness with his "game" (v. 64). She is, in fact, so overjoyed that she announces that Perrin has never served her so well. Perrin arrives on the scene just in time to realize what has happened and accuses Ermoison of shaming him. She protests that she has merely offered company to the knight (v. 76). Table 5.1 provides the piece in full.[28]

Two features of the text suggest that it takes place somewhere near Occitania. The first is linguistic. A sense of "Occitaneity" is conveyed primarily through suffixes in *-az*, only two of which are correct Occitan forms (*levaz*, v. 1, and *montaz*, v. 2). All of the others, such as *seraz* (Occitan *seretz*) and *avatz* (Occitan *avetz*), are incorrect (Paden 1996, 310). The only two other Occitanisms in the text are the forms *honorade* (v. 16, cf. Occitan *onrata* or *onorata*) and *troberaz* (v. 19; *trouverez/trouveroiz* in Old French; *trobaretz* in Occitan).[29] These linguistic features are not concentrated in either character's speech (Paden 1996, 310). Some occur in the knight's narration, some in his direct speech, and some in the shepherdess's direct speech. The other feature of "L'autrier m'iere levaz" that suggests a relationship to Occitania is that it is situated somewhere near Limoges (v. 50), just on the southern side of the linguistic boundary. At one point, the shepherdess announces rather cryptically that she was there the previous Tuesday. Only she, therefore, is concretely associated with Occitan geography; the knight, for his part, seems to be merely "passing through," if we are to take the opening lines of the poem seriously. What is more, the Occitan linguistic traits of the piece disappear conspicuously at the moment of the shepherdess's rape.[30] Thus, if the knight's "game" has "cured" the shepherdess (v. 64), the only symptom of this transformation is the absence of Occitan in the rest of the piece. The knight's sexual conquest is thus mapped onto a linguistic one. It is telling, however, that neither character is explicitly associated with France or Occitania, and neither's language is completely mappable onto either French or Occitan. While the shepherdess is associated with Occitania and Occitan

28. Edition by Bill Paden (1987). I have lightly adapted his translation.

29. "Creanterie" (v. 51) may be an attempt at an Occitan conditional in *-ia*. Rivière, one of the piece's recent editors, remarks on the clumsiness with which these Occitanisms are applied: "La langue de cette pièce est teintée de provençal, ce qui dénote l'influence que les pastourelles d'oc pouvaient avoir au Nord de la Loire. Mais, comme l'a remarqué Bartsch, le poète—ou le scribe—n'avait qu'une connaissance superficielle de cette langue; en effet, si certaines formes, comme 'levaz, montaz, praz, amaz', peuvent passer pour occitanes, d'autres, comme 'entendaz, avaz, les futurs seraz, ameraz, troberaz', ne l'ont jamais été; il s'agit d'adjonction mécanique de désinences qui, pour l'auteur, avaient une consonance occitane" (Rivière 1974, 85).

30. The last form ending in *-az* appears at v. 48. It is possible that the direct object pronoun *lou* (v. 68) is an (incorrect) attempt at Occitan, but this form was found in Lorraine (Frank 1952a, 63). It is also present in Bern 389, which otherwise bears no trace of Occitanisms.

Table 5.1 L'autrier m'iere levaz(PC 461,148)[1]

I.	L'autrier m'iere levaz;	The other day I had got up;
	sor mon cheval montaz,	Mounted on my horse,
	sui por deduire alaz	I went for amusement
	laz une praierie.	along a meadow.
	Ne fui gaires esloignaz	I had not gone far
	can me sui arrestaz	when I stopped
	et dessendi en praz	and dismounted in the meadow
	soz une ante florie.	beneath a grafted tree in bloom,
	S'ai Ermoison choisie:	And I saw Ermoison—
	c'onkes rose espennie	Never was blooming rose
	ne fu tals ne cristals.	Or crystal the like of her.
	Vers li vois liez et baus	Cheerful and happy I went toward her,
	que sa beltaz m'agrie.	since her beauty pleased me.
II.	Quant la fui aprochaz	When I had come near
	dis li: 'Suer, car m'amaz,	I said: "Sister, please love me!
	honorade en seraz	You will be honored
	en tote vostre vie.'	for all your life."
	—'Signer, ne moi gabaz;	—"Sir, don't make fun of me;
	bien sai, prou troberaz	I know well that you'll find many
	fenne cui ameraz,	a woman you will love,
	plus riche et meuz vestie.'	richer and better dressed."
	—'Bele, je ne quier mie	—"Pretty one, I don't seek
	en amor seignorie;	mastery in love;
	senz mi plaiz et beltaz	I like good sense and beauty
	dont grant plantaz avaz	(of which you have an abundance)
	et dolce conpaignie.'	And sweet companionship."
III.	De folie parlaz	—"You speak out of madness,
	car ren n'en porteraz,	for you won't get a thing,
	c'autres est affiaz	since another has been promised
	d'avoir ma druderie.	to have my love.
	Se tost ne remontaz	If you don't quickly mount again
	et de ci non tornaz	and go away from here,
	ja seraz malmenaz,	soon you will be beaten,
	que Perrins nos espie,	for Perrin is watching us,
	et s'a plus grant aïe	and he'll have greater help
	des bergiers s'il s'escrie.'	from the shepherds, if he cries out."
	—'Bele, ja n'en dotaz,	—"Pretty one, never fear,
	mais a mei entandaz;	but listen to me:
	vos dites grant folie!'	You're talking great nonsense!"
IV.	—'Sire, al moins je vos pri,	—"Sir, I beg of you at least
	kar je remaindrai ci,	(since I shall remain here)
	k'aiez de moi merci;	to have mercy on me
	si serai mal baillie.'	(since I'll have no protection)."
	—'Bele, je vos affi,	—"Pretty one, I promise you,
	se m'avez a ami,	if you take me as your friend,
	n'i aura si hardi	no one will be so brave
	qui oltrage vos die.'	as to insult you."
	—'Sire, n'en parlaz mie;	—"Sir, don't speak of it;
	por de quanques je vi	for all I saw
	a Limoiges mardi,	at Limoges on Tuesday
	nel vos creanterie.'	I would not give you my promise."
V.	—'Bergiere, or est ensi;	—"Shepherdess, this is how it is:
	fols sui quant plus vos pri,	I'm a fool to beg you any more,

	c'ainz nul n'en vi joïr	for I've never seen anyone enjoy
	de longe roterie.'	a long melody played on the rote."
	Lors la trais pres de mi;	Then I drew her near to me;
	elle geta un cri	she gave out a cry
	c'unques nuns ne l'oï.	but no one ever heard it.
	Ne fu pas trop estrie,	She was not very hostile,
	ainz m'a dit cortesie:	rather she gave me a compliment:
	'Sire, g'iere marrie	—"Sir, I was sad
	qant vos venistes ci.	when you came here.
	Or ai lo cuer joli,	Now my heart is glad;
	vostres geus m'a garie.'	your game has cured me.
VI.	Perrins m'ait engingnie,	Perrin has deceived me,
	car onkes en sa vie	for never in his life
	si bel ne me servi;	has he served me so well;
	por ceu se lou defi	therefore I condemn him
	d'un mes de coupperie.'	to a month of cuckoldry!"
	Et Perrins haut c'escrie:	And Perrin cried aloud,
	'Je t'ai trop bien servie,	"I served you too well!
	tu lou m'ais mal meri.	You've paid me back badly—
	Davant moi m'ais honi;	You've put me to shame before my eyes.
	jamaix n'avrai amie.'	I will never have a sweetheart!"
	Tais, gairs, Deus te maldie!'	—"Quiet, boy, God curse you!
	—'Se j'ai fait trop compaignie	If I've offered company
	a cest chevalier si,	to this knight,
	de coi t'ai je honi?	how have I shamed you?
	Il ne m'en porte mie.'	He's not taking me away!"

1. Translation based on William D. Paden's (1987: I.58-63)

linguistic traits to a greater degree, the piece refuses to construct a clear boundary between French and Occitan identity by supplying clear representatives of each. Instead, it blurs the line, while simultaneously depending on the existence of the line in its conceit of corrective rape as linguistic panacea.

If we do read the piece with such a line in mind, France-as-knight's desire for Ermoison is naturalized as erotic attraction. He moves toward her as if compelled, the shepherdess's beauty providing an impetus and excuse for his advances ("que sa beltaz m'agrie" [since her beauty pleased me], v. 13). The shepherdess's resistance is couched not as the result of any lack of interest on her part, but as embarrassment over her indigence (vv. 18–21). Her sexual union with the knight—though initially resisted—ultimately proves salutary to her, lifting her from the emotional doldrums into happiness (vv. 62–63) and even healing her (v. 64). The ministrations of the (presumably Occitan) shepherd Perrin, by contrast, are found inadequate (vv. 65–66). The desire of francophone audiences for Occitan song, and by extension for Occitania, is cast in this scene as natural, inevitable, *and* wholly positive. The Occitan shepherdess is thoroughly grateful, by the end of the song, for the knight's attention. While acknowledging the underlying desire of francophone audiences for Occitan song, the piece absolves these audiences of guilt, suggesting that the status of rustic Occitania can only be improved by the attention of French interlopers. Indeed, though the piece acknowledges shame, the shame is not that of the theft of Occitan sex or song (a theft naturalized as erotic and even praised as civilizing) but that of the shepherdess's companion, whose beloved has been irrevocably defiled. That Occitania is ultimately degraded by the knight's theft of the shepherdess's sexual favors is, however, simultaneously acknowledged: the knight's claim that the shepherdess will be honored all her life if she grants him sexual access (vv. 16–17) rings hollow to all those familiar with the generic *pastourelle* plot, in which the interloping knight always rides away. The knight's promises are suspected, by the shepherdess, of being worthless (vv. 48–51). The poem thus weaves an elaborate lie about the relationship between France and Occitania, all the while acknowledging the fraudulence of its account.

That this story of theft of sexual favors is also about the theft of song is clear in the piece's simultaneous overemphasis on and elision of vocal production, especially song. Though in many *pastourelles* it is the shepherdess's song that attracts the knight to her, in this one the grounds for the knight's choice of Ermoison are never explained. Song is thus conspicuous in its absence in the opening lines. But elsewhere song is strangely present: the shepherdess's mounting resistance is cast as melodic production that is, on all counts, deficient. It is too long ("longe roterie," v. 55) and inaudible; the shepherdess's scream (at the moment of rape) remains unheard and unheeded (vv. 55–56). These ineffective vocal productions, alongside her prerape Occitan linguistic traits, may serve to demote, *en filigrane*, the vocal productions of Occitania as a whole. And, indeed, in the framework of the poem the shepherdess's speech is profoundly ineffective, failing as it does to stop the knight's advances. By the end of the poem, however, the shepherdess sings to the "right" tune in praising the knight, in a French devoid of all Occitanisms, for his sexual prowess (vv. 61–64).

Another poem in the Occitanizing corpus, "Volez vos que je vous chant," provides a different take on the relationship between Occitan and French, both linguistically and culturally. If "L'autrier" frames Occitan as rustic, "Volez vos" positions it as part of France's own linguistic past. Both poems, however, imagine Occitan not as a distinct language but as a linguistic coloring. Moreover, both stage the relationship between French and Occitan as an eroticized heterosexual encounter. I quote the poem in full in table 5.2.

The delineation of cultural identity is clearer here than in "L'autrier," though the poem obfuscates on the question of the knight's identity. The mystical female creature, for her part, is clearly associated with France, a

Table 5.2 Volez vos que je vous chante

I.	Volez vous que je vous chant	Would you like me to sing
	Un son d'amors avenant?	a beautiful song of love?
	Vilain ne.l fist mie,	It was not composed by a peasant,
	Ainz le fist un chevalier	but rather by a knight
	Souz l'onbre d'un olivier	under the shade of an olive tree
	Entre les braz s'amie.	between the arms of his beloved.
II.	Chemisete avoit de lin	She was wearing a shirt of linen,
	En blanc peliçon hermin	in a white fur-lined coat of ermine,
	Et blïaut de soie,	an overgarment of silk,
	Chauces ot de jaglolai	slippers of gladiolus,
	Et sollers de flors de mai	and shoes of mayflowers
	Estroitement chauçade.	were tightly on her feet.
III.	Çainturete avoit de fueille	She had a belt of leaves,
	Qui verdist quant li tens mueille;	which became green in times of rain.
	D'or ert boutonade.	Her buttons were of gold.
	L'aumosniere estoit d'amor;	Her purse was made of love
	Li pendant furent de flor.	and the ties were of flowers.
	Par amors fu donade.	It had been given to her in love.
IV.	Si chevauchoit une mule;	She rode a mule
	D'argent ert la ferreüre,	whose shoes were of silver
	La sele ert dorade;	and whose saddle was entirely golden.
	Seur la crope par derrier	On the croup behind her,
	Avoit planté trois rosiers	she had planted three rosebushes,
	Por fere li honbrage.	so that she would have shade.
V.	Si s'en vet aval la pree;	She goes throughout the fields.
	Chevaliers l'ont encontree,	Knights have met her there.
	Biau l'ont saluade:	They greet her courteously:
	- Bele, dont estes vous nee?	"Beautiful one, where were you born?"
	- De France sui, la loee,	"I am from France the praised,
	Du plus haut parage.	of the highest extraction."
VI.	Li Rosignous est mon pere	"My father is the nightingale
	Qui chante seur la ramee	who sings in the branches
	El plus haut boscage;	of the highest woods.
	La seraine, ele est ma mere	My mother is the siren
	Qui chante en la mer salee	who sings in the salty sea
	El plus haut rivage.	on the highest bank."
VII.	Bele, bon fussiez vous nee,	"Oh, beautiful one, you were born well,
	Bien estes enparentee	and have a good parentage
	Et de haut parage;	and [are] of high extraction;
	Pleüst a Dieu nostre pere	Might it please God the Father
	Que vous me fussiez donee	that you were given to me
	A fame espouade.	as my wedded wife."

space whose reputation is imagined to precede it ("France the praised," v. 29). That the sentence revealing the creature's home is also the first sentence she utters further associates her with the space, as does the fact that France is foregrounded through topicalization ("De France sui" rather than, for instance, "si sui de France"). Though the knight's identity is not explicit, it is telling that the Occitanisms that punctuate the song appear only in his speech. These Occitanisms all take the form of (inappropriate) suffixes in *-ade,* a suffix based on Occitan *-ada* (and still evident in terms such as *tapenade*). The suffix appears six times in the poem. In most of these instances, one would expect to find the feminine adjectival ending *-ée* or a past participle ("chauçade," "donade," "dorade," "saluade"). No Occitanisms appear in the female creature's speech, and indeed, the nine lines of speech attributed to her are conspicuous in their failure to use the suffix, which has appeared almost every three lines in stanzas 2 through 5. The preferred suffix in the woman's speech, *-age*—only one consonant away from *-ade*—aurally harks back to it. This hint of a linguistic division between the knight/narrator and the lady subtly frames him as Occitan, while still not explicitly acknowledging any kind of linguistic division between the two characters. The knight's language is not presented as a foreign language but contains instead Occitan linguistic coloring *within French*. Like the Occitan language, the setting of the poem is, for its part, unnamed but nevertheless discernable. First of all, for the lady's statement that she is from France to make sense, the poem must be set in a space outside of France. Unlike in "L'autrier," the geographical framework of the poem is not circumscribed through a toponym, but we do learn that the poem was composed "under an olive tree" (v. 5), and this detail alone is enough to conjure up the space of the Midi (Lods 1984, 312).[31]

The form of the song reinforces a view of Occitan not as a distinct language but as a part of French, one dating back to the birth of song, or so the poem suggests. It does this by changing the status of the Occitanisms it includes, which move from being a graphic fiction that must be pronounced as French for the rhyme scheme to cohere, to being pronounced as written, but only in a context of assonance rather than strict rhyme. Because this shift corresponds to a temporal one in the poem, with the knight and creature's union under a tree appearing before the story of their encounter (i.e., to a movement from present to past), Occitan is depicted as an etymological remnant of French in the present moment (of composition) and as a part of the French language at the moment of its "birth" in song. The shift to assonance corresponds to a movement backward in the history of French poetics, because of assonance's association with the earliest verse production in French.

I turn first to the evolution of the Occitanisms, which transform from a graphic fiction to a phonetic reality over the course of the poem. In stanza 1, the rhyme scheme is clearly discernable as *aabccb*. This is confirmed in the

31. Cf. Drzewicka (1974, 451), who links the olive tree to the *chanson de geste*.

second stanza, but only on the condition that we read *-ade* as rhyming with *soie* and *jaglolai*, that is, if we sound it as the expected Old French form. Here is stanza 2 in full:

> Chemisete avoit de l*in*
> En blanc peliçon herm*in*
> Et blïaut de s*oie*,
> Chauces ot de jaglol*ai*
> Et sollers de flors de m*ai*
> Estroitement chauç*ade*.

If we fail to pronounce the Occitanism *-ade* as if it merely stood for French, the poem fails to cohere as a poem; its rhyme scheme dissolves. If, on the other hand, we pronounce the word *chauçade* as if it rhymed with *soie* (i.e., if we substitute the French cognate), the rhyme scheme remains intact.

In the next stanza, the status of the Occitanisms pivots from graphic fiction to reality. Here the *aabccb* rhyme scheme is maintained but only on two conditions: if the Occitan suffix is pronounced as its spelling suggests it should be pronounced, and if we treat assonance as a substitute for rhyme.

> Si chevauchoit une m*ule*;
> D'argent ert la ferre*üre*,
> La sele ert dor*ade*;
> Seur la crope par derr*ier*
> Avoit planté trois ros*iers*
> Por fere li honbr*age*.

The endings *-ule* and *-üre* can only be linked through assonance, and the same is true for *-ier* and *-iers* and for the coupling of *-ade* and *-age*, the Occitanism having evolved from a graphic representation into something like [adə]. The formal structure of the poem thus accomplishes the ideological work of making French and Occitan one language—the language out of which the union of France and Occitania is born in the poem. Occitan "dialect" in this song is deployed to narrate the origins not just of this song but of *all* song, and in such a way as to suggest that the event it recounts—the union of "France the praised" and an unnamed Occitan other—produced as if by natural parturition the formal means appropriate to it.

These two shifts in the poem—from Occitanisms as graphic fiction to Occitanisms as phonetic reality, and from rhyme to assonance—correspond to a temporal regression in the poem. The piece moves from the present moment of performance (vv. 1–6) to a description of the initial encounter between the female creature and the knight (vv. 7–15) and then subtly, with the backstory to her purse, into a description of the female creature's past and lineage (vv. 16–18, 31–36). As the poem moves back in time, its own form regresses in such a way as to mimic the formal evolution of French poetry, moving from rhyme to assonance. Assonance was, of course, the earliest form of versification used in the French vernacular, with rhyme taking over as the predominant mode only over the course of the twelfth century (Kibler 1995, 1793). The poem thus encodes within its own form a historical poetics, one in which Occitan has always been part of the French language, but in which Occitan shifts from a phonetic reality to a graphic fiction—something akin, perhaps, to spurious silent letters. The Occitanisms become, within the "recent" French of the poem's initial stanzas, akin to the etymological silent letters left over from Latin in English (e.g., island, doubt).

Just as Occitan is woven into the history of the French language, it is woven into the history of song. Though song is associated with the knight, who also doubles as a troubadour, in the sense that it is he who composes the poem that comes down to us (vv. 3–4), it is most emphatically associated with the female creature. Indeed, symbols of song and poetry proliferate not in association with the troubadour but instead with the creature from France. Both the nightingale and siren—the creature's parents (stanza VI)—are long-standing symbols of song. Moreover, the creature's illustrious lineage—and thus France's fictional past—is constructed through these symbols of song. The "heights" of the creature's ancestry are thus not merely metaphorical buttressing to her superiority: her father's song cascades from the branches of the highest forest while her mother's serenade emanates from the highest bank. This creature's genealogy—and, by extension, that of "France the praised"—is illustrious *because* of its association with the act of song. Indeed, song is the genealogical core that stabilizes French identity. The miraculousness of the chimeric lineage recounted therein (nightingale and siren, mysterious female creature) is acknowledged both in the song's image of impossible roots—a rose tree planted on a mule? (v. 23) and in its abundance of (presumably sterile) hybrids (nightingale-siren, mule) but nevertheless insisted upon. Indeed, the formal hybridity of the poem (rhyme and assonance, French and Occitan) *is* what allows for the lineage of hybrid creatures recounted therein. It is only by imagining the capacity for song as a congenital trait bequeathed from one generation to the next that the contours of the song's lineage cohere.

We saw in the introduction to this book that the idea of a "gift of song" being passed from generation to generation appears elsewhere. In Philippe Mousket's *Chronique rimée* this gift is attributed not to the French but to the "Provençaux." As we have already seen, according to Mousket, Charlemagne bequeathed Provence to the minstrels who followed his army, which explains why they produce better songs than anyone else:

> Dont departi Karles les tieres,
> Qu'il avoit conquises par gierre [. . .]
> Li manestrel et li jougleur
> Orent Prouvence, si fu leur.
> Par nature encor çou trouvons,
> Font Provenciel et cans et sons
> Millors que gent d'autres païs
> Pour çaus dont il furent nays.

> When Charlemagne divided the lands he had conquered through war [. . .] the minstrels and jongleurs had Provence. Through nature still we find this, that the Provençaux make better melodies and lyrics than people from other countries, because of those from whom they were born. (Mousket 1836, vv. 6274–75, 6298–6303)

"Volez vos" appropriates the cultural legacy—lyric poetry—that was most strongly associated with Occitania, using it as the genealogical core through which the very essence of Frenchness is articulated. Indeed, the poem's French identification through song is further shored up via performances already inscribed in it as part of its narrative framework: "Would you like me to sing you a beautiful song of love?" asks the narrator of his audience, interpellated through an indirect object pronoun, thereby perpetuating the lyric lineage imagined in the poem. The text thus imagines a future lineage in which France and Occitania are one. This union, however, is also the poem's necessary past, since, for the rhyme scheme of the piece to make sense, the conjoining of France and Occitania must already have occurred. In this sense, the poem is the condition of its own writing.

As in "L'autrier m'iere levaz," the power hierarchy in "Volez vos" is unequivocal. The French creature's association with the siren frames her as a dangerous seductress. The siren was not a neutral symbol of song; she was most often described as a morally perilous force who exerted an extreme sexual power on her male victims, whom she often consumed after luring them with her song (Leach 2006, 2007). While there is nothing overtly ominous about the encounter in "Volez vos" (the knight apparently escapes unscathed, if he is able to compose the poem), I think we should read the siren symbol as the arrogation of a power that was traditionally Occitan. It was Occitan, and not French, that was the language most widely used to voice desire in love lyric, and it is precisely this power to voice desire that the mysterious creature arrogates. It is she, and not the troubadour, who controls the sexual scenario of the poem. It is she who chooses the knight from among many possible suitors (vv. 26–27).

Paradoxically, however, it is the encounter with the troubadour that allows the woman (and, by extension, France?) to find a subject position: Frenchness can only be articulated via its Occitan other, as when the troubadour's question—"Beautiful, where were you born?" (v. 28)—elicits both the initial instance of first-person speech *and* the revelation of the creature's French identity. Up until this point, she is an immaterial creature whose body can only be inferred from the luxurious clothing heaped on it. In the Old French, no subject pronoun is used to describe the creature until the fifth stanza of the poem. The absence of both corporeal description and reification through subject pronouns further conflates the creature with France and lends her additional mystique. It is only through her encounter with the troubadour that she seems to come fully into being. The troubadour continues to provide the vehicle for French identification when he devotes the last stanza of the poem to a gushing description of the creature's noble descent.

The Occitanizing songs "L'autrier" and "Volez vos," though superficially quite different, fundamentally represent similar rescriptings of the desire of francophone writers and audiences for troubadour song. Both poems transpose these dynamics of desire into an erotic scenario, though both also obfuscate the cultural and linguistic identity of the character they most associate with Occitania or the Occitan language. In "L'autrier" the Occitan-identified character is rustic—a shepherdess who proclaims to the world her simplicity and poverty, absolving the French character from having to disparage her himself. In "Volez vos" the prestige of Occitan is recognized in that the knight's status is emphasized ("no peasant, he!" vv. 3–4) but nevertheless overshadowed by the illustrious status of the female creature, a status conveyed symbolically through her luxurious raiments and then through an exposition of her bloodline. In both songs, the French character controls the erotic scenario. In "L'autrier" this control extends to the right to rape, while in "Volez vos" the Occitan knight is selected from an array of handsome and worthy suitors (v. 26). The impact of the sexual union is, in both cases, at least partially linguistic: in "L'autrier" the shepherdess is cured of her Occitanisms, while in "Volez vos" the song—presumably born in a moment of postcoital bliss (vv. 5–6)—sees a shift from Occitanism as graphic fiction to phonetic reality (an inverted trajectory of what the poem imagines to be a historical development). And finally, though the Occitan character is imagined to be improved by his or her encounter with France in both instances (the shepherdess is "cured" of an unnamed ailment and the troubadour-knight marries into an eminent lineage), both songs also acknowledge the monstrosity or at least the excessiveness of French lust—in "L'autrier" via the reader's awareness that the French knight is not just a rapist but one whose promises ring hollow, and in "Volez vos," in the association of the French creature with the infamous siren.

Occitanizing Song: A Mirage of Origins

There is, unfortunately, no medieval evidence for the way in which the Occitanizing corpus was read or interpreted, beyond the way in which it is transmitted in manuscript. There, nothing suggests that the songs were registered as being distinctive in any way, and they are often transmitted alongside Gallicized troubadour songs and/or lyric in *langue d'oïl*. But one very strong indicator of the powerful ideological work accomplished in the Occitanizing corpus is the frequency with which it serves as the pièce de résistance in nineteenth-century arguments regarding the "origin" of French poetry. Many nineteenth-century readers, and perhaps medieval ones as well, took seriously the fantasy of origins spun in the Occitanizing corpus—one in which the Occitanizing corpus was held up as the most archaic and, for some critics, one in which Occitan and French poetic histories have been intertwined since their inceptions. Writing in 1889, for instance, Alfred Jeanroy, though skeptical of the folkloric veneer of many songs, describes the Occitanizing "A l'entrade del tens clar" as the only truly "folk" piece preserved in French and Occitan songbooks: "dans tous les chansonniers, tant provençaux que français, il n'y a peut-être qu'une seule pièce vraiment populaire, la célèbre ballade: *A l'entrada del tems clar*" (in all songbooks, both Occitan and French, there is maybe only one piece truly of the people, the famous ballade *A l'entrada del tems clar*) (Jeanroy 1889b, xix). Since he makes no mention of the linguistic characteristics of the piece, it is not clear whose folkloric tradition he thinks it belongs to—Occitania's or France's. "A l'entrada" is the only remnant, according to Jeanroy, of what he imagines to be the earliest stage of lyric composition. It was this phase of lyric composition, Jeanroy argues, that went on to exert an influence on medieval literature elsewhere in Europe. In the closing pages of the work, he turns to another Occitanizing song, this time "Volez vos," holding it up as a piece that resembles the phase of archaic French folk poetry no longer extant (except, as just discussed, for "A l'entrada"). Though he realizes that "Volez vos" is not, in fact, archaic, he points to it as an example of what this corpus looked like, asking: "Cette fée au costume fantastique et printanier, cette fille du rossignol et de la sirène, qui est 'de France la loée,' ne ressemble-t-elle pas un peu à notre poésie populaire du moyen âge?" (This fairy with a fantastic, springtime costume, this girl born of the nightingale and siren, who is from 'France the praised,' does she not resemble a little our folk poetry of the Middle Ages?) (Jeanroy 1889b, 449). It is telling that Jeanroy does not indicate the song by its incipit but instead conflates it with one of its protagonists, the French female creature. Indeed, Jeanroy, thoroughly seduced by the mythical accounts of the origins of French song in "Volez vos," conflates the female protagonist with the entire history of French folk lyric production: "cette fée [. . .] ne ressemble-t-elle pas un peu à notre poésie populaire du moyen âge?" (this fairy [. . .], does she not resemble a little our popular/folkloric poetry of the Middle Ages?). It is unclear how a character in a poem could be thought to resemble an entire body of "folk" poetry—or any body of poetry at all, for that matter—but Jeanroy's very willingness to see the poem as a synecdoche for all of French folk production testifies to the success of the myth of origins it spins. Moreover, just as he was on "A l'entrada," Jeanroy remains silent on the linguistic characteristics of "Volez vos," and this time there is no doubt that he views the piece as analogous to the oldest tradition of French song. The temporal *fata morgana* of the Occitanizing corpus works, in Jeanroy's case, and despite his apparent partial awareness of being duped (he concedes that the piece is *analogous* to the oldest specimens, not an example of them), to frame the songs as anterior to all others. In "Volez vos," Jeanroy implies (through his inclusion of the piece in the closing lines of his book), lie the true *Origines de la poésie lyrique en France*—an originary moment whose Frenchness, at least for Jeanroy, cannot be unseated by its Occitanizing traits.

Like Alfred Jeanroy, Paul Meyer succumbed to the lure of the Occitanizing corpus, pointing to various Occitanizing songs as both archaic and rustic. Regarding both the triplum and motetus of "Li jalous par tout sunt fustat / Tuit cil qui sunt enamourat / Veritatem" and "A l'entrade," he declared: "Il est à croire que dans les deux cas nous avons affaire à un de ces chants de mai, à une de ces *kalendas maias*" (It seems that in the two cases we are dealing with one of those May songs, one of the *kalendas maias*) (Meyer 1872, 405). Meyer's suggestion of a relationship between two Occitanizing songs and May festivals situates the Occitanizing songs in what he imagines to be one of the oldest venues for the composition of poetry in medieval Europe. Unlike Alfred Jeanroy, however, Paul Meyer viewed the Occitanizing corpus (or at least this portion of it) as Occitan rather than French, despite indications he himself documents that would suggest otherwise. "Il est curieux," comments Meyer, "que les deux chants de mai les plus caractérisés que possède la littérature provençale nous aient été conservés par deux chansonniers français. C'est une preuve de plus du peu de cas que les méridionaux faisaient de leur littérature populaire" (It is curious that the two most characteristic May songs in Occitan literature were preserved for us in two French songbooks. This is an additional piece of proof for the disregard that southerners had for their popular literature) (405). Meyer's comment on the provenance of the songs is all the more remarkable given that he argues, in the lines that precede this statement, that linguistically a French origin seems more likely than an Occitan one. All the while acknowledging that a French regularization of the motet is easier than a transposition into Occitan, Meyer posits Occitan origin on the grounds that "l'ensemble a une saveur provençale qu'il est impossible de méconnaître" (the whole thing has a *provençal* flavor that is impossible to miss) (406). Perhaps, he concedes, the piece is from a border territory such as Auvergne or Limousin. Like Jeanroy, Meyer is taken in by the songs' pseudo-archaic quality and also by their demotion of the status of the Occitan language. As we have already seen, Meyer comments on the curious fact that this most "populaire" (folkloric, rustic) of Occitan specimens is preserved only in France. In light of my discussion above, I would note that it is likely no coincidence that the part of the Occitanizing corpus Meyer views as Occitan (or perhaps from a border region) is the part of the Occitanizing corpus from a lower register—in this case songs associated with dancing.

Following Meyer's and Jeanroy's leads, Gaston Paris (1892) used "Volez vos" as the linchpin in his hypothesis that all European poetry could be traced to springtime dances, or *fêtes de mai* (12). Like Jeanroy, Paris thought that "Volez vos" represented the traces of the earliest moments of French lyric history, a history he associated with annual festivals. In his words, "Volez vos" is "le chef-d'œuvre de cette poésie printanière" (14). Unlike Jeanroy, however, Paris notes the Occitan features of the text and initially seems to suggest that the text has been altered: "elle est malheureusement altérée et sans doute incomplète; elle est en outre écrite dans une langue étrangement hybride, où des formes du Midi s'allient avec des formes du Nord" (it is unfortunately altered and undoubtedly incomplete; it is moreover written in a strangely hybrid language, in which forms from the Midi are joined to forms from the North) (14). Paris makes no effort to account for the strange linguistic status of the song, which does not seem, in any case, to alter his stance on French provenance. Also archaic, in Paris's view (perhaps following Jeanroy's), is "A l'entrade del tems" (51), although the Occitan coloring of this piece makes Paris suspect provenance in the Limousin, a region of France where he situates the oldest "French" poetry (50).[32] Determined to document the existence of a period of French lyric history that antedates

32. For Paris's theory on the Limousin, see Paris (1892, 27–28).

the influence of the troubadours, the hypothesis of this border region allows Paris to circumvent the problem of linguistic coloring.

Paris's theory of primitive French poetry is based, in part, on form. Since he assumes that more "simple" poetry must come before more complex forms, he posits that his *chansons de maieroles* antedate the troubadours:

> Je voudrais rendre vraisemblable cette thèse que la poésie des troubadours proprement dite, imitée dans le Nord à partir du milieu du XIIe siècle, et qui est essentiellement la poésie courtoise, a son point de départ dans les chansons de danse et notamment de danses printanières. (G. Paris 1892, 58)

> I would like to make plausible (i.e., defend) the thesis that the proper poetry of the troubadours, imitated in the North starting in the middle of the twelfth century, and which is essentially courtly poetry, had its origins in dance songs and notably in springtime dances.

Although Paris concedes that much later trouvère poetry was conceived in imitation of the troubadours, it is pieces such as "Volez vos" and "A l'entrade" that allow him to hypothesize the existence of a primitive period in which French lyric remained untouched by the troubadour repertoire. This allows him to reverse, or at least to complicate, traditional accounts of the direction of influence between Occitan and French lyric, which viewed trouvère lyric as an imitation (usually a paltry one at that) of Occitan poetry. In Paris's schema, springtime French folk lyric sparked troubadour lyric, which, in turn, was the impetus for later French imitations.

Writing in 1896, Joseph Bédier seems to agree with the basic idea of Paris's *fêtes de mai* hypothesis. Like Paris, he also assumes that the "simplest" poetry—a corpus in which he includes at least one Occitanizing song—must come before the more complex: "Il suffit de poser ces définitions et de mettre en regard les chansons de maieroles et ces pièces courtoises [. . .] pour faire pressentir aussitôt que ceci est sorti de cela" (It is enough to define the terms and to contrast May songs with courtly songs [. . .] to realize immediately that the latter emerged from the former) (Bédier 1896, 160). Like Paris, he concludes that these "archaic" *maieroles* were written before 1140, a date he associates with the oldest troubadour poetry (161). It is difficult to tell precisely which "chansons de maieroles" Bédier has in mind, but it is clear that "Volez vos" is one of them. He initially echoes Paris's description of this poem as charming in its very strangeness before going on to describe it as both a point of origin for French literary history *and* a link to the springtime rituals still practiced in nineteenth-century France. About the female figure in this poem, he asks: "Qui est-elle? Vêtue de fleurs, portant ceinture qui reverdit à la rosée, n'est-ce pas elle qu'honorent et figurent les reines de mai de nos villages? N'est-elle pas l'Esprit même de la végétation renaissante et comme la Muse de toute cette gracieuse poésie archaïque?" (Who is she? Dressed in flowers, wearing a belt that grows green in dew, is it not she whom the queens of May in our villages honor and represent? Is she not the very Spirit of renewed vegetation and the Muse of all of this graceful, archaic poetry?) (164). Bédier, even more than the handful of philologists who paved the way for him, buys hook, line, and sinker into the conjuring trick of "Volez vos." Responding to the interpellation of its opening lines ("Would you like me to sing you a beautiful song of love?"), Bédier sees the female protagonist of the song both as the ancestor of the female practitioners of lyric still active in France in the late nineteenth century and as the fertile yet only quasi-human point of origin (a muse!) for all of French lyric history. As we saw above, the basis for this fiction is spun in the poem itself. All of these philologists take seriously the promise of the female creature of "Volez vos," a quasi-incarnation of France, that all lyric poetry descends from her. If she is the source of this body of Occitanizing texts, they are framed not as Occitan but as French.

Though there is no real evidence to suggest that the Occitanizing pieces to which these nineteenth-century philologists turn, again and again, are actually from an earlier phase of French lyric history than the other pieces with which they are compiled, their faux-archaic qualities successfully duped a succession of eminent critics. All make claims for the particular simplicity of pieces from the corpus, a simplicity that in their view lends credence to the hypothesis of their temporally and culturally primitive status. Their disagreements on the provenance of the various songs in the corpus conform to the theory of genre outlined earlier in this chapter: those Occitanizing songs in a low register, those at the greatest remove from the prestigious *canso*, are the ones philologists speculate may in fact be genuinely Occitan (for Paul Meyer, the triplum and motetus of "Li jalous par tout sunt fustat / Tuit cil qui sunt enamourat / Veritatem" and the dance song "A l'entrade") or else from the border regions between France and Occitania (Paris speculates that "A l'entrade" is from the Limousin, and Meyer acknowledges this possibility for both this piece and the motet as well). By contrast, the higher-style "Volez vos" is routinely held up as French (e.g., by Jeanroy, Bédier, and Paris) with its unusual linguistic status either omitted from discussion or else acknowledged and dismissed with no attempt at explanation.

Epilogue

It will hardly come as news to medievalists that thirteenth-century francophone authors, compilers, and composers were interested in the troubadours. Indeed, the traditional story, which situates the troubadours as the forerunners to the trouvères, postulates just such a relationship of imitation. What I hope to have shown in *Stolen Song*, however, is not just that early French audiences were interested in the troubadours, but that, in its early French transmission, troubadour lyric was separated from its original language, region of origin, compositional circumstances, and authorial voice. To illustrate this point, we might imagine a scenario in which we were forced to construct all of our knowledge about the troubadours from the French sources discussed here. Let's imagine, hypothetically, that a natural disaster wiped out all Catalan, Italian, and Occitan manuscripts and narratives with any relationship to the troubadours. In such a scenario, I would argue, we would not even have enough material to conceptualize such a thing as "troubadour song." First of all, there would be very few actual troubadours in sight. Without the help of fr. 844, we would only know of one troubadour, Folquet de Marselha, thanks to an author attribution in Bern 389. If we had some idea of what Occitan sounded like as a language, we might notice that some anonymous pieces—usually scattered here and there rather than compiled in a self-contained section—had Occitan traits. If we were to imagine, logically, that some Occitan pieces had found their way into French sources, the pieces we would turn to first would be *not* the genuine troubadour lyrics discussed in chapters 1–4 but instead the Occitanizing corpus outlined in chapter 5. It is these pieces, after all, that contain the highest degree of Occitan coloring on the whole. If we were to try to reconstruct the origin of the other pieces with Occitan coloring—those in which this coloring is much fainter—we would be led to believe that they were mostly from Poitou, on the border between French- and Occitan-speaking territories. Thus, if we were to draw a line from northern France downward, in the very north we would have a broad range of genres, including *grands chants courtois*, by named trouvères. Moving south, toward the linguistic border with Occitania, but still on the northern side, we would have some anonymous pieces, mostly in a high register (these are the pieces we know from elsewhere to be genuine troubadour lyrics). Still farther south, finally, we would have a handful of low-register pieces, all anonymous (the Occitanizing corpus). Thus, if the fate of the troubadours had been left to early French readers and compilers, there would be no troubadours. There would only be a body of anonymous lyric with various shades of Occitan coloring, some of it adapted from actual troubadours and some newly composed.

Some parts of the troubadour corpus, as this book shows, were transmitted in a form that bordered on incomprehensibility. Writers and manuscript compilers had different ways of accounting for the semantic opacity of the texts with which they were confronted. For the compiler of BnF MS fr. 844, troubadour song became akin to the raving of the mentally deranged or to birdsong. A subtle comparison to birdsong became a key strategy for explaining the strange breakdown of referential language in the texts. This, as we saw, was one of Jean Renart's strategies, alongside other framings that account for a failure of denotative language: song overheard from a distance and song as part of a larger sonic spectacle in which multiple texts compete. Gerbert de Montreuil takes this comparison of Occitan lyric to birdsong to its acme, quoting two troubadour songs in the romance—and only those songs—after evocations of birdsong. His rewriting of Bernart de Ventadorn's famous lark song to include an allusion to the vocalizations of the lark and not just to its image against the sun further strengthens the connection between troubadour and avian song. But if such comparisons rationalize the compromised intelligibility of Occitan song in Gallicized form, they also threaten to undermine its status as song, at least as defined in medieval treatises. Such treatises specify that song must be composed of *vox articulata*—meaningful speech. As Elizabeth Leach (2007) has explained, for song to be song and not just noise, a rational agent needed to lie behind its production. Troubadour song was thus imagined in its francophone reception less as a rational human product and more as anonymous, garbled, and, sometimes, avian. Curiously, though, in some imaginings—the *Violette* and "Volez vos"—avian status is not restricted to Occitan; in the *Violette* Euriaut is aligned with songbirds, and in "Volez vos" it is the female creature who identifies herself with France whose status as human seems the most questionable. Some songs of the Occitanizing corpus also demote the status of Occitan lyric. Those that ventriloquize Occitan to the highest degree are also those that are the most oriented toward the rustic and folkloric, with scenes of dancing and sex. Although such songs are, in some sense, at a far remove from "Volez vos," with its troubadour-as-knight, both parts of the Occitanizing corpus's attempt to provide speech to an imagined (and subordinate) Occitan other—an other whose Occitan identity is only hinted at and never explicitly acknowledged. The genuine voices of the troubadours, those transmitted in their songs, were meanwhile garbled through Gallicization, rendered anonymous, and quoted and compiled in such a way as to efface nearly all remnants of their cultural and linguistic alterity. Occitan was not, as it was in Italy and Catalonia, an object of intense philological study, but rather, in francophone territories, a language that could be pastiched with little to no concern for attested morphology. Indeed, a brief survey of the two main strands of reception besides the one discussed in *Stolen Song*, Italian and Catalan, throws into greater contrast the particularities of the corpus's francophone reception.

The Catalan reception of troubadour song treated it as a prestige object worthy of study, memorization, and imitation. As discussed in the introduction, a series of Catalan writers wrote language handbooks for aspiring composers to learn Occitan and emphasize the cachet of composition in the language.[1] Raimon Vidal, for example, famously announces how fashionable Occitan composition has become throughout all sectors of society:

> Totas genz cristianas, iusieuas et sarazinas, emperador, princeps, rei, duc, conte, vesconte, contor, valvasor, clergue, borgues, vilans, paucs et granz, meton totz iorns lor entendiment en trobar et en chantar, o q'en volon trobar o q'en volon entendre o q'en volon dire o q'en volon auzir; que greu seres en loc negun tan privat ni tant sol, pos gens i a paucas o moutas, qe ades non auias cantar un o autre o tot ensems, que neis li pastor de la montagana lo maior sollatz qe ill aiant an de chantar. (Marshall 1972, 2)

1. These are, in chronological order, Raimon Vidal de Besalú (*Las Razos de trobar*), Jofre de Foixà (*Las Regles de trobar*), the anonymous author who wrote the *Doctrina de compondre dictats*, and the anonymous author of the two Ripoll treatises.

> All Christian people, Jews, Saracens, emperors, princes, kings, dukes, counts, viscounts, tale-tellers, vavasseurs, clerks, bourgeois, peasants, small and great, devote their efforts every day to composing and singing (in Occitan). They either want to compose songs or understand them, or they want to sing them or hear them—to the point that you can hardly go to any secluded spot, no matter how solitary, whether there be few people or many, without hearing someone or another, or all of them together, sing, for even the shepherds of the mountain take their greatest delight in singing.

Although Raimon's endorsement of Occitan is, in all likelihood, hyperbolic, as self-interest would dictate, the manuscript evidence from Catalonia does suggest that the consumption of Occitan song was a popular pursuit. Raimon's framing of Occitan as an object worthy of study, and the act of Occitan composition as a trendy pursuit find no analogs in the francophone reception of the troubadours. Although troubadour song demonstrably enjoyed popularity in francophone territories, as is clear from its manuscript diffusion, no francophone author from the earliest phase of reception clearly imagines Occitan as a discrete language, let alone a discrete language worthy of study (it is intriguing, however, that by the fifteenth century, the prose *remanieur* of the *Roman de la violette* characterizes the "langue prouvençal" as "moult dificile a entendre" ("very difficult to understand").[2] This is all the more noteworthy given the proximity of Catalan and Occitan. Catalan was in fact closer to Occitan than any dialect of Old French, but rather than using Occitan as a kind of sound coloring, as we saw in the francophone reception of troubadour song, Catalan authors move in the opposite direction, going to great pains to distinguish "proper" Occitan forms from similar forms in other romance languages.

The same treatise tradition diverges from the francophone reception of the troubadours not just in its treatment of the Occitan language but also in its treatment of individual troubadours. Many of the treatises emphasize the existence of individual poets behind the corpus of Occitan song, and sometimes even the distinctive styles of these poets. In his *Razos de trobar*, Raimon quotes troubadour lyric thirty-two times, and in each instance he

2. Curiously, he describes the whole of the original verse *Violette* as being in Occitan—a testament to the strength of the association between Occitan and lyric composition: "[je] me suis ingeré et avachyé de moy traveillier a aplicquier mon petit sens et entendement a mettre et rediger par escript ce petit livret lequel *par avant estoit en langage prouvençal* et moult dificile a entendre" (I have exerted all of my effort in applying my small intellect and understanding to put into writing thi little book which before was written in the Provençal language and was very difficult to understand) (Lowe 1928, 2).

attributes the pieces to a troubadour by name, often prefaced by the honorific "En." For his part, Jofre de Foixà quotes the corpus eleven times and cites individual troubadours in all but three instances. And in the anonymous Ripoll treatises, which contain eighteen quotations, all but six are attributed (and the six unattributed pieces are all dance pieces, a genre that is rarely accompanied by author attributions). Raimon, author of the earliest grammatical treatise on Occitan, also penned two short stories or *novas* in which individual troubadours are quoted and, usually, named. His treatment of French material also diverges from the pattern of francophone reception in that this material is flagged as foreign. In one of his *novas*, "En aquel temps c'om era gais," one French quotation is flagged as such: "Anc non auzis ni aprezes / So que dis us Franses d'amor? / *Cosselhetz mi, senhor*" ("have you never heard or learned what a Frenchman says about love? *Advise me, Lord*") (Raimon Vidal de Besalú 1989, vv. 666–68), asks one character.

Some Italian speakers also composed grammatical treatises on Occitan, and their treatises share the same features—a normative sense of Occitan as a distinct language and an interest in and awareness of individual troubadours—as those discussed above. The latter feature was also emphasized in the Italian transmission of troubadour song, where composers were sometimes given *vidas* or short biographies and/or author portraits.[3] Moreover, most Italian songbooks are structured in sections devoted to particular composers (even when these are subsumed into a broader structure that groups according to genre), and the rubrics of the songbooks emphasize this author-centered structure. The songbook known as *I*, for example, emphasizes not just its authorial organization but the proper names of the troubadours whose works are compiled therein: "Aqui son escrig li noms dels trobadors qui / son enaq*ue*st livre que ant trobadors laç ca*n* / sos lun apres lautre" (Here are written the names of the troubadours who are in this book who have who composed songs one after the other).[4]

It would be easy to take the argument I have sketched in *Stolen Song* as one of conscious oppression of Occitan culture. Such stories are legion. The Albigensian Crusade is still remembered with emotion in some circles, and much scholarship on the Midi has been colored by the fact that many historians of the region are also political activists. Most famously, Robert Lafont

3. The songbooks that include *vidas* are from the second half of the thirteenth century and are thus roughly contemporary with many of the songbooks and narratives discussed in this book. The earliest group of songbooks date from the period between 1254 and 1300 (*AIKDDaHST*) (Burgwinkle 1999, 246).

4. I follow Marisa Galvez (2012, 230) in reading the second *trobadors* as a misreading of the verb form *trobadas*, which is what the same songbook gives elsewhere in its index.

was a vocal supporter of Occitan separatism. As Emmanuel Le Roy Ladurie (1977, 22) points out, this has created a situation in which "there is the danger of writing history that is Manichean, paranoiac, that would impute all that is evil to the France of *Oïl*." It is not at all my intent to write such a history. If I have evoked the Albigensian Crusade in passing throughout this study, it is only to suggest that it was, in some sense, a nonevent for these French authors and compilers—even those who depict historical knights who actually participated in the Crusade. Chapters 2 and 3 show that the Battle of Bouvines was the much more critical historical event for Jean Renart and Gerbert de Montreuil. Both writers, as we saw, are far more concerned with the border of Capetian territories with the Holy Roman Empire (to the east) than the border with Occitania (to the south). Indeed, although in the midst and the aftermath of the Albigensian Crusade the ground was ripe for cross-cultural hostility between French and Occitan speakers, there is, on the part of francophone writers, no explicit condemnation of the sort penned by the troubadours who, as we saw in the introduction, used poetry as a means of political resistance against their new French oppressors. However, even in the absence of overt hostility, *Stolen Song* has shown that troubadour songs were not celebrated and circulated in francophone territories as part of a linguistically and culturally distinct movement. They were, instead, either treated as if they were—or made to be—francophone.

That this *francophonie* of the troubadours does not map onto any actual political space very easily should make us wary of reading the assimilation of the troubadours in their early francophone reception as a concerted and conscious act of oppression. While Gerbert de Montreuil certainly wrote in pro-Capetian circles, the provenance of some of the songbooks that assimilate troubadour song is in fact the Holy Roman Empire. That the troubadours can "pass" in any francophone space, however this space is politicized (or not), suggests that the processes I have charted in this study are the result of widespread adulation and envy, both unconscious and conscious, extending beyond the bounds of any one political center. This envy is clearest in "Volez vos," which shows how the very act of song—culturally associated with Occitania—has been appropriated as the foundation of French identity, whatever "French" might have meant to the composer.

This is not to say that the "Frenchness" of the troubadours was secured once and for all for posterity. Literary canons are in constant flux, and the battle over ownership of the troubadours continued long past the thirteenth century. For Jean de Nostredame, brother of the famous astrologer, they illustrated the glory of Languedoc and Provence. As in the early French songbooks and narratives discussed in this study, the provenance of troubadours who were not actually from these regions was creatively reinvented in Nostredame's *Vies des plus célèbres et anciens poètes provençaux* (1575). Nostredame also concocted some troubadours who bore a suspicious resemblance to his contemporaries, including his famous brother (Haines 2004, 53; Kendrick 1995). For him, there was nothing remotely French about the troubadours. The same was true for the Italian Renaissance scholar Pietro Bembo, who viewed troubadour lyric primarily as the source for the Sicilian school at Frederick II's court and, consequently, as the origin of *Italian* rather than French poetry. To drum up the Italianness of the troubadours, Bembo (1989, 91) grasped at biographical details from the *vidas*, such as the fact that Folquet de Marselha's family purportedly came from Genoa.[5] Even the language of troubadour poetry took on an Italianate hue for Bembo, who posited (correctly) that Occitan was more closely related to the Tuscan language than to French.

Faced with this Italian appropriation, after having fallen into a period of critical oblivion, the troubadours and the Occitan language suddenly became very French in the hands of scholars such as Henri Estienne and Étienne Pasquier (Cohen 2001, 547).[6] According to Estienne, the prestige of Italian culture was the result of linguistic borrowing from Occitan. Estienne (1914) responds to Bembo's comments on the Occitan influence on Tuscan by recasting the Italians' appropriation as an act of theft. After listing page after page of borrowings from Occitan (and French), he declares: "S'ils [the Italians] sont riches, c'est de nos bienfaicts" (if the Italians are rich, it is from our gifts) (348). The glory of the Italian language would not exist, in his estimation, were it not for these acts of linguistic pilfering from French and Occitan. Likewise, for Pasquier (1996), there was no question of the Frenchness of the troubadours, probably because they provided an easy method of arguing for French influence on Italian poetry. The scholar devotes a full chapter to troubadour verse in *De l'origine de nostre Poësie Françoise*, hammering in the fact that even Petrarch and Dante explicitly acknowledged their debt to Occitan poets (1395). If Pasquier thought the troubadours were the forerunners of the trouvères, he

5. According to Bembo (1989, 89), the Occitans stole from the Tuscans: "De' Provenzali non si può dire così; anzi se ne leggono, per chi vuole, molti, da' quali si vede che hanno apparate e tolte molte cose gli antichi Toscani, che fra tutti gl'italiani popoli a dare opera alle rime sono senza dubbio stati primieri, della qual cosa vi posso io buona testimonianza dare, che alquanti anni della mia fanciullezza ho fatti nella Provenza, e posso dire che io cresciuto mi sono in quella contrada. Perché errare non si può a credere che il rimare primieramente per noi da quella nazione, più che da altra, si sia preso."

6. This oblivion is best illustrated by Claude Fauchet's famous *Recueil de l'origine de la langue et poésie françoise* (1581), which makes no mention of the troubadours, focusing instead on French-language production.

does not say so, framing them instead as the springboard for Italian lyric: "La fin de cette Poësie fut le commencement de celle des Italiens" (1398). Cultural "ownership" of the troubadours remains contested to this day, with their poetry still featuring in both French and Italian literary surveys.

Today, we tend to think of troubadour and trouvère lyric as two separate—even if mutually influential—repertoires. This is not the picture that emerges from the French songbooks and narratives that feature troubadour lyric. Despite plenty of evidence that French and Occitan were sometimes perceived as distinct languages in the thirteenth and fourteenth centuries, troubadour lyric was not imagined in its francophone reception as a foreign or linguistically other corpus. It was instead transformed to bring it closer to French. Fictively relocated to the boundary between France and Occitania, anonymized, and linguistically Gallicized, troubadour song became nearly indistinguishable as such in francophone songbooks and narratives.

Works Cited

Primary

Adam de la Halle. 1995. *Œuvres Complètes*. Edited by Pierre Yves Badel. Paris: Livre *de poche*.

Aimeric de Peguilhan. 1950. *Poems*. Edited by William P. Shepard and Frank M. Chambers. Evanston, Ill.: Northwestern University Press.

Albertet de Sestaro. "Les poésies du troubadour Albertet." Edited by Jean Boutière. *Studi medievali* 10 (1937): 1–129.

Appel, Carl, ed. 1892. *Provenzalische Inedita aus Pariser Handschriften*. O.R. Reisland.

Arnaut Daniel. 1961. *Canzoni*. Edited by Gianluigi Toja. Firenze: G. G. Sansoni.

Bartsch, Karl, ed. 1904. *Chrestomathie provençale (Xe-XVe siècles)*. N.G. Elwert.

Beatriz de Dia. See Rieger 1991.

Beck, Jean, and Louise Beck, eds. 1970. *Le manuscrit du roi: fonds français n. 844 de la Bibliothèque nationale, publié [en facsimile] avec une introduction par Jean Beck et Louise Beck*. 2 vols. New York: Broude Brothers.

Bembo, Pietro. 1989. *Prose della volgar lingua* edited by C. Dionisotti. Turin: TEA.

Bernart de Ventadorn. 1915. *Bernart von Ventadorn: seine Lieder, mit Einleitung und Glossar*. Edited by Carl Appel. Halle a.S.: M. Niemeyer.

——. 1966. *Chansons d'amour*. Edited by Moshé Lazar. Paris: C. Klincksieck.

Blacasset. Otto Klein, "Der Trobadour Blacassetz." In *Städtische Realschule zu Wiesbaden Jahres-Bericht*, 1886–87. Wiesbaden: Ritter, 1887.

Boethius. 2010. *On Aristotle, On Interpretation 1–3*. Translated by Andrew Smith. London: Duckworth.

Bruckner, Matilda Tomaryn, Laurie Shepard, and Sarah White, eds. 1995. *Songs of the Women Troubadours*. New York: Garland.

Casapullo, Rosa. 1997. *Lo diretano bando: Conforto et rimedio delli veraci e leali amadori*. Florence: Accademia della Crusca.

Castets, Ferdinand, ed. 1909. *La chanson des Quatre fils Aymon*. Montpellier: Coulet et fils.

Chabaneau, C. 1888. "Descort anonyme inédit." *Revue des langues romanes*, 32: 575–78.

Coltelli, Cristina. 2014. *Bestiaire d'amours, Richard de Fournival—La redazione franco-italiana: Studio comparativo ed edizione dei testi*. Saarbrücken: Edizioni Accademiche Italiane.

Croizy-Naquet, Catherine, ed. 2014. *L'Estoire de la guerre sainte*. Paris: H. Champion.

Dante Alighieri. 1979. *Convivio*. In *Opere Minori*, edited by Cesare Vasoli and Domenico De Robertis. Vol. 3. Milan and Naples: Riccardo Ricciardi.

——. 1996. *De vulgari eloquentia*. Translated by Steven Botterill. Cambridge: Cambridge University Press.

Daude de Pradas. 1933. *Poésies de Daude de Pradas*. Edited by Alexander Schutz. Toulouse: E. Privat.

——. 2016. *Per sen de trobar: l'opera lirica di Daude de Pradas*. Edited by Silvio Melani. Turnhout, Belgium: Brepols.

Elias Fonsalada. See Raupach 1974.

Epstein, Marcia, ed. 1997. *Prions en chantant: Devotional Songs of the Trouvères*. University of Toronto Press.

Estienne, Henri. 1914. *La défense et illustration de la langue française par Joachim du Bellay, suivie du Projet de l'œuvre intitulée De la précellence du langage françois, par Henri Estienne*. Edited by Louis Humbert. Paris: Garnier frères.

Folquet de Marseille. 1910. *Le Troubadour Folquet de Marseille*. Edited by Stanisław Stroński. Krakow: Académie des sciences.

Frank, István. 1950. "Ce qui reste d'inédit de l'ancienne poésie lyrique provençale." *Boletín de la Real Academia de Buenas Letras de Barcelona*, 23: 69–81.

——. 1954. "*Tuit cil qui sunt enamourat.*" *Romania*, 75: 98–108.

Gambino, Francesca, ed. 2003. *Canzoni anonime di trovatori e trobairitz: edizione critica con commento e glossario*. Alessandria: Edizioni dell'Orso.

Gaucelm Faidit. 1965. *Les poèmes de Gaucelm Faidit, troubadour du XIIe siècle*. Edited by Jean Mouzat. Paris: A. G. Nizet.

Gennrich 319. See Aubrey 1997: 24.

Gerbert de Montreuil. 1928. *Roman de la violette ou de Gerart de Nevers*. Edited by Douglas Buffum. Paris: Honoré Champion.

Gui d'Ussel. In *Les poésies des quatre troubadours d'Ussel*. Edited by Jean Audiau. Paris: Delagrave, 1922.

Guilhem Augier Novella. *Gedichte des Guillem Augier Novella, eines provenzalischen Trobadors aus dem Anfange des XIII. Jahrhunderts*. Edited by Johannes Müller. Halle: Niemeyer, 1899.

Guillaume de Lorris and Jean de Meun. 1992. *Le Roman de la rose: édition d'après les manuscrits BN 12786 et BN 378*. Edited by Armand Strubel. Paris: Librairie Générale Française.

Guillaume le Breton. 1825. *Philippide*. Collection des mémoires relatifs à l'histoire de France depuis la fondation de la monarchie française jusqu'au XIIIe siècle, vol. 12. Paris: J.-L.-J. Brière.

Guillem Magret. "Der Trobador Guillem Magret." Edited by Fritz Naudieth. *Beihefte zur Zeitschrift für romanische Philologie* 52 (1914): 78–144.

Guiraut d'Espanha. *Die Lieder des Trobadors Guiraut d'Espanha*. Edited by O. Hoby. Freiburg, Switzerland: St. Paulus–Drückerei, 1915.

Harrison, Frank L. J., ed. 1956. *Polyphonic Music of the Fourteenth Century*. Vol. 5. Monaco: Editions de l'Oiseau-Lyre.

Harvey, Ruth, and Linda Paterson, eds. 2010. *The Troubadour Tensos and Partimens*. Rochester, N.Y.: D. S. Brewer.

Jacobsthal, G. 1879–80. "Die Texte der Liederhandschrift von Montpellier H. 196." *Zeitschrift für romanische Philologie*, 3: 526–56 and 4: 35–64, 278–317.

Jaufre Rudel. 1985. *Il canzoniere di Jaufre Rudel*. Edited by Giorgio Chiarini. Romanica vulgarica. Rome: Japadre.

Jean Renart. 1893. *Le Roman de la rose ou de Guillaume de Dole*. Edited by Gustave Marie Joseph Servois. Société des anciens textes français. Paris: Firmin Didot.

——. 1995. *The Romance of the Rose or of Guillaume de Dole*. Edited by Regina Psaki. Garland Library of Medieval Literature. New York: Garland.

——. 2008. *Le Roman de la rose ou de Guillaume de Dole*. Edited by Jean Dufournet and Félix Lecoy. Paris: Honoré Champion.

Jeanroy, Alfred, and Arthur Långfors, eds. 1921. *Chansons satiriques et bachiques du XIIIe siècle*. Paris: H. Champion.

Johannes de Grocheio. 1993. "Johannes de Grocheio on Secular Music: A Corrected Text and a New Translation." Edited by Christopher Page. *Plainsong and Medieval Music* 2 (1): 17–41.

Jordan Bonel de Cofolen. In C. A. F. Mahn, *Die Werke der Troubadours in provenzalische Sprache*, 3:311. Geneva: Slatkine Reprints, 1977.

Kolsen, Adolf. 1919. *Zwei provenzalische sirventese nebst einer Anzahl Einzelstrophen*. M. Niemeyer.

Lecoy, Felix. 1962. *Jean Renart: Le Roman de la Rose ou de Guillaume de Dole*. Paris: Champion.

Leroux de Lincy, Antoine, ed. 1841. *Recueil de chants historiques française depuis le XIIe jusqu'au XVIIIe siècle*. C. Gosselin.

Lowe, Lawrence, ed. 1928. *Gérard de Nevers: Prose Version of the Roman de la Violette*. Princeton: Princeton University Press; Paris: Presses universitaires de France.

Marcabru. *Marcabru: A Critical Edition*. Edited by Simon Gaunt, Ruth Harvey, and Linda Paterson. Woodbridge: D. S. Brewer, 2000.

Marshall, John, ed. 1972. *The Razos de trobar of Raimon Vidal and Associated Texts*. London: Oxford University Press.

Meyer, Paul. 1872. "Mélanges de littérature provençale." *Romania*, 1: 401–19.

Molinier, Guillem. 1977. *Las Flors del gay saber: estier dichas, Las Leys d'amors*. Edited by Gatien-Arnoult. Geneva: Slatkine.

Mousket, Philippe. 1836. *Chronique rimée*. Edited by Frédéric-Auguste-Ferdinand-Thomas Reiffenberg. Brussels: M. Hayez.

Muratova, Xenia, and Bruno Roy. 2006. *Le Bestiaire d'amour de Richard de Fournival: Kommentarband zum Vollfaksimile*. Ramsen: Antiquariat Bibermühle.

Oroz Arizcuren, Francisco J, ed. 1972. *La lírica religiosa en la literatura provenzal antigua: edición crítica, traducción, notas y glosario*. Pamplona: Institución Principe de Viana.

Ovid. 1972. *Ovid's Metamorphoses, Books 6–10*. Edited by William S. Anderson. Norman: University of Oklahoma Press.

Paden, William D., ed. 1987. *The Medieval Pastourelle*, 2 vols. New York: Garland.

Pasquier, Etienne. 1996. *Les recherches de la France*. Edited by Marie-Luce Demonet. Paris: H. Champion.

PC 461.9. See Gauchat 1893: 399 and Gambino 2003: 121–24.

PC 461.12 See Leroux de Lincy 1841: 79 and Bartsch 1904: 121.

PC 461.13. See Gauchat 1893: 396, Appel 1892: 316, Rostaing 1973: 643 and Gambino 2003: 111–20.

PC 461.17. See Gauchat 1893: 401 and Appel 1892: 318.

PC 461.20a. See Frank 1950: 78 and Gambino 2003: 87–90.

PC 461.35a. See Frank 1950: 80 and Gambino 2003: 133–36.

PC 461.37. See Chabaneau 1888: 575.

PC 461.41. See Gauchat 1893: 400 and Kolsen 1919: 13.

PC 461.67. See Aimeric de Peguilhan 1950: 214 and Zingarelli 1899: 72.
PC 461.92. See Appel 1892: 322.
PC 461.100. See Gauchat 1893: 397 and Appel 1892: 323.
PC 461.102. See Gauchat 1893: 402, Varvaro 1960: 217, Bartsch 1904: 252 and Gambino 2003: 125–32.
PC 461.103a. See Buffum 1928: 16.
PC 461.122. See Billy 1995a.
PC 461.124. See Billy 1995a.
PC 461.146. See Billy 1995b.
PC 461.148. See Rivière 1974 and Paden 1987.
PC 461.150. See Gauchat 1893: 403 and Appel 1892: 326.
PC 461.152. See Gauchat 1893: 402 and Appel 1892: 326.
PC 461.169a. See Gauchat 1893: 392 and Frank 1953 II: 219.
PC 461.170a. See Saint-Cricq, Doss-Quinby and Rosenberg 2017: li–lii and Tischler 1978: 43.
PC 461.170c. n/a
PC 461.192. See Oroz Arizcuren 1972: 454–59 and Epstein 1997: 278–81.
PC 461.196. See Appel 1892: 328.
PC 461.197. See Gauchat 1893: 393, Appel 1892: 329, Anglade 1923: 152 and Gambino 2003: 91–109.
PC 461.206. See Gauchat 1893: 400, Bartsch 1904: 249 and Gambino 2003: 207–16.
PC 461.230. See Appel 1892: 331.
PC 461.240a/vdB 1822. See Jacobsthal 1879–1880: 4.61, Meyer 1872: 405, Frank 1954: 100.
Peire Cardenal. 1957. *Poésies complètes du troubadour Peire Cardenal*. Edited by René Lavaud. Toulouse: É. Privat.
Peire d'Alvernhe. 1955. *Liriche; testo, traduzione e note a cura di Alberto del Monte*. Edited by Alberto del Monte. Torino: Loescher-Chiantore.
——. 1996. *Poesie*. Edited by Aniello Fratta. Rome: Vecchiarelli.
Peire Vidal. 1913. *Les poésies de Peire Vidal*. Edited by Joseph Anglade. Paris: H. Champion.
——. 1960. *Poesie*. Edited by D'Arco Silvio Avalle. Documenti di filologia 4. Milan: Ricciardi.
Peirol. 1953. *Peirol, Troubadour of Auvergne*. Edited by Stanley Collin Aston. Cambridge: Cambridge University Press.
Perdigon. 1926. *Les chansons de Perdigon*. Edited by H. J. Chaytor. Paris: H. Champion.
Pierre de Beauvais. 2010. *Le bestiaire*. Edited by Craig Baker. Paris: Champion.
Pistoleta. "Der Trobador Pistoleta." Edited by E. Niestroy. *Beihefte zur Zeitschrift für romanische Philologie* 52 (1914): 1–77.
Pons de Capdoill. *Leben und Werke des Trobadors Ponz de Capduoill*. Edited by Max von Napolski. Halle: M. Niemeyer, 1879.
Priscian. 2010. *Institutiones grammaticae*. Edited by Jakob Henrichmann. Library of Latin Texts – Series B. n.p.: Brepols. https://about.brepolis.net/library-of-latin-texts-series-b.
pseudo-Richard de Fournival. 1975. *La Poissance d'amours*. Edited by Gian Battista Speroni. Florence: La nuova Italia.
Radaelli, Anna, ed. 2004. *Dansas provenzali del 13. secolo: appunti sul genere ed edizione critica*. Florence: Alinea.

Raimbaut d'Aurenga. 1952. *The Life and Works of the Troubadour Raimbaut d'Orange.* Edited by Walter Thomas Pattison. Minneapolis: University of Minnesota Press.

Raimbaut de Vaqueiras. 1964. *The Poems of the Troubadour, Raimbaut de Vaqueiras.* Edited by Joseph Linskill. The Hague: Mouton.

Raimon Jordan. 1990. *Il trovatore Raimon Jordan.* Ed. Stefano Asperti. Modena: Mucchi.

Raimon Vidal de Besalú. 1989. "So fo el temps." In vol. 2 of *Obra poètica*, edited by Hugh Field, 6–173. Barcelona: Curial.

Raupach, Manfred, ed. 1974. "Elias Fonsalada. Kritische Ausgabe." *Zeitschrift für romanische Philologie* 90: 141–73.

Reinhard, John, ed. 1926. *Amadas et Ydoine.* Paris: Champion.

Richard de Fournival. 1874. "Biblionomia." In *Le cabinet des manuscrits de la Bibliothèque impériale*, edited by Léopold Delisle, 2:518–35. Paris: Imprimperie impériale.

——. 1957. *Li bestiaires d'amours di Maistre Richart de Fornival e Li response du Bestiaire.* Edited by Cesare Segre. Milan: R. Ricciardi.

——. 1972. "Li Commens d'amours de Richard de Fournival (?)." Edited by Antoinette Saly. *Travaux de linguistique et de littérature* 10 (2): 21–55.

——. 1974. "Il 'Consaus d'amours' di Richard de Fournival." Edited by Gian Battista Speroni. *Medioevo romanzo* 1: 217–78.

——. 1981. *L'Œuvre lyrique de Richard de Fournival.* Edited by Yvan G. Lepage. Ottawa: Editions de l'Université d'Ottawa.

——. 2009. *Le Bestiaire d'amour et la Réponse du bestiaire.* Edited by Gabriel Bianciotto. Champion Classiques. Paris: H. Champion.

Rieger, Angelica, ed. 1991. *Trobairitz: der Beitrag der Frau in der altokzitanischen höfischen Lyrik. Edition des Gesamtkorpus.* Tübingen: M. Niemeyer.

Rigaut de Berbezilh. 1960. *Liriche [di] Rigaut de Barbezilh.* Edited by Alberto Varvaro. Bari: Adriatica.

Riquer, Martín de, ed. 1975. *Los trovadores: historia literaria y textos,* 3 vols. Barcelona: Editorial Planeta.

Rivière, Jean-Claude, ed. 1974. *Pastourelles.* Geneva: Droz.

Rosenberg, Samuel N., and Hans Tischler, eds., with the collaboration of Marie-Geneviève Grossel. 1995. *Chansons des trouvères: chanter m'estuet.* Paris: Librairie générale française.

Rostaing, Charles. 1973. "Une chanson de troubadour anonyme, *A l'entrada del tans florit*, BdT 461,13." *Travaux de Linguistique et de Littérature*, 11: 643–48.

RS 318. See Rosenberg and Tischler 1995: 122–27.

Saint-Cricq, Gaël, Eglal Doss-Quinby and Samuel N. Rosenberg, eds. 2017. *Motets from the Chansonnier de Noailles* Middleton, WI: A-R Editions.

Strubel, Armand, ed. 2012. *Le roman de Fauvel.* Paris: Librairie Générale Française.

Taylor, Pauline, ed. 1952. *Gerbert de Metz: chanson de geste du XIIe siècle.* Namur: Presses universitaires de Namur.

Thiolier-Méjean, Suzanne, and Marie-Françoise Notz-Grob, eds. 1997. *Nouvelles courtoises occitanes et françaises.* Lettres Gothiques. Paris: Librairie Générale Française.

Tischler, Hans, ed. 1997. *Trouvère Lyrics with Melodies: Complete Comparative Edition.* Neuhausen: Hänssler-Verlag.

——. 1978. *The Montpellier Codex.* Madison, Wisc.: A-R Editions.

Vallerie, Josephine Elvira, ed. 1947. *Garin le Loherain.* Ann Arbor, Mich.: Edwards Brothers.

Wailly, Natalis de, ed. 1876. *Récits d'un ménestrel de Reims au treizième siècle*. Paris: Librairie Renouard.

Zingarelli, Nicola. 1899. *Intorno a due trovatori in Italia*. Sansoni.

Zink, Michel, ed. 1989. *Chanson de la croisade albigeoise*. Lettres gothiques. Paris: Librairie générale française.

Secondary

Abeele, Baudouin van den. 1988. "L'Escoufle. Portrait littéraire d'un oiseau." *Reinardus: Yearbook of the International Reynard Society/Annuaire de la Société Internationale Renardienne* 1: 5–15.

Adams, Edward Larrabee. 1913. *Word-Formation in Provençal*. New York: Macmillan.

Anderson, Gordon A. 1973. "Motets of the Thirteenth-Century Manuscript La Clayette: The Repertory and Its Historical Significance." *Musica Disciplina* 27: 11–40.

Arseneau, Isabelle. 2010. "La condition du pastiche dans le roman lyrico-narratif de Jean Renart (*Le Roman de la Rose* ou de *Guillaume de Dole*)." *Études françaises* 46 (3): 99–122.

Asperti, Stefano. 1991. "Contrafacta provenzali di modelli francesi." *Messina* 13: 5–49.

——. 1995. *Carlo I d'Angiò e i trovatori: componenti "provenzali" e angioine nella tradizione manoscritta della lirica trobadorica*. Ravenna: Longo.

Aubrey, Elizabeth. 1997. "The Dialectic between Occitania and France in the Thirteenth Century." *Early Music History* 16: 1–53.

Aurell, Martin. 1989. *La vielle et l'épée: troubadours et politique en Provence au XIIIe siècle*. Paris: Aubier.

Baldwin, John W. 1986. *The Government of Philip Augustus: Foundations of French Royal Power in the Middle Ages*. Berkeley: University of California Press.

——. 1997. "'Once There Was an Emperor . . .': A Political Reading of the Romances of Jean Renart." In *Jean Renart and the Art of Romance: Essays on Guillaume de Dole*, edited by Nancy Vine Durling, 45–82. Gainesville: University Press of Florida.

——. 2000. *Aristocratic Life in Medieval France: The Romances of Jean Renart and Gerbert de Montreuil, 1190–1230*. Baltimore: Johns Hopkins University Press.

Bartsch, Karl. 1872. *Grundriss zur Geschichte der provenzalischen Literatur*. Elberfeld: R. L. Friderichs.

Battelli, Maria Carla. 1992. "La ricezione della lirica provencale nei codici M (B.N. f. fr. 844) e U (B.N. f. fr. 20050): Alcune considerazioni." In *Contacts de langues, de civilisations et intertextualité (IIIème Congrès international de l'Association Internationale d'Études Occitanes, Montpellier, 20–26 septembre 1990)*, edited by Gérard Gouiran, 2:595–605. Montpellier: Centre d'études occitanes de l'Université de Montpellier.

——. 1993. "Il codice Parigi B.N.F. fr. 844: un canzoniere disordinato." In *La filologia romanza e i codici. Atti del Convegno, Messina-Università degli Studi, 19–22 dicembre 1991*, I:273–308. Messina: Sicania.

——. 2001. "Ancora sui testi trobadorici a tradizione francese: variazioni sul vocabulario cortese." In *Le Rayonnement de la civilisation occitane à l'aube d'un nouveau millénaire. Sixième congrès international de l'AIEO (12–19 septembre 1999)*, 157–70. Vienna: Praesens Wissenschaftverlag.

Baumgartner, Emmanuèle. 1981. "Les Citations lyriques dans le *Roman de la Rose* de Jean Renart." *Romance Philology* 35 (1): 260–66.

Beaman, Mark, and Steve Madge. 1998. *The Handbook of Bird Identification: For Europe and the Western Palearctic*. London: Christopher Helm.

Bec, Pierre. 1973. "L'aube francaise Gaite de la Tor: Pièce de ballet ou poème lyrique?" *Cahiers de Civilisation Médiévale (Xe–XIIe Siècles)* 16: 17–33.

——. 1977. *La lyrique française au Moyen Age, XIIe–XIIIe siècles: contribution à une typologie des genres poétiques médiévaux: études et textes*. 2 vols. Paris: A. & J. Picard.

——. 1986. "Troubadours, trouvères et espace Plantagenêt." *Cahiers de Civilisation Médiévale (Xe–XIIe Siècles)* 29 (1–2): 9–14.

——. 1998. "Bernard de Ventadour et Thibaut de Champagne. Essai de bilan comparatif." In *Le Rayonnement des Troubadours: Actes du colloque de l'AIEO, Association internationale d'études occitanes, Amsterdam, 16–18 octobre 1995*, edited by Anton Touber, 163–72. Amsterdam: Rodopi.

Bédier, Joseph. 1896. "Les fêtes de mai et les commencements de la poésie lyrique au Moyen Age." *Revue des deux mondes*, 135 (1): 146–72.

Beer, Jeanette. 1991. "A Fourteenth-century *Bestiaire d'amour*." *Reinardus: Yearbook of the International Reynard Society/Annuaire de la Société Internationale Renardienne* 4: 19–26.

——. 2003. *Beasts of Love: Richard de Fournival's Bestiaire d'amour and a Woman's Response*. Toronto: University of Toronto Press.

——. 2007. "Le *Bestiaire d'amour* in Lombardy." *Florilegium* 24: 1–10.

Bellos, David. 2011. *Is That a Fish in Your Ear? Translation and the Meaning of Everything*. New York: Faber & Faber.

Bent, Margaret. 2015. *Magister Jacobus de Ispania, Author of the Speculum Musicae*. Burlington, Vt.: Ashgate.

Beretta, Margherita Spampinato. 1998. "Le citazioni trobadoriche nel *Roman de la Rose* di Jean Renart." In *Atti del XXI Congresso Internazionale di Linguistica e Filologia Romanza, VI: Sezione 7: Edizione e analisi linguistica dei testi letterari e documentari del Medioevo*, 748–57. Tübingen: Niemeyer.

Berman, Antoine. 1999. *La traduction et la lettre, ou, L'auberge du lointain*. L'ordre philosophique. Paris: Seuil.

Bertoni, Giulio. 1913. "Servâdzo." *Bulletin du Glossaire des patois de la Suisse romande* 12: 33–39.

——. 1917. "La sezione francese del manoscritto provenzale estense." *Archivum romanicum* 1: 307–410.

Billy, Dominique. 1995a. *Deux lais en langue mixte: le lai Markiol et le lai Nompar*. Tübingen: M. Niemeyer.

——. 1995b. "Anonyme. L'autrier cuidai aber druda (BdT 461.146). *Lecturae tropatorum* 8: 1–30.

Birkenmajer, Alexandre. 1949. "Pierre de Limoges commentateur de Richard de Fournival." *Isis: A Journal of the History of Science* 40: 18–31.

Bond, Gerald A. 1985. "The Last Unpublished Troubadour Songs." *Speculum* 60 (4): 827–49.

Bonse, Billee A. 2003. "'Singing to Another Tune': Contrafacture and Attribution in Troubadour Song." Ph.D. diss., Ohio State University.

Boorman, Stanley, John A. Emerson, David Hiley, David Fallows, Thomas B. Payne, Elizabeth Aubrey, Lorenz Welker, et al. n.d. "Sources, MS." *Grove Music Online*. https://www.oxfordmusiconline.com/grovemusic/view/10.1093/gmo/9781561592630.001.0001/omo-9781561592630-e-0000050158.

Boulton, Maureen Barry McCann. 1993. *The Song in the Story: Lyric Insertions in French Narrative Fiction, 1200–1400*. Philadelphia: University of Pennsylvania Press.

Bracken, Paul. 2002. "The Myth of the Medieval Minstrel: An Interdisciplinary Approach to the Performers of the Chansonnier Repertory." *Viator* 33: 100–116.

Brown, Elizabeth A. R. 1980. "The Ceremonial of Royal Succession in Capetian France: The Funeral of Philip V." *Speculum* 55 (2): 266–93. https://doi.org/10.2307/2847288.

Brownlee, Kevin. 1984. *Poetic Identity in Guillaume de Machaut*. Madison: University of Wisconsin Press.

Buffum, Douglas. 1911. "The Songs of the *Roman de la Violette*." In *Studies in Honor of A. Marshall Elliott*, 1:129–57. Baltimore: Johns Hopkins University Press.

Bumke, Joachim. 1967. *Die romanisch-deutschen Literaturbeziehungen im Mittelalter. Ein Überblick*. Heidelberg: Winter.

Burgwinkle, William. 1999. "The Chansonniers as Books." In *The Troubadours: An Introduction*, edited by Simon Gaunt and Sarah Kay, 246–62. Cambridge: Cambridge University Press.

Burns, E. Jane. 2009. *Sea of Silk: A Textile Geography of Women's Work in Medieval French Literature*. Philadelphia: University of Pennsylvania Press.

Butterfield, Ardis. 2002. *Poetry and Music in Medieval France: From Jean Renart to Guillaume de Machaut*. Cambridge: Cambridge University Press.

——. 2009. *The Familiar Enemy: Chaucer, Language, and Nation in the Hundred Years War*. Oxford: Oxford University Press.

Cain Van D'Elden, Stephanie. 1995. "The Minnesingers." In *A Handbook of the Troubadours*, edited by F. R. Akehurst and Judith Davis, 262–70. Berkeley: University of California Press.

Callahan, Christopher. 1990. "The Evolution of the Lyric Insertion in Thirteenth-Century Narrative." *Essays in Medieval Studies* 7: 29–40.

——. 2002. "Hybrid Discourse and Performance in the Old French Pastourelle." *French Forum* 27 (1): 1–22.

——. 2012. "Troubadour Songs in Trouvère Codices: Mouvance in the Transmission of Courtly Lyric." *Variants* 9: 31–48.

Cannon, Christopher. 2004. "The Owl and the Nightingale and the Meaning of Life." *Journal of Medieval and Early Modern Studies* 34 (2): 251–78.

Carapezza, Francesco. 2012. "Un'ipotesi sul son poitevin." *Medioevo romanzo* 36 (2): 390–405.

Cerquiglini, Bernard. 1983. "Une langue, une littérature." In *Précis de littérature française du moyen âge*, edited by Daniel Poirion, 17–31. Paris: Presses universitaires de France.

Chambers, Frank. 1952. "Imitation of Form in the Old Provençal Lyric." *Romance Philology* 6: 104–20.

——. 1979. "Three Troubadour Poems with Historical Overtones." *Speculum* 54 (1): 42–54.

——. 1985. *An Introduction to Old Provençal Versification*. Philadelphia: American Philosophical Society.

"Chatter, V." n.d. *OED Online*. Oxford University Press. http://www.oed.com/view/Entry/30971.

Chion, Michel. 2012. "The Three Listening Modes." In *The Sound Studies Reader*, edited by Jonathan Sterne, 48–53. New York: Routledge.

Cohen, Paul. 2001. "Courtly French, Learned Latin, and Peasant Patois: The Making of a National Language in Early Modern France." Ph.D. diss., Princeton University.

Coldwell, Maria V. 1981. "*Guillaume de Dole* and Medieval Romances with Musical Interpolations." *Musica Disciplina* 35: 55–86.

Crespo, Roberto. 1991. "Una strofa 'sentenziosa' di Richard de Fournival." *Romania* 112: 544–52.

Curtius, Ernst Robert. 1953. *European Literature and the Latin Middle Ages*. Translated by Willard R. Trask. London: Routledge & Kegan Paul.

Davis, Christopher. 2015. "'Chascus en lor lati': Guilhem IX, Birdsong, and the Language of Poetry." *Tenso: Bulletin de la Société Guillaume IX* 30 (1–2): 2–24.

DEAFplusonline, garir, https://deaf-server.adw.uni-heidelberg.de/lemme/garir.

——. tïeschier, https://deaf-server.adw.uni-heidelberg.de/lemme/tieschier?expand=true#tieschier.

Demaules, Mireille. 2000. "L'art de la ruse dans le *Roman de la Violette* de Gerbert de Montreuil." *Revue des Langues Romanes* 104 (1): 143–61.

Dijkstra, Cathrynke. 1998. "Troubadours, trouvères and crusade lyrics." In *Le Rayonnement des Troubadours: Actes du colloque de l'AIEO, Association internationale d'études occitanes, Amsterdam, 16–18 octobre 1995*, edited by Anton Touber, 173–84. Amsterdam: Rodopi.

Dillon, Emma. 2012. *The Sense of Sound: Musical Meaning in France, 1260–1330*. New York: Oxford University Press.

——. 2016. "Sensing Sound." In *A Feast for the Senses: Art and Experience in Medieval Europe*, edited by Martina Bagnoli, 95–114. Baltimore: Walters Art Museum.

Dolar, Mladen. 2006. *A Voice and Nothing More*. Cambridge, Mass.: MIT Press.

Dragonetti, Roger. 1960. *La technique poétique des trouvères dans la chanson courtoise. Contribution à l'étude de la rhétorique médiévale*. Brugge: De Tempel.

Drzewicka, Anna. 1974. "Fantaisie et originalité dans la poésie lyrique médiévale: la chanson 'Volez vos que je vos chant?'" *Kwartalnik Neofilologiczny* 21: 441–58.

Duby, Georges. 1973. *Le Dimanche de Bouvines; 27 juillet 1214*. Paris: Gallimard.

Duport, Danièle. 1993. "Les chansons dans le *Guillaume de Dole*." In *Et c'est la fin pour quoy sommes ensemble: Hommage à Jean Dufournet professeur à la Sorbonne Nouvelle: Littérature, histoire et langue du Moyen Age, I–III*, edited by Jean-Claude Aubailly, 2:513–24. Paris: Champion.

Eckard, G. 1999. "'Li oiseaus dit en son latin'. Chant et langage des oiseaux dans trois nouvelles courtoises du Moyen Age français." *Critica del testo* 2 (2): 677–93.

Eco, Umberto, Roberto Lambertini, Costantino Marmo, Andrea Tabarroni. 1989. "On Animal Language in the Medieval Classification of Signs." In *On the Medieval Theory of Signs*, edited by Umberto Eco and Constantino Marmo, 3–41. Amsterdam: John Benjamins.

Everist, Mark. 1994. *French Motets in the Thirteenth Century: Music, Poetry, and Genre*. New York: Cambridge University Press.

Fourrier, Anthime. 1969. "Les armoiries de l'empereur dans *Guillaume de Dole*." In *Mélanges offerts à Rita Lejeune, Professeur à l'Université de Liège*, edited by Fred Dethier, 2:1211–1226. Gembloux: J. Duculot.

Frank, István. 1952a. "Le Chansonnier Y: fragments provençaux du manuscrit français 795 de la Bibliotheque Nationale." *Symposium: A Journal Devoted to Modern Foreign Languages and Literature* 6 (1): 51–87.

——, ed. 1952b. *Trouvères et Minnesänger: recueil de textes pour servir à l'étude des rapports entre la poésie lyrique romane et le Minnesang au XIIe siècle*. Saarbrücken: West-Ost Verlag.

——. 1953. *Répertoire métrique de la poésie des troubadours*. Paris: Champion.

——. 1954. "'Tuit cil qui sunt enamourat.'" *Romania* 75: 98–108.

Fritz, Jean-Marie. 2011. *La cloche et la lyre: pour une poétique médiévale du paysage sonore*. Geneva: Droz.

Gal, Susan, and Judith T. Irvine. 1995. "The Boundaries of Languages and Disciplines: How Ideologies Construct Difference." *Social Research* 62 (4): 967–1001.

——. 2000. "Language Ideology and Linguistic Differentiation." In *Regimes of Language: Ideologies, Polities, and Identities*, edited by Paul V. Kroskrity. Santa Fe, N.M.: School of American Research Press; Oxford: J. Currey.

Gally, Michèle. 2002. "Entre *fin'amor* et Ovide: Richard de Fournival's 'Soutius parliers' d'amour." *Cahiers de recherches médiévales et humanistes* 9: 1–9.

Galvez, Marisa. 2012. *Songbook: How Lyrics Became Poetry in Medieval Europe*. University of Chicago Press.

Gambino, Francesca. 2000. "L'anonymat dans la tradition manuscrite de la lyrique troubadouresque." *Cahiers de civilisation médiévale* 43 (169): 33–90.

Gauchat, Louis. 1893. "Les poésies provençales conservées par des chansonniers français." *Romania* 22: 364–404.

Gaunt, Simon. 2002. "'Desnaturat son li Frances': Language and Identity in the Twelfth-Century Occitan Epic." *Tenso* 17: 10–31.

——. 2013. *Marco Polo's* Le Devisement du monde*: Narrative Voice, Language and Diversity*. Cambridge: D. S. Brewer.

Gégou, Fabienne. 1973. "Jean Renart et la lyrique occitane." In *Mélanges de langue et de littérature médiévales offerts à Pierre Le Gentil, par ses collègues, ses élèves et ses amis*, 319–23. Paris: S.E.D.E.S.

Gennrich, Friedrich. 1926. "Der deutsche Minnesang in seinem Verhaltnis zur Troubadour-und Trouvère-Kunst." *Zeitschrift für deutsche Bildung* 2: 536–632.

Godefroy, Frédéric. 2002. *Dictionnaire de l'ancienne langue française*. Classiques Garnier Numérique. https: / / www-classiques-garnier-com.

Gregory, Stewart, William Rothwell, D. A. Trotter, Michael Beddow, and Modern Humanities Research Association, eds. 2005. *Anglo-Norman Dictionary*. 2nd ed. Publications of the Modern Humanities Research Association, v. 17. London: Maney Publishing for the Modern Humanities Research Association.

Gröber, Gustav. 1877. "Die Liedersammlungen der Troubadours." *Romanische Studien* 2: 337–668.

Haines, John. 1998. "The Transformations of the 'Manuscrit du Roi.'" *Musica Disciplina* 52: 5–43.

——. 2004. *Eight Centuries of Troubadours and Trouvères: The Changing Identity of Medieval Music*. Cambridge: Cambridge University Press.

——. 2013. "A Songbook for William of Villehardouin, Prince of the Morea (Paris, Bibliothèque Nationale de France, Fonds Français 844): A Crucial Case in the History of Vernacular Song Collections." In *Viewing the Morea: Land and People in the Late Medieval Peloponnese*, edited by Sharon E. J. Gerstel, 56–109. Washington, D.C.: Dumbarton Oaks.

Hamilton, Bernard. 2008. "The Albigensian Crusade and Heresy." In *The New Cambridge Medieval History c. 1198–1300*, vol. 5, edited by David Abulafia. Cambridge: Cambridge University Press.

Harvey, Ruth. 1995. "Languages, Lyrics and the Knightly Classes." In *Medieval Knighthood V: Papers from the Sixth Strawberry Hill Conference 1994*, edited by Stephen Church and Ruth Harvey, 197–220. Woodbridge: Boydell.

——. 2005. "Eleanor of Aquitaine and the Troubadours." In *The World of Eleanor of Aquitaine: Literature and Society in Southern France between the Eleventh and Thirteenth Centuries*, edited by Marcus Graham Bull and Catherine Léglu, 101–14. Rochester, N.Y.: Boydell.

Haye, Thomas. 2010. "Canon ou catalogue? Perspectives historico-littéraires dans la *Biblionomia* de Richard de Fournival." *Romania* 128: 213–33.

Heller-Roazen, Daniel. 2013. *Dark Tongues: The Art of Rogues and Riddlers*. New York: Zone Books.

Hollier, Denis, ed. 1994. *A New History of French Literature*. Cambridge, M.A.: Harvard University Press.

Huot, Sylvia. 1987. *From Song to Book: The Poetics of Writing in Old French Lyric and Lyrical Narrative Poetry*. Ithaca, N.Y.: Cornell University Press.

——. 2003. *Madness in Medieval French Literature: Identities Found and Lost*. Oxford: Oxford University Press.

Ibos-Augé, Anne. 2006. "'Noter biaus chans por ramenbrance de chançon': les auteurs narratifs font-ils oeuvre de témoins de leur temps musical?" *Cahiers de recherches médiévales et humanistes* 13: 257–70.

Ineichen, Gustav. 1969. "Autour du graphisme des chansons françaises à tradition provençale." *Travaux de linguistique et de littérature* 7 (1): 203–18.

Jeanroy, Alfred. 1889a. *De nostratibus Medii Aevi poetis qui primum lyrica Aquitaniae carmina imitati sint*. Paris: Hachette.

——. 1889b. *Les origines de la poésie lyrique en France au moyen âge; études de littérature française et comparée suivies de textes inédits*. Paris: E. Champion.

——. 1891. "[Review.] Carl Appel: Provenzalische Inedita aus Pariser Handschriften." *Annales du Midi* 3 (9): 84–88.

——. 1898. "Une imitation d'Albert de Sisteron par Mahieu le Juif." *Romania* 27: 148–50.

——. 1916. *Bibliographie sommaire des chansonniers provençaux (manuscrits et éditions)*. Paris: H. Champion.

Jewers, Caroline. 1996. "Fabric and Fabrication: Lyric and Narrative in Jean Renart's *Roman de la Rose*." *Speculum* 71 (4): 907–24.

Johnson, Glenn Pierr. 1991. "Aspects of Late Medieval Music at the Cathedral of Amiens." Ph.D. diss., Yale University.

Jung, Marc-René. 1986. "A propos de la poésie lyrique courtoise d'oc et d'oïl." *Studi francesi e provenzali* 84/5: 5–36.

——. 1992. "Rencontres entre troubadours et trouvères." In *Contacts de langue, de civilisations et intertextualité: IIIe Congrès international de l'Association internationale d'études occitanes, Montpellier, 20–26 septembre 1990*, 3:991–1000. Montpellier: Centre d'études occitanes de l'Université de Montpellier.

Karp, Theodore. n.d. "Gace Brulé." *Grove Music Online*. https://www.oxfordmusiconline.com/grovemusic/view/10.1093/gmo/9781561592630.001.0001/omo-9781561592630-e-0000010463.

Kasten, Ingrid. 1986. *Frauendienst bei Trobadors und Minnesängern im 12. Jahrhundert. Zur Entwicklung und Adaption eines Literarischen Konzepts*. Heidelberg: Universitätsverlag Winter.

Kasten, Ingrid, Werner Paravicini, and René Pérennec, eds. 1998. *Kultureller Austausch und Literaturgeschichte im Mittelalter / Transferts culturels et histoire littéraire au Moyen Âge*. Sigmaringen: Jan Thorbecke Verlag.

Kay, Sarah. 2010. "The Monolingualism of the Parrot, or the Prosthesis of Origins, in *Las Novas del Papagay*." *Romanic Review* 101 (1/2): 23–35.

——. 2011. "La seconde main et les secondes langues dans la France médiévale." In *Translations médiévales: Cinq siècles de traductions en français (XIe–XVe siècles)*, edited by Claudio Galderisi, 1:461–85. Turnhout, Belgium: Brepols.

——. 2013. *Parrots and Nightingales: Troubadour Quotation and the Development of European Poetry*. Philadelphia: University of Pennsylvania Press.

Kendrick, Laura. 1995. "The Science of Imposture and the Professionalization of Medieval Occitan Literary Studies." In *Medievalism and the Modernist Temper*, edited by R. Howard Bloch and Stephen G. Nichols, 95–126. Baltimore: Johns Hopkins University Press.

Kibler, William W., ed. 1995. "Versification." In *Medieval France: An Encyclopedia*, 1793–96. New York: Garland.

Kordecki, Lesley Catherine. 2011. *Ecofeminist Subjectivities: Chaucer's Talking Birds*. New York: Palgrave Macmillan.

Krause, Kathy. 2007. "Géographie et héritage: Les Manuscrits du *Roman de la Violette*." *Babel: Langages, Imaginaires, Civilisations* 16: 81–99.

Lacy, Norris J. 1980. "'Amer par oïr dire.' Guillaume and the Drama of Language." *French Review* 54 (6): 779–87.

Ladurie, Emmanuel Le Roy. 1977. "Occitania in Historical Perspective." *Review (Fernand Braudel Center)* 1 (1): 20–30.

Lagarde, André and Laurent Michard. 1962. *Moyen Age; les grands auteurs français du programme*. Paris: Bordas.

Leach, Elizabeth Eva. 2006. "'The Little Pipe Sings Sweetly while the Fowler Deceives the Bird': Sirens in the Later Middle Ages." *Music and Letters* 87 (2): 187–211.

——. 2007. *Sung Birds: Music, Nature, and Poetry in the Later Middle Ages*. Ithaca, N.Y.: Cornell University Press.

——. 2009. "Grammar and Music in the Medieval Song-School." *New Medieval Literatures* 11: 195–211.

Leach, Elizabeth Eva, and Jonathan Morton. 2017. "Intertextual and Intersonic Resonance in the *Bestiaire d'amour*." *Romania* 135: 313–51.

Léglu, Catherine, Rebecca Rist, and Claire Taylor, eds. 2014. *The Cathars and the Albigensian Crusade: A Sourcebook*. London: Routledge.

Lejeune, Rita. 1935. *LŒuvre de Jean Renart: contribution à l'étude du genre romanesque au moyen âge*. Liège/Paris: Faculté de Philosophie et Lettres/Droz.

——. 1954. "Rôle littéraire d'Aliénor d'Aquitaine et de sa famille." *Cultura Neolatina* 14: 5–57.

——. 1958. "Rôle littéraire de la famille d'Aliénor d'Aquitaine." *Cahiers de Civilisation Médiévale (Xe–XIIe Siecles)* 1 (3): 319–37.

——. 1974. "Le Roman de *Guillaume de Dole* et la principauté de Liège." *Cahiers de civilisation médiévale* 17: 1–24.

——. 1978. "Jean Renart et le roman réaliste au XIIIe siècle." In *Le roman jusqu'à la fin du XIIIe siècle*, edited by Jean Frappier and Reinhold R. Grimm, 400–446. Grundriss der romanischen Literatur des Mittelalters. Heidelberg: Winter.

Leonardi, Lino. 2006. "'Nuovi' manoscritti della *Mort le Roi Artu.*" In *Studi di filologia romanza offerti a Valeria Bertolucci Pizzorusso*, 883–98. Pisa: Pacini.

Lepage, Yvan G. 1982. "Richard de Fournival et Le Mythe de Narcisse." *Revue de l'Université d'Ottawa* 52 (2): 238–46.

Limentani, Alberto. 1980. "Effetti di specularità nella narrative medievale." *Romanische Zeitschrift für Literaturgeschichte* 4: 307–21.

Linker, Robert White. 1979. *A Bibliography of Old French Lyrics*. University, Miss.: Romance Monographs.

Lodge, R. Anthony. 1993. *French, from Dialect to Standard*. London: Routledge.

Lods, Jeanne. 1984. "Une étrange petite fée." In *Mélanges de langue et de littératures médiévales offerts à Alice Planche*, edited by Maurice Accarie and Ambroise Queffélec, 2:311–17. Paris: Les Belles Lettres.

Longnon, Jean. 1939. "Le prince de Morée chansonnier." *Romania* 65: 95–100.

Lops, R. L. H. 1982. "La Huppe: Histoire littéraire et légendaire d'un oiseau." In *Mélanges de linguistique, de littérature et de philologie médiévales offerts à J. R. Smeets*, edited by Q. Mok, I. Spiele, and P. Verhuyck, 171–85. Leiden: Instituut Frans.

Louison, Lydie. 2009. "Escoufle, hüa, milan, nieble: Analyse lexicologique." *Le Moyen Age* 115 (1): 109.

Lucken, Christopher. 1999. "L'Écho du poème ('ki sert de recorder che k'autres dist')." In *Par la vue et l'ouïe: littérature du Moyen Age et de la Renaissance*, 26–58. Paris: ENS.

——. 2002. "'Onqes n'amai tant que jou fui amee': La chanson de femme à l'épreuve de la fin'amor." *Perspectives médiévales* 28: 33–68.

——. 2010. "Les manuscrits du *Bestiaire d'Amours* de Richard de Fournival." In *Le recueil au Moyen Âge. Le Moyen Âge central*, edited by Yasmina Foehr-Janssens and Olivier Collet, 113–38. Turnhout, Belgium: Brepols.

Lug, Robert. 2000. "Katharer und Waldenser in Metz: Zur Herkunft der altesten Sammlung von Trobador-Liedern (1231)." In *Okzitanistik, Altokzitanistik und Provenzalistik: Geschichte und Auftrag einer europäischen Philologie*, edited by Angelica Rieger. Frankfurt am Main: P. Lang.

——. 2012. "Politique et littérature à Metz autour de la guerre des amis (1231–1234): Le témoignage du chansonnier de Saint-Germain-des-Prés." In *Lettres, musique et société en Lorraine médiévale: autour du Tournoi de Chauvency*, edited by Nancy F. Regalado, 451–86. Geneva: Droz.

Madureira, Margarida. 2009. "La mort de l'oiseau chanteur et la poétique amoureuse du *Bestiaire d'amour* de Richard de Fournival." In *Déduits d'oiseaux au Moyen Âge*, 193–204. Aix-en-Provence: Publications de l'Université de Provence.

Marshall, John. 1979. "The descort of Albertet and Its Old French Imitations." *Zeitschrift für romanische Philologie* 95: 290–306.

——. 1982. "[Review of Raupach & Raupach 1979]." *Romance Philology* 36 (1): 83–93.

——. 1987. "Une versification lyrique popularisante en ancien provençal." In *Actes du premier congrès international de l'Association internationale d'études occitanes*, edited by P. T. Ricketts, 35–66. London: London University Press.

Mason, Paul, and Jake Allsop. 2010. *The Golden Oriole*. London: A&C Black.

McCormick, Stephen. 2011. "Remapping the Story: Franco-Italian Epic and Lombardia as a Narrative Community." Ph.D. diss., University of Oregon.

Meneghetti, Maria Luisa. 1984. *Il pubblico dei trovatori: ricezione e riuso dei testi lirici cortesi fino al XIV secolo*. Modena: Mucchi.

Meyer, Paul. 1872. "Mélanges de littérature provençale." *Romania* 1: 401–19.

——. 1884. "La chanson de *Doon de Nanteuil*: Fragments inédits." *Romania* 13: 1–26.

——. 1890. "Des rapports de la poésie lyrique des trouvères avec ceux des troubadours." *Romania* 19: 1–42.

Mölk, Ulrich. 1968. *Trobar Clus, Trobar Leu; Studien zur Dichtungstheorie der Trobadors*. Munich: W. Fink.

Morawski, Joseph. 1925. *Proverbes français antérieurs au XVe siècle*. Paris: É. Champion.

Mouzat, Jean. 1958. "Quelques hypothèses sur les poèmes perdus d'Eble II Vicomte de Ventadorn." *Cultura Neolatina* 18: 111–20.

Nelson, Deborah. 1995. "Northern France." In *A Handbook of the Troubadours*, edited by F. R. Akehurst and Judith Davis. Berkeley: University of California Press.

Paden, William D. 1993. "Old Occitan as a Lyric Language: The Insertions from Occitan in Three Thirteenth-Century French Romances." *Speculum* 68 (1): 36–53.

——. 1996. "Flight from Authority in the Pastourelle." In *The Medieval "Opus": Imitation, Rewriting and Transmission in the French Tradition*, 299–326. Amsterdam: Rodopi.

——. 2005. "Troubadours and History." In *The World of Eleanor of Aquitaine: Literature and Society in Southern France between the Eleventh and Thirteenth Centuries*, edited by Marcus Graham Bull and Catherine Léglu, 157–82. Rochester, N.Y.: Boydell.

Page, Christopher. 1987. *Voices and Instruments of the Middle Ages: Instrumental Practice and Songs in France, 1100–1300*. London: J. M. Dent.

Parducci, Amos, ed. 1920. "Bonifazio di Castellana." *Romania* 46: 478–511.

Paris, Gaston. 1892. *Les origines de la poésie lyrique en France au moyen âge*. Paris: Imprimerie nationale.

Paris, Paulin. 1856. "Richard de Furnival." In *Histoire littéraire de la France*, 23:708–33. Paris: Firmin Didot.

Paterson, Linda. 1993. *The World of the Troubadours: Medieval Occitan Society, c. 1100–c. 1300*. Cambridge: Cambridge University Press.

——. 2011. "Was There an Occitan Identity in the Middle Ages?" In *Culture and Society in Medieval Occitania*. Farnham, Surrey, and Burlington, Vt.: Ashgate.

Peraino, Judith A. 2011. *Giving Voice to Love: Song and Self-Expression from the Troubadours to Guillaume de Machaut*. Oxford: Oxford University Press.

Perloff, Marjorie, and Craig Douglas Dworkin, eds. 2009. *The Sound of Poetry, the Poetry of Sound*. Chicago: University of Chicago Press.

Pfeffer, Wendy. 1985. *The Change of Philomel: The Nightingale in Medieval Literature.* New York: P. Lang.

Pillet, Alfred, and Henry Carstens. 1933. *Bibliographie der Troubadours.* Halle: M. Niemeyer.

Power, Daniel. 2004. "Capetian Government in the Franco-Norman Marches." In *The Norman Frontier in the Twelfth and Early Thirteenth Centuries.* Cambridge: Cambridge University Press.

Räkel, Hans-Herbert S. 1977. *Die musikalische Erscheinungsform der Trouverepoesie.* Bern: P. Haupt.

Ranawake, Silvia. 1976. *Höfische Strophenkunst: vergleichende Untersuchungen zur Formentypologie von Minnesang und Trouvèrelied an der Wende zum Spätmittelalter.* Munich: Beck.

Raupach, Manfred, and Margret Raupach. 1979. *Französierte Trobadorlyrik: zur Überlieferung provenzalischer Lieder in französischen Handschriften.* Tübingen: M. Niemeyer.

Raynouard, François, ed. 1836. *Lexique roman, ou, dictionnaire de la langue des troubadours: comparée avec les autres langues de l'Europe latine.* Paris: Silvestre.

Restori, Antonio. 1904. *La Gaite de la Tor.* Messina: A. Trimarchi.

Ricketts, Peter T. 2001. *Concordance de l'Occitan Médiéval [Electronic Resource] = The Concordance of Medieval Occitan.* Turnhout, Belgium: Brepols.

Rieger, Dietmar. 1976. *Gattungen und Gattungsbezeichnungen der Trobadorlyrik.* Tübingen: Niemeyer.

Roncaglia, Aurelio. 1969. "Trobar clus-discussione aperta." *Cultura Neolatina* 29: 5–53.

Rosenberg, Samuel N. 1998. "French Songs in Occitan Chansonniers: An Introductory Report." *Tenso: Bulletin de la Société Guillaume IX* 13 (2): 18–32.

——. 2005. "French Songs in Occitan Chansonniers: Mahieu Le Juif in Ms. O (Rome, Biblioteca Apostolica Vaticana Vaticani Latini 3208)." In *"De Sens Rassis": Essays in Honor of Robert T. Pickens*, edited by Keith Busby, Bernard Guidot, and Logan E. Whalen, 567–76. Amsterdam: Rodopi.

Rosenstein, Roy. 1995. "Translation." In *A Handbook of the Troubadours*, edited by F. R. P. Akehurst and Judith M. Davis. Berkeley: University of California Press.

Rossi, Luciano. 1979. "Mout m'alegra douza vos per boscaje." *Cultura Neolatina* 39: 69–76.

Roy, Bruno. 2006. "Un nouveau manuscrit du *Bestiaire d'amour.*" In *Qui tant savoit d'engin et d'art: mélanges de philologie médiévale offerts à Gabriel Bianciotto*, edited by Claudio Galderisi and Jean Maurice, 205–13. Poitiers: Université de Poitiers, Centre d'études supérieures de civilisation médiévale.

Scott, Clive. 2012. *Translating the Perception of Text: Literary Translation and Phenomenology.* London: Legenda/Modern Humanities Research Association and Maney.

Silverstein, Michael. 1979. "Language Structure and Linguistic Ideology." In *The Elements: Parasession on Units and Levels*, edited by R. Clyne, 193–247. Chicago: Chicago Linguistics Society.

Sivéry, Gérard. 1995. *Louis VIII le Lion.* Paris: Fayard.

Snowe, Joseph. 1839. *The Rhine, Legends, Traditions, History, from Cologne to Mainz.* 2 vols. London: F. C. Westley.

Spanke, Hans. 1955. *G. Raynauds Bibliographie des altfranzösischen Liedes. Neu bearbeitet und ergänzt von Hans Spanke*. Leiden: E. J. Brill.

Spiegel, Gabrielle M. 1975. "The Cult of Saint Denis and Kingship." *Journal of Medieval History* 1 (1): 43–70.

Stevens, John, Ardis Butterfield, and Theodore Karp. 2009. "Troubadours, Trouvères." *Grove Music Online*. https://www.oxfordmusiconline.com/grovemusic/view/10.1093/gmo/9781561592630.001.0001/omo-9781561592630-e-0000028468?rskey=Xn5e8d&result=1.

Strayer, Joseph R. 1992. *The Albigensian Crusades*. Ann Arbor: University of Michigan Press.

Symes, Carol. 2007. *A Common Stage: Theater and Public Life in Medieval Arras*. Ithaca, N.Y.: Cornell University Press.

Taylor, Robert A. 1986. "'L'altrier cuidai aber druda' (PC 461,146): Edition and Study of a Hybrid-Language Parody Lyric." In *Studia Occitanica in Memoriam Paul Remy*, edited by Hans-Erich Keller, 2:189–201. Kalamazoo: Medieval Institute Publications, Western Michigan University.

——. 1993. "Barbarolexis Revisited: The Poetic Use of Hybrid Language in Old Occitan/Old French Lyric." In *The Centre and Its Compass: Studies in Medieval Literature in Honor of Professor John Leyerle*, 457–74, edited by Robert J. Taylor, James F. Burke, Patricia J. Eberle, Ian Lancashire, and Brian S. Merrilees. Kalamazoo: Western Michigan University Press.

Tobler, Adolf. 1925. *Altfranzösisches Wörterbuch*. Berlin: Weidmann.

Toch, Michael. 1995. "Welfs, Hohenstaufen and Habsburgs." In *New Cambridge Medieval History*, edited by David Abulafia, 5:375–404. New York: Cambridge University Press.

Usher, Jonathan. 1997. "Poetry." In *The Cambridge History of Italian Literature*, edited by Peter Brand and Lino Pertile, 5–27. Cambridge: Cambridge University Press.

van den Boogaard, Nico. 1969. *Rondeaux et refrains du XIIe siècle au début du XIVe*. Klincksieck.

van der Werf, Hendrik. 1997. "Jean Renart and Medieval Song." In *Jean Renart and the Art of Romance: Essays on Guillaume de Dole*, edited by Nancy Vine Durling, 157–87. Gainesville: University Press of Florida.

Venuti, Lawrence. 1998. *The Scandals of Translation: Towards an Ethics of Difference*. New York: Routledge.

Vuagnoux-Uhlig, Marion. 2009. *Le couple en herbe: Galeran de Bretagne et l'Escoufle à la lumière du roman idyllique médiéval*. Geneva: Droz.

——. 2011. "Saint-Gilles." In *Dictionnaire des lieux et pays mythiques*, edited by Olivier Battistini and Jean Dominique Poli, 1050–53, Paris: Broché.

Walter, Philippe. 1989. *La mémoire du temps: fêtes et calendriers de Chrétien de Troyes à La mort Artu*. Genève: Slatkine.

Walters, Lori. 1994. "Reading the Rose: Literacy and the Presentation of the *Roman de la Rose* in Medieval Manuscripts." *Romanic Review* 85 (1): 1–26.

Wittig, Monique. 1992. "The Category of Sex." In *The Straight Mind and Other Essays*. Boston: Beacon.

Woledge, B. 1965. "Old Provençal and Old French." In *Eos: An Enquiry into the Theme of Lovers' Meetings and Partings at Dawn in Poetry*, edited by A. T. Hatto, 344–89. London: Mouton.

Wolinski, Mary E. 1992. "The Compilation of the Montpellier Codex." *Early Music History* 11: 263–301. https://doi.org/10.1017/S0261127900001248.

Woolard, Kathryn Ann. 1998. "Introduction: Language Ideology as a Field of Inquiry." In *Language Ideologies: Practice and Theory*, edited by Bambi B. Schieffelin, Kathryn Ann Woolard, and Paul V. Kroskrity, 3–47. Oxford: Oxford University Press.

Woolard, Kathryn, and Bambi Schieffelin. 1994. "Language Ideology." *Annual Review of Anthropology* 23: 55–82.

Zingesser, Eliza. 2012. "French Troubadours: Assimilating Occitan Literature in France (1200–1400)." Ph.D. diss., Princeton University.

——. 2015. "Remembering to Forget Richard de Fournival's *Bestiaire d'amour* in Italy: The Case of Pierpont Morgan Ms 459." *French Studies* 69 (4): 439–48.

——. 2017. "Pidgin Poetics: Bird Talk in Medieval France and Occitania." *New Medieval Literatures* 17: 62–80.

Zink, Michel. 1979. *Roman rose et rose rouge: Le Roman de la Rose ou de Guillaume de Dole, de Jean Renart*. Paris: Nizet.

Zufferey, François. 1987. *Recherches linguistiques sur les chansonniers provençaux*. Geneva: Droz.

Zumthor, Paul. 1960. "Un problème d'esthétique médiévale: l'utilisation poétique du bilinguisme." *Le Moyen Âge* 66: 301–36, 561–94.

——. 1972. *Essai de poétique médiévale*. Paris: Seuil.

INDEX

Printed in the USA
CPSIA information can be obtained
at www.ICGtesting.com
LVHW090833030424
776067LV00018B/22/J

9 781501 747571